Dedicated to my family.

Sociological Perspectives on Substance Use and College Life:

An Ethnographic Investigation

Patrick O'Brien, Ph.D.

Note: Chapters 2 and 3 are comprised of the concepts and theories that are used throughout the data Chapters 5 through 9. As you read through the data chapters, please use Chapters 2 and 3 as a reference and refer back to them often to understand the presentation and analysis of the data.

Preface

This book is specifically designed to be used in a variety of my sociology courses, including Introduction to Sociology and Social Problems. It is an example of a sociological monograph, a detailed written study on a specialized scholarly subject. Throughout the semester it will provide us with an example of how original sociological research is conducted, analyzed, and written.

Throughout this text we will examine a wide variety of sociological concepts and theories while analyzing college life and a distinct period of the life-course known as emerging adulthood. This unique developmental stage occurs between the adolescent and adult years within the age range of 18 to 29. The result of widespread secondary education and a later age of marriage in late-modern societies, emerging adulthood involves a life stage of self-exploration, risk-taking, identity formation, changing affiliations (i.e., peers and romantic attachments), and shifts toward independence and adult sufficiency that frequently occurs in the college environment. For college students and emerging adults, self and identity exploration often entail a high degree of experimentation, including meeting different kinds of people, questioning their belief system, deciding on a college major or field of study, and engaging in risky behaviors such as substance use.

While reading this text, we will examine the social controls that operate among and upon emerging adults as they navigate college, substance use, and social life. The data are drawn from six years of participant-observation and 100 in-depth interviews with college students. In chapter 1, we are introduced to the concept of emerging adulthood and examine what exactly makes this a unique period of life in modern society. Specifically, we see that substance use, especially alcohol use, is quite prevalent in the emerging adult years and we will critically examine these forms of experimentation. Is substance use among college students a social problem? Or, is substance use simply a part of the risk-taking of emerging adulthood, one that is overstated by media, researchers, and worried adults?

In chapters 2 and 3, we are introduced to a central concept in the field of sociology known as social control. Social control, or all the mechanisms and resources by which members of society attempt to assure others follow norms, rules, and laws, is almost as old as the discipline of sociology itself. Social controls are essential for understanding culture, crime / deviance, gender, social interaction, and modern life. In these chapters we will see how social controls operate to ensure compliance with norms, or guidelines for behavior. We will learn how informal social controls operate through socialization, culture, and group memberships. We will also examine formal social controls manifested in the criminal justice system, medicalization, and via other social institutions. In chapter 4 we will examine ethnographic research methods, focusing on qualitative observation of natural situations or settings. Throughout the chapter we will see how qualitative data is gathered via participant observation and in-depth interviews, analyzed via conceptual coding, and written up to contribute to sociological knowledge.

In chapters 5 through 9 we will analyze the data gathered from these ethnographic research methods. In chapter 5 we are introduced to students' first years of college and the structural, cultural, and interactional dynamics that often contribute irresponsible risk-taking and educational floundering. We also investigate the formal and medical university sanctions used to manage student substance use and discuss the manifest and latent consequences of these punitive control mechanisms. Chapter 6 introduces us to the *dual career*, or the intertwined paths of school and partying that constituted college life and emerging adulthood. We will see how students' transitioned into their final years of college with a burgeoning understanding that their success was contingent on a reciprocal balance between their academic responsibilities and their social lives. Chapter 7 examines alcohol intoxication as it relates to social psychology and focuses on changes in self that college students experience during and after a drinking episode. Chapter 8 focuses on the accomplishment of femininity and the "doing" of gender to exhibit the potency of informal regulations through peer groups. In chapter 9 we examine the transformation in social control for students, the law, the community, and the State fostered by a thriving legal-medical marijuana dispensary system. Specifically, exploring the motivations students have to become marijuana cardholders and the ramifications this emerging social process has on students' perceptions of agency, responsibility, and the conventional social order. Finally, we examine how students learn to regulate and moderate their drug and alcohol use through informal control processes such as peer networks, gender norms, and academic demands. Overall, throughout this book we will discuss how informal methods of social regulation, fostered through cultural or structural shifts or learned through peers and individual experience, provide more effective guidance and socialization than formal controls for emerging adults throughout their collegiate careers.

Chapter One

Sorry for Partying

I am sitting in a mandated treatment class at Campus University. This 13-week harm reduction/substance abuse course is the final strike for students who have been cited or arrested for drug and/or alcohol use on more than one occasion. It's the first day of class, and these ten strangers sit in chairs, in a circle, looking uncomfortable and displeased. Certainly, none of them are thrilled taking two hours out of their Wednesday night, not to mention the mandatory course costs them each $450. Furthermore, most are on mandatory drug testing and have paid hundreds upon hundreds of dollars in fines, court costs, and class fees. Since it's the first night of class, the health practitioner in charge, Amanda, who works for the university health center, asks the students to give their name, a brief bio, and what charges brought them to this treatment class. There are ten students, and they begin their stories.

Jacob is a young, white male, just like the rest of the "patients" in this treatment class. There is only one woman in the group of ten. He is a tall, lanky sophomore and a mechanical engineering major. He seems outgoing; he likes to go out with his friends, but seems very dedicated to his studies. Two weeks into his freshman year, campus police caught him smoking a bowl on the quad outside of his dorm with friends. Later that semester, he hosted a beer pong party in his room with a few friends and was caught by his Resident Assistant and cited for an alcohol violation. During his second semester, Campus Safety Officers came to his room claiming they smelled weed. Jacob told the group that no one was actually smoking in his room, and at this point, I really do not see why he would lie. But, the CSOs called campus police and he was arrested and taken to jail for possession after his room was searched and a small amount of marijuana and paraphernalia was found.

Jacob is currently on probation for a year. He is drug tested three times a month for a semester[1] has paid for and taken three other substance abuse classes, and with conduct fees and drug testing has paid around $1200. He claims he is currently maintaining complete sobriety.

Marc is a shy, sophomore engineering major. He typically looks at the ground when he talks, but laughed a lot and opened up by the end of the session. He says that he doesn't like to get wasted or go out to big parties, but would rather stay in his room, chill with friends, and smoke some weed and have a few beers. Marc was cited for three separate marijuana incidents in the dorms his freshman year. Although he possesses a medical marijuana license, he decided to live in the dorms so as not to miss out on the social aspects of being a freshman. He wanted to meet friends and thought the dorms would offer that outlet. Bad idea. He was cited twice for having marijuana in his dorm room, and once for having an open beer can. The same Campus Safety Officer called the police for all three of his offenses. He is convinced they targeted his room by peering through his first-floor windows and red-flagged him because he had his medical card. Marc is on drug testing three times a month, has logged countless hours of community service, $700 in fines and fees, and is currently on probation.

Tate, a sophomore and environmental studies major is very much into the outdoors and spends much of his time camping and rock climbing. He was caught having a beer in his dorm by his RA, cited for smoking a bowl on the campus quad by university police, and then cited for having weed in his dorm room. All during his freshman year. For his third offense, the Campus Safety Officers knocked on his door insisting they smelled weed emanating from his room. He was not smoking. They called the police, his room was searched, and he offered up a small amount of weed he had hidden so the officers would stop ransacking his dormitory. He was arrested. Currently he is on four months of testing and he is tested three times a month. He has taken and paid for three substance abuse classes for around $1000, done sixty hours of community service, and is on suspension in abeyance.[2]

Jordan, is a skier from the east coast, he is the most outgoing of the group and gets the others laughing and talking. He is a sophomore and a business major who also has his medical marijuana card, but chose to live in the dorms to meet friends. His first citation was because his roommate was charged with an alcohol violation when Jordan was not in the room or even involved. For his second offense, he was returning to his dorm room late at night when his RA approached him in the hallway as he was unlocking his door, asked if he was high, and told him to empty his pockets. For some reason he complied to his RAs request and was written up for possession of marijuana. For his third offense, he was on a campus parking lot before a concert smoking a joint. He was approached by a person who asked for a "hit." He obliged. Too bad he didn't recognize his RA. Although he claimed entrapment (jokingly), he was written up for a third time. Luckily he was not arrested. Currently, he is being drug tested every day, has countless hours of community service, and has paid $1000 in class fees and fines. When Amanda asks Jordon how quickly he got into trouble after arriving at the university, he laughs and shakes his head in disbelief: "I was suspended in four days, all I can say is, sorry for partying."

(Field Notes August 28, 2012).

---

[1] Regardless of whether students are drug tested intermittently or daily, they are required to call the off-campus testing center every morning (Monday through Friday) to hear if their assigned color requires them to be tested that day. Tests range from breathalyzers, to urines testing, and sensitive EtG (Ethyl Glucuronide) tests.

[2] Suspension in abeyance means that a student is technically suspended from the university, but due to mitigating circumstances the suspension is deferred, and the student is allowed to continue university activities. According to the university, suspension in abeyance is a student's final chance to prove he or she can operate responsible within the community.

Sorry For Partying

The college years fall within a unique developmental stage referred to as **emerging adulthood,** a distinct period of the life course (18 to 29) occurring between the adolescent and adult years (Arnett 2000, 2004). The result of widespread secondary education and a later age of marriage in late-modern societies, emerging adulthood involves a life stage of self-exploration, risk taking, identity formation, changing affiliations (i.e., peers and romantic attachments), and shifts toward independence and adult sufficiency that frequently occurs in the college environment (Arnett 2000; 2004; Ravert 2009; Shulenberg et al. 2004; 2006).

The developmental stage of emerging adulthood is a useful conceptual framework in which to understand substance use during the college years (Arnett 2005). The central features of emerging adulthood (the age of identity explorations, the age of instability, the age of self focus, the age of feeling in-between, and the age of possibilities) all offer explanations on why substance use and abuse may be prevalent during this time period.

Identity exploration: It is during emerging adulthood when young adults are figuring out their own identity (particularly in the realm of love and work). With love and relationships, individuals "begin to ask themselves more seriously what kind of person they wish to form a long-term relationship with, which requires them to know who they really are and what qualities are most important to them in a (hopefully) life-long romantic partner" (Arnett 2005:239). With work, emerging adults ponder their long term goals and career paths, which requires them to know themselves, their abilities, interests, and work they might aspire to as adults. During this time substance use may increase with an absence of commitment to love and work. Students may use alcohol and other substances to cope with identity confusion and students may crave "experience" or "sensation" seeking as they try out different identities and lifestyle options before settling into adult roles and relationships (Arnett 2005).

The age of instability: The college years are associated with great instability and is arguably the most unstable period of life (Arnett 2005). As students experiment with different identities, this stage is associated with "frequent changes in their lives in terms of love partners, jobs, and educational status (dropping in and out of college, changing college majors)" (Arnett 2005:241). The anxiety, stress, and even sadness associated with such instability often elevates substance use as students use to alleviate negative moods as a form of self-medication.

The self-focused age: To say emerging adults are self-focused does not mean they are selfish or egocentric (Arnett 2005). It is the fact that college students often gain independence from family, teachers, and past obligations and commitments of adolescence. Students are free to make independent decisions regarding their money, time, leisure, and relationships. In this context, free from family and past social groups, social controls that once constrained risk behaviors may weaken. Furthermore, students may spend more time with friends who promote substance use.

Feeling in-between: Students may have a "foot in both worlds," feeling neither fully adolescent or fully adult. Thus, emerging adults may feel that "because they are no longer adolescents, they are capable of deciding for themselves whether or not to use substances. But if they also feel that they are not yet adults, they may not feel committed to adult standards of behavior and an adult level of responsibility" (Arnett 2005:246). In this context, students may experience a feeling of freedom or "time-out" to engage in heavy alcohol use and other substances that will be less acceptable later in adulthood.

The age of possibilities: Emerging adulthood is a time when students can make dramatic changes in their lives, the future looks bright, and they experience optimism for success and happiness. In this context, students may participate in risky substance use because they do not understand or foresee the potential negative consequences of their present behavior.

Thus, for college students and emerging adults, self and identity exploration often entails a high degree of experimentation, including meeting different kinds of people, questioning their belief system, engaging in promiscuous sex, and using drugs (Arnett 2000; Dworkin 2005). Experimentation with drugs and alcohol is often considered bad, or behavior to be avoided, but as Ravert (2009:531) and numerous scholars note, "some degree of risk-taking can be functional, goal-directed, and necessary in order to establish autonomy and successfully transition to adulthood" (Dworkin 2005; Jessor 1991; Shulenberg and Zarrett 2006).

Given such purposeful experimentation (Dworkin 2005; Ravert 2009), risk-taking behavior (Arnett 2000), and time spent with peers, it should come as no surprise that the 18 to 29 age group reports the highest levels of all types of drug use (Johnston, O'Malley, and Bachman 2003). According to Schulenberg et al. (2004), an abundance of free time, new found freedoms, meeting people through school and work, and experiencing life as an adult for the first time tends to promote widespread experimentation, including with drugs.

Illicit polydrug use is a common behavior among American college students (Feigelman, Gorman, and Lee 1998; Martin, Clifford and Clapper 1992; McCabe et al. 2006; Quintero 2009; Schorling et al. 1994). Recent studies suggest that increasing numbers of university students are experimenting with a variety of psychoactive substances such as marijuana, cocaine, hallucinogens, and prescription drugs (Ford and Schroeder 2009; Gledhill-Hoyt et al. 2000; Mohler-Kuo, Lee, and Wechsler 2003; O'Grady et al. 2008; O'Malley and Johnston 2002).

Illegal drug use among college students pales in comparison to alcohol consumption. Researchers have traditionally reported high rates of drinking, termed "binge" or "heavy episodic" drinking among young adults on college campuses across the United States (Jackson, Sher, and Park 2006; Sher and Rutledge 2007; Wechsler and Austin 1998; Wechsler and Wuethrich 2002). Other studies have reported that binge drinking is associated with the use of a variety of illicit drugs, reporting a strong relationship between the frequency of binge drinking and past-year use of marijuana, cigarettes, amphetamines, LSD, and other hallucinogens (Strote, Lee, and Wechsler 2002).

Researchers argue (Dworkin 2005; Jessor and Jessor 1977; Ravert 2009; Schulenberg and Zarrett 2006) that some level of substance use during the years of emerging adulthood is normative, expected, and positive in the developmental process. Along the life-course, experimentation and risky behaviors involving drug and alcohol use are primarily located in this 18 to 29 year-old range that comprises a period between adolescence and young adulthood (Arnett 1991, 2000, 2004). The emerging adult years are a result of cultural and structural shifts in late modern society such as widespread enrollment in secondary education, later age of marriage, and minimal family obligations. Due to such changes, emerging adulthood is considered a unique and distinct period of life that postpones the transition to adult roles and responsibilities. These youthful years involve developmental endeavors related to educational attainment and career advancement, establishing social networks and romantic relationships, and experimenting with identities and exploring the self (Arnett 2000, 2004; Schulenberg, Bryant, and O'Malley 2004; Schulenberg and Zarrett 2006). In this period of the life course, emerging adults shift from the dependence and control of adolescence toward, but not into, the independence, freedom, and self-sufficiency of adulthood.

It is during these exploratory and self-directed years that college/ university students engage in experimentation with drugs and alcohol. Arnett (2000:475) posits that 'emerging adults' risk behaviors can be understood as part of their identity exploration, that is, as one reflection of the desire to obtain a wide range of experiences before settling down into roles and responsibilities of adult life." The transition to university life fosters experimentation as students experience greater independence and freedom from parental constraints. Furthermore, the collegiate culture encourages risky behavior as students report all night parties, promiscuous sex, and drug use. In this context, college students are susceptible to cross the unclear boundaries between healthy experimentation and hazardous risk taking behavior (Dworkin 2005).

It is important to note that college students can experience both positive benefits and negative consequences as a result of their drug and alcohol use. For emerging adults, testing limits, partaking in risky activities, and finding the streams of consciousness they value is important to their identity development and adult maturation. For example, research has shown that occasional heavy drinking can increase social bonds and intimacy between students, but frequent heavy drinking is associated with relationship problems, less intimacy, and other negative consequences (Nezlek et al. 1994; Vander Ven 2011). Alcohol may act as a medium of exchange where college students come to form bonds, friendship, and identity. While consistent heavy drinking may be damaging to mental health, relationships, and social bonds, the occasional "night out" may in fact integrate an individual into certain social circles while building camaraderie and solidarity with others.

Thus, the line between beneficial and dangerous is often blurred (Jessor and Jessor 1977; Jessor 1991; Lightfoot 1997). As Dworkin (2005:221) states: "Experimentation behaviors are not inherently dangerous or problematic, rather, negative outcomes occur under certain conditions. It is unlikely that a behavior will be either entirely problematic or conventional. It is possible to engage in both behaviors simultaneously." For example, not all drug using behavior is equivalent. There is a distinction between smoking marijuana as a reward for finishing homework and hitting a bong ten times a day between classes. There is a difference between casually drinking beers over a game of pool and shot-gunning beers, doing keg stands, and competing in case races. The divergent nature of these drug using behaviors must be understood within the cultural contexts they occur and in relation to normative social controls mediated through social learning processes. To understand how college students come to increasingly control their drug and alcohol use, the structural, cultural, and interactional changes they experience through the college years must be examined. The social controls that students both develop and experience in relation to their substance use are important because they reflect how emerging adults relate to formal and informal control mechanisms, and how they might socialize their peers or even their children to balance their social or recreational activities with obligations of education and employment. The control shifts students experience throughout their college years are varied and distinct among different students and their primary networks. However, fundamental patterns emerge as students' transition into freshman year and progress through college and the emerging adult years.

Binge Drinking Criticisms

As noted in the previous section, illegal drug use among college students pales in comparison to alcohol consumption. Researchers have traditionally reported high rates of drinking, termed "binge" or "heavy episodic" drinking among young adults on college campuses across the United States (Jackson, Sher, and Park 2006; Sher and Rutledge 2007; Wechsler and Austin 1998; Wechsler and Wuethrich 2002). Other studies have reported that binge drinking is associated with the use of a variety of illicit drugs, reporting a strong relationship between the frequency of binge drinking and past-year use of marijuana, cigarettes, amphetamines, LSD, and other hallucinogens (Strote, Lee, and Wechsler 2002).

These studies generally report alarming rates of binge drinking. For example, Henry Wechsler and his colleagues from the Harvard College Alcohol Study (CAS) noted that over 44 percent of students reported binge drinking in the previous two weeks, and these binge drinkers accounted for 91 percent of all the alcohol consumed by college students (Wechsler et al. 1999). Other studies suggest that nearly 85 percent of college students reported a binge-drinking episode in the previous 90 days (Vik et al. 2000) and others indicate that two in five college students are binge drinkers (O'Malley and Johnston 2002; Wechsler et al. 1998).

These studies generally define university drinking as major public health concern, focusing on the negative consequences (e.g., blackouts, hangovers, missing class, falling grades, regrettable behavior, physical fights, and police encounters) of student binge drinking practices (Durkin, Wolfe, and Clark 2005; Ham and Hope 2003; Wechsler and Wuethrich 2002). For example, in the first CAS study, and similarly thereafter, Wechsler and colleagues (1994) reported that frequent binge drinkers were 25 times more likely than non-binge drinkers to have experienced five or more alcohol-related consequences such as getting a hangover, missing class, getting injured, doing something regretful, falling behind in school work, forgetting what they did, arguing with friends, engaging in unprotected sexual activity, damaging property, getting in trouble with the law, or requiring treatment for an alcohol overdose. In 2002, Hingson and colleagues reported more startling binge drinking consequences. In their "Call to Action" press release they stated that 1,400 college students between the ages of 18-24 die each year from alcohol-related unintentional injuries, including motor vehicle crashes. The researchers went on to state that 500,000 students are injured, 600,000 are assaulted, 70,000 are victims of sexual assault, 25 percent have academic problems, and 150,000 have health-related problems.

These statistics are particularly troubling, and if accurate, college applications should contain a Surgeon General's Warning. However, these numbers and the manner in which these studies have been reported have come under fire from students, university officials, alcohol educators, and treatment specialists. To begin, the manner in which these number are reported by researchers and discussed by the media, are subject of controversy, as (Haines 1996:12-13) explains:

When alcohol research and assessment data are presented, the media
frequently spin stories in a negative light, making undesirable behavior seem
more prominent than it actually is and reinforcing misperceptions that support
binge drinking. For example, the Wall Street Journal, December 7, 1994, ran the
following headline and lead sentence in response to the press release
distributed by the Harvard School of Public Health announcing the results of
Wechsler's research (1994).

"Binge" Drinking at Nation's Colleges Is Widespread, a Harvard Study Finds
BOSTON–Almost half of all students surveyed at 140 U.S. colleges admitted to
"binge" drinking, leading to everything from fights to vandalism according
to ...

Instead, the study could have resulted in this headline and story lead:

Majority of College Students Drink Moderately or Not at All, a Harvard
Study Finds BOSTON–More than half of all students surveyed at 140
U.S. colleges reported moderate drinking as the campus norm, resulting
in relatively small numbers (only 9 percent) who get hurt or vandalize,
according to...

It should also be noted that these numbers seem alarming due to the
operationalization of binge drinking as a quantitative measure. Binge
drinking is defined as 4 or 5 standard drinks for men, and 3 to 4 for
women, in a single session within the previous two weeks (Wechsler et al.
1994). This definition problematizes a common behavior across the United
States. It sounds much more frightening to state that 44 percent of college
students are binge drinkers, as opposed to stating that 44 percent of college
students consumed 4 or 5 drinks in a row, sometime in the past two weeks.
Furthermore, binge drinking is quite common among most strata of U.S.
adults, including those 26 years or older (Naimi et al. 2003). Naimi and

colleagues (2003:73) reported that while those aged 18 to 29 years reported the highest number of binge drinking episodes per capita, "70 percent of binge drinking episodes were reported among those 26 years or older, and approximately half of binge drinking episodes were reported among moderate drinkers." It is this *normalcy* of drinking five or more drinks in a session across the U.S. population that scholars and practitioners find problematic (Dimeff et al. 1995). Furthermore, when scientists and researchers **operationalize** the concept of binge drinking, there has been wide ranging definitions. As (Kennedy and Kennedy 2010:108) illustrate:

- Sipping more than five alcoholic drinks in a row at least three times in a month.

- Consuming over half the government's recommended number of units for a week in one session (thus, binge drinking would be defined as drinking, in one session, 10 units for men and seven units for women).

- Consuming more than five drinks on a single occasion.

- Consuming eight or more units for men and six or more units for women on at least one day in a week.

- Consuming two-thirds of a bottle of wine for women or four pints of beer for men.

- An extended period of time, usually two days or more, during which a person repeatedly drinks to intoxication, giving up usual activities and obligations.

- Consumption of five drinks for males and four drinks for females during one drinking experience in the previous two-week period.

Finally, scholars also find that binge drinking as a phrase is not one that students identify or agree with; instead students regard drinking frequency, level of intoxication, and drunken outcomes as indicative of potential problems rather than the number of drinks they consume (Goodhart et al. 2003). Also, when binge drinking refers simply to a set number of drinks, it fails as a measure to account for the social contexts where drinking occurs, gender differences, strength and types of drinks, drinking games, and the norms and informal rules that influence student drinking. Critics of the term also argue that it fails to account for the size of the drink, body weight of the drinker, and number of drinks consumed in relation to the length (i.e., number of hours) of the drinking session.

These studies have consistently been scrutinized for problems related to validity, methodology, data mining, and reporting practices. For example, Ralph Hingson and colleagues have been discredited as reporting "guesswork" due to poor methodology.[1] As Blimling (2009:4) reported, "anyone reading the newspaper article[2] would conclude that the nation was annually losing 1,400 college-age students to drunk driving or alcohol poisoning and that some enterprising researcher had taken the time to actually count the college students who had died due to misuse of alcohol. That's not what happened; no one actually counted anything." A more methodologically sound study, conducted by *USA Today* (Davis and DeBarros 2006) found that only 36 alcohol-related deaths occur annually. According to David J. Hanson:[3]

> USA Today newspaper conducted an analysis of college student deaths in the United States over a five-year period beginning January 1, 2000. After a careful investigation, it identified 786 college student deaths. It then eliminated from analysis those whose deaths were completely unrelated to their status as college students, reducing the number to 620. Overall, illness, homicides and traffic accidents are the leading causes of death among four-year college students, as they are for all young people age 15 to 24.

Suicide apparently causes as many deaths as alcohol abuse and drugs, although suicide is often not disclosed. The analysis found that the number of deaths among freshmen was disproportionately high. This included deaths from natural causes, suicide, and falls from windows, balconies and rooftops. Twenty percent of the freshman deaths were alcohol-related. It appears that about 25 college students at four-year institutions die each year in alcohol-related incidents. If that number is expanded at the same rate to include students at both two- and four-year colleges, it becomes 36.

Henry Wechsler has been coined as "Doctor Doom" (Hoover 2002), and researchers and university officials have challenged the validity of his findings, called attention to his data mining practices, questioned his use of marketing firms for maximizing publicity, and argued that his interpretations exaggerate the severity of the college alcohol problem.

Such startling and frightening statistics regarding college youth attach emotion to the term binge drinking, inflate the actual harm college students experience, and create panic among parents and administrators. According to Hoover (2002:6), "binge drinking labels too many students as problem drinkers, creating an exaggerated picture of alcohol abuse on campus. A number of researchers and colleges, as well as the Journal of Studies of Alcohol, have refused to use or endorse the term; they say it is misleading." By focusing only the problems and consequences students sometimes experience from heavy drinking, researchers ignore the benefits (Dworkin 2005; Ravert 2009; Vander Ven 2011) students experience through substance use and make negative consequences seem the rule rather than the exception. Exaggerating the rates, risks, and negative outcomes of students' partying behaviors neglects the fact that harmful consequences associated with heavy drinking are *not* occurring for the majority of students (Perkins 2002). Finally, by stigmatizing alcohol use, researchers and the public fail to recognize that alcohol itself is not the problem, but the abuse of alcohol. The punitive zero-tolerance approaches that result from alarming studies and the emotional fervor attached to the term binge drinking hinder practical alcohol education and lessons of moderation. As David J. Hanson explains:

> Teaching about responsible use does not require student consumption of alcohol any more than teaching them world geography requires them to visit Nepal, or teaching them civics requires that they run for office or vote in presidential elections. We teach students civics to prepare them for the day when they can vote and assume other civic responsibilities if they choose to do so. Because either drinking in moderation or abstaining should both be equally acceptable options for adults, we must prepare students for either choice. To do otherwise is both irresponsible and ineffective if not counterproductive.

Binge Drinking as a Social Problem

Although "binge drinking" has a somewhat controversial history, this is not to say that risky alcohol use is without negative consequences. On the contrary, years of research has illustrated the myriad problems related to heavy episodic drinking among college students. Heavy episodic drinking (HED), commonly known as "binge drinking," is common across America's colleges and universities and still gains much attention among parents, administrators, professors, researchers, and the general public. Numerous surveys such as the Monitoring the Future Study, the Harvard College Alcohol Study, the National Epidemiological Survey on Alcohol and Related Conditions, the National Survey on Drug Use and Health, and the Core Institute Project (CORE), provide a picture of the scope and consequences of college drinking.

- According to the Core Alcohol and Drug Survey (2010), 83.9% of students surveyed consumed alcohol in the past year, 71.2% consumed alcohol in the past 30 days, 65.7% of underage students consumed alcohol in the previous 30 days, and 45.9% of students reported binge drinking in the previous two weeks.

- It has been estimated that 35% of college students (43% of men and 30% of women) meet the criteria for binge drinking over a two-week period. Other national surveys report higher rates with 44% of college students (49% of men and 41% of men) meeting the standard criteria as heavy episodic drinkers (Johnston et al. 2013; Wechsler 2002).

- Research has found that youth and college students are drinking much more than the traditional binge drinking threshold. In a sample of college freshmen it was found that 33.7% of women (consumed 4+ drinks) and 40.6% of men (consumed 5+ drinks) in a row in the previous two weeks. The standard definition of binge drinking. But, 8.2% of women (consumed 8+ drinks) and 19.9% of men (consumed 10+ drinks) in a row in the previous two weeks. Furthermore, 1.8% of women (consumed 12+ drinks) and 7.6% of men (consumed 15+ drinks) in a row in the previous two weeks (Patrick et al. 2013; Read et al. 2008; White et al. 2006).

Heavy episodic drinking results in negative consequences for both students who consume alcohol and those students who do not:

- Frequent bing drinkers are seventeen times more likely to miss class, ten times more likely to vandalize property, and eight times more likely to get hurt or injured as a result of their drinking when compared to students who drink, but do not binge (Wechsler 2002). Furthermore, "60% of heavy binge drinkers miss class and 42% get behind in their schoolwork…and consuming more than five drinks per occasions is associated with a half grade lower GPA" (Wechsler 2002:158).

- According to Hingson et al. 2009, approximately 646,000 physical assaults, 97,000 sexual assaults, 599,000 unintentional injuries can be linked to alcohol use among college students every year. It is also possible that more than 1,800 college students between the ages of 18-24 die annually from alcohol-related unintentional injuries, including motor-vehicle crashes (Krieger et al. 2018; Merrill and Carey 2016).

- According to national estimates 10 percent of non-binge drinkers, 27 percent of occasional binge drinkers, and 54 percent of frequent binge drinkers reported at least one incident of blacking out within the past year; forgetting where they were or what they were doing while drinking (Hingson et al. 2002; Krieger et al. 2018; Merrill and Carey 2016; White and Hingson 2013; Wechsler 2002).

- Approximately 5 percent of 4-year college students are involved with police or campus security as a result of drinking. It is also estimated that 110,000 students between the ages of 18-24 are arrested for an alcohol-related violation every year (Hingson et al. 2002; Krieger et al. 2018; Merrill and Carey 2016; Wechsler 2002).

- Overall, drinking levels on college campuses have remained relatively stable over the last 30 years. For college students, the consequences of excessive drinking can include: overdoses and death, sexual and physical assaults, injuries, car crashes, lower grades, mental health issues, and abuse and dependence. Furthermore, secondhand effects of binge drinking also impact students who do not binge drink or are nondrinkers (Hingson et al. 2009; White and Hingson 2013).

Binge Drinking as a Moral Panic

Another sociological lens in which to view the immense concern over binge drinking is through the concept of a moral panic. A central topic in the field of sociology, a **moral panic** describes a process whereby society becomes captivated by a moral threat from the actions or behaviors of a particular social group. During a moral panic a significant number of people come to believe that a group of "evil-doers" poses a threat to the moral order and must be stopped (Cohen 1972; Goode and Ben-Yehuda 1994). A moral panic is based upon widespread fear, often irrational, over the behavior of a certain group seen as threatening the values and/or safety of the community. During a moral panic the media focuses on sensational, atypical and "horror" grabbing stories arousing public attention and stoking public fear. Politicians and lawmakers become involved and new laws and regulations are often passed targeting those responsible for the moral panic. Thus, moral panics result in new forms of social control.

The concept of moral panic was coined by Jock Young in his 1971 study of 'drug-takers,' that examined the bohemian counterculture in 1960s Notting Hill, England and how police labeling and enforcement of hippies increased their crime and drug use. The concept was further popularized by sociologist Stanley Cohen, who, in his 1972 book *Folk Devils and Moral Panics* studied public reactions to fights between "mod" and "rocker" youth subcultures of 1960s and 1970s England. Cohen used the term moral panic as a way to describe the reactions of the media, the public, and social control agents to the youthful subcultures he was studying. Referring to moral panics, he stated:

> A condition, episode, person or group of persons emerges to become defined as a threat to societal values and interests; its nature presented in a stylized and stereotypical fashion by the mass media; the moral barricades are manned by editors, bishops, politicians, and other right-thinking people; socially accredited experts pronounce their diagnoses and solutions; ways of coping are evolved or...resorted to; the condition then disappears, submerges, or deteriorates and becomes more visible. Sometimes the subject of the panic is quite novel and at other times it is

something which has been in existence long enough, but suddenly appears in the limelight. Sometimes the panic passes over and is forgotten, except in folklore and collective memory; at other times it has more serious and long-lasting repercussions and might produce such changes as those in legal and social policy or even in the way society conceives itself (Cohen 1971:9).

To breakdown Cohen's original thoughts on moral panics we see a processual model unfold:

- The initial behavior is labeled deviant by claimsmakers.

- Information is diffused to wider society via the primary definers and media.

- There is a negative social reaction amongst the general public.

- The deviant group become isolated resisting the claims about the moral panic, often becoming more deviant.

- Increased social control, harsher punishments, new laws.

- The situations spirals out of control, or disappears, and is potentially forgotten. However, moral panics can also be pervasive, enduring and result in social change.

Cohen identifies four groups that are integral in constructing the moral panic: **mass media**, **moral entrepreneurs**, the **control culture** and the **public** (Critcher 2008). Of central concern to Cohen (1972) was the role of the mass media in creating moral panics, **folk devils** and **deviance amplification**. **Folk devils** comprise the 'deviant' group in the moral panic, representing the threat to the moral order, labelled as subversive, and often scapegoated or blamed for social problems. The role of the media and social control agents also results in **deviance amplification** as relatively minor deviant behavior is amplified into increasingly severe forms of criminality and/or deviance. As the mass media reports continuous stories on this deviant behavior, often stories that would not be news worthy in the past, the behavior becomes seen as typical and epidemic in the mind of the public. The public demands action from social control agents, who, through new laws, harsh enforcement, and increased resources further criminalize the 'deviant' group pushing their behavior further to the fringes of legitimate society. These elements involve a positive feedback loop where the initial deviance is amplified and spirals out of control as media coverage, social control agents, and public outcry feed off one another perpetuating the moral panic.

In 1994, Erich Goode and Nachkann Ben-Yehuda expanded on Cohen's original formulations and identified five defining 'elements of criteria' of a moral panic (1994:33):

•   **Concern:** There is a heightened level of concern over the behavior of a certain group or category of people. In this stage we begin to see media magnification, public opinion polls, anecdotal statistics, and lobbying by special interest groups (Goode and Ben-Yehuda 1994).

•   **Hostility**: There is increased hostility toward the group engaging in the behavior. These individuals are considered a threat and an enemy of respectable society. An identifiable group or segment of society comes to be viewed as responsible for the threat. (Goode and Ben-Yehuda 1994).

•   **Consensus**: To qualify as a moral panic, there must be widespread agreement or consensus that this is a real, serious threat related to the misbehaving and wrongdoing of the defined group. The entire population of a society does not need to feel this way, moral panics are a matter of degree, "some gripping the vast majority of the members of a given society at a given time, others creating concern only among certain groups or categories" (Goode and Ben-Yehuda 1994:39). However, the number needs to be substantial to be considered a moral panic.

- **Disproportionality**: There is a belief among society that there are more individuals involved in the deviant behavior or the behavior in question than actually are. There is common agreement that the "threat, danger, or damage said to be caused by the behavior is far more substantial than…what a realistic appraisal could sustain" (Goode and Ben-Yehuda 1994:40).

- **Volatility**: Moral panics appear fairly suddenly, disappear, reappear, and then can suddenly subside forever. However, some "moral panics may become routinized or institutionalized, that is, after the panic has run its course, the moral concern about the target behavior results in, or remains in place in the form of social movement organizations, legislation, enforcement practices…or practices punishing transgressors" (Goode and Ben-Yehuda 1994:41).

Conclusion

Although substance use can have adverse outcomes and consequences, and high-risk drinking is dangerous, the majority of young people do not experience negative consequences as result of participating in risky behavior (Arnett 1991). Furthermore, experimental substance use during late adolescence and early adulthood can hold developmental benefits for students in areas of peer bonding, independence, and identity experimentation (Chassin, Presson, and Sherman 1989; Shulenberg, Maggs and O'Malley 2003; Shulenberg et al. 2004). Some degree of substance use for young adults during the college years is argued to be expected and normative (Shulenberg and Zarrett 2006). Ravert (2009) found that social outings such as "partying" and "drinking" as an aspect of emerging adult college life were associated with establishing and maintaining relationships, both social and romantic.

The university years are marked by educational pursuit, identity development, self-exploration, risk-taking, substance use, and its *potential* for negative outcomes and consequences. Throughout this text we will examine the various modes of social control that mediate students' positive and negative drug experiences. We will also analyze their social demands and academic responsibilities and explore the formal and informal social controls that influence their substance use during the university years of emerging adulthood.

---

[1] For a thorough critique of Hingson et al. (2002) study, see (Blimling 2009).

[2] In 2002, USA Today ran an article by Michelle Healy with the headline "College Drinking Kills 1,400 a Year, Study Finds." The article was based on a report by Hingson et al. 2002 and the NIAAA, "A Call to Action: Changing the Culture of Drinking at U.S. Colleges." (Blimling 2009).

[3] For more on alcohol myths and facts, problems with current definitions of binge drinking, and media depictions of student alcohol use, please see the fantastic website create by David J. Hanson, Ph.D., Professor Emeritus Sociology of the State University of New York at Potsdam: http://www2.potsdam.edu/hansondj/AboutYourHost.html

Notes and Discussion Questions:

References

Arnett, Jeffrey Jensen. 2000. "Emerging Adulthood: A Theory of Development from the Late Teens Through the Twenties." *American Psychologist* 55(5):469–80.

Arnett, Jeffrey Jensen. 2004. "Emerging Adulthood: The Winding Road from the Late Teens Through the Twenties." New York: Oxford University Press.

Arnett, Jeffrey Jensen. 2005. " The Developmental Context of Substance Use in Emerging Adulthood." The Journal of Drug Issues 33(2): 235-254.

Arnett, Jeffrey Jensen. 2016. "College Students as Emerging Adults: The Developmental Implications of the College Context." *Emerging Adulthood* 4(3):219–22.

Blimling, Gregory S. 2009. "White Blankets May Make You Smarter and Other Questionable Social Science Findings." *About Campus* 9(3):2–9.

Chassin, Laurie L., Clark C. Presson, and Steven J. Sherman. 1989. "Constructive versus Destructive Deviance in Adolescent Health-Related Behaviors." *Journal of Youth and Adolescence* 18(3):245-62.

Cohen, Stanley. 1972. *Folk Devils and Moral Panics*. London: MacGibbon and Kee.
Davis, Robert and Anthony DeBarros. 2006. "First Year in College is the Riskiest." *USA Today*.

Core Institute. Core Alcohol and Drug Survey Long From—Form 194: Executive Summary. Carbondale, IL: Southern Illinois University Carbondale: 2010.

Critcher, Chas. 2008. "Moral Panic Analysis: Past, Present, and Future." *Sociology Compass* 2(4): 1127-1144.

Dimeff, Linda A., Kilmer J., John S. Baer, and Alan G. Marlatt. 1995. "Binge Drinking in College." *Journal of the American Medical Association* 273:1904–03.

Durkin, Keith F., Timothy W. Wolfe, and Gregory A. Clark. 2005. "College Students and Binge Drinking: An Evaluation of Social Learning Theory." *Sociological Spectrum* 25(3):255–72.

Dworkin, Jodi. 2005. "Risk Taking as Developmentally Appropriate Experimentation for College Students." *Journal of Adolescent Research* 20(2): 219–41.

Feigelman, William, Bernard S. Gorman, and Julia A. Lee. 1998. "Binge Drinkers, Illicit Drug Users, and Polydrug Users: An Epidemiological Study of American Collegians." *Journal of Alcohol and Drug Education* 44(1): 47-69.

Ford, Jason A. and Ryan D. Schroeder. 2009. "Academic Strain and Non-Medical Use of Prescription Stimulants Among College Students." *Deviant Behavior* 30(1):26-53.

Gledhill-Hoyt, Jeana, Hang Lee, Jared Strote, and Henry Wechsler. 2000. "Increased Use of Marijuana and Other Illicit Drugs at U.S. Colleges in the 1990s: Results of Three National Surveys." *Addiction* 95(11):1655-67.

Goodhart, Fern Walter, Linda C. Lederman, Lea P. Stewart, and Lisa Laitman. 2003. "Binge Drinking: Not the Word of Choice." *Journal of American College Health* 52(1):44–46.

Haines, Michael. P. 1996. *A Social Norms Approach to Preventing Binge Drinking at Colleges and Universities.* Higher Education Center for Alcohol and Other Drug Prevention Newton, MA.

Ham, Lindsay S. and Debra A. Hope. 2003. "College students and problematic drinking: A review of the literature." *Clinical Psychology Review* 23(5):719–59.

Hingson, Ralph W., Wenxing Zha, and Elissa R. Weitzman. 2009. "Magnitude of and Trends in Alcohol-Related Mortality and Morbidity among U.S. College Students Ages 18-24, 1998-2005." *J. Stud. Alcohol Drugs Suppl.* (16):12–20.

Hingson, Ralph W., Timothy Heeren, Ronda C. Zakocs, Andrea Kopstein, and Henry Wechsler. 2002. "Magnitude of Alcohol-Related Mortality and Morbidity among US College Students Ages 18-24." *J. Stud. Alcohol* 63(2): 136–144.

Hoover, Eric. 2002. "Binge Thinking." *Chronicle of Higher Education* 49(11):1–11.

Jackson, Kristina M., Kenneth J. Sher, and Aesoon Park. 2005. "Drinking among College Students: Consumption and Consequences." *Recent Developments in Alcoholism* 17:85–117.

Janowitz, Morris. 1975. "Sociological Theory and Social Control." *American Journal of Sociology* 81(1):82-108.

Jessor, Richard and Shirley L. Jessor. 1977. *Problem Behavior and Psychosocial Development: a Longitudinal Study of Youth.* Waltham, MA: Academic Press.

Jessor, Richard. 1991. "Risk Behavior in Adolescence: A Psychosocial Framework for Understanding and Action." *Journal of Adolescent Health* 12(8):597–605.

Johnston, Lloyd D., Patrick M. O'Malley, and Jerald G. Bachman. 2003. *Demographic Subgroup Trends for Various Licit And Illicit Drugs 1975-2002.* Ann Arbor, MI: Institute for Social Research.

Johnston, Lloyd D., Patrick M. O'Malley, Jerald G. Bachman, and John E. Schulenberg. 2013. "Monitoring the Future National Results on Adolescent Drug Use: Overview of Key Findings, 2012."

Kennedy, Peter and Carole Kennedy. 2010. *Using Theory to Explore Health, Medicine and Society.* Policy Press.

Krieger, Heather, Chelsie M. Young, Amber M. Anthenien, and Clayton Neighbors. 2018. "The Epidemiology of Binge Drinking Among College-Age Individuals in the United States." *Alcohol Res.* 39(1):23–30.

Lightfoot, Cynthia. 1997. *The Culture of Adolescent Risk-Taking.* New York, NY: Guilford Press.

Martin, Christopher S., Patrick R. Clifford, and Rock L. Clapper. 1992. "Patterns and Predictors of Simultaneous and Concurrent Use of Alcohol, Tobacco, Marijuana, and Hallucinogens in First-Year College Students." *Journal of Substance Use* 4(3):319-26.

McCabe, Sean Estaban, James A. Cranford, Michele Morales, and Amy Young. 2006. "Simultaneous and Concurrent Polydrug Use of Alcohol and Prescription: Prevalence, Correlates, and Consequences." *Journal of Studies on Alcohol* 67(4):529-37.

Meier, Robert F. 1982. "Perspectives on the Concept of Social Control." *Annual Review of Sociology* 8:35-55.

Merrill, Jennifer E. and Kate B. Carey. 2016. "Drinking Over the Lifespan: Focus on College Ages." *Alcohol Res.* 38(1):103–114.

Mohler-Kuo, Meicho, Jae Eun Lee, and Henry Wechsler. 2003. "Trends in Marijuana and Other Illicit Drug Use Among College Students: Results From 4 Harvard School of Public Health College Alcohol Surveys: 1993-2001." *Journal of American College Health* 52: 17-24.

Naimi, Timothy S., Robert D. Brewer, Ali Mokdad, Clark Denny, Mary K. Serdula, and James S. Marks. 2003. "Binge Drinking Among U.S. Adults." *Journal of the American Medical Association* 289: 70-75.

Nezlek, J.B., Pilkington, C.J. & Bilbro, K.G. 1994. "Moderation in Excess: Bing Drinking And Social Interaction among College Students." *The Journal of Studies on Alcohol.* 55: 342-351.

O'Grady, Kevin E., Amelia M. Arria, Dawn M.B. Fitzelle, and Eric D. Wish. 2008. "Heavy Drinking and Polydrug Use Among College Students." *Journal of Drug Issues* 38(2):445-66.

O'Malley, Patrick M. and Lloyd D. Johnston. 2002. "Epidemiology of Alcohol and Other Drug Use Among American College Students." *Journal of Studies on Alcohol* 14:23-39.

Patrick, Megan E., John E. Schulenberg, Meghan E. Martz, Jennifer L. Maggs, Patrick M. O'Malley, and Lloyd D. Johnston. 2013. "Extreme Binge Drinking among 12th-Grade Students in the United States: Prevalence and Predictors." *JAMA Pediatr.* 167(11):1019–1025.

Perkins, H. Wesley. 2002. "Social Norms and the Prevention of Alcohol Misuse in Collegiate Contexts." *Journal of Studies on Alcohol* 63(14):164–72.

Quintero, Gilbert. 2009. "Controlled Release: A Cultural Analysis of Collegiate Polydrug Use." *Journal of Psychoactive Drugs* 41(1):39-47.

Ravert, Russell D. 2009. "'You're Only Young Once' Things College Students Report Doing Now Before It Is Too Late." *Journal of Adolescent Research* 24(3):376–96.

Read, Jennifer P., Melissa Beattie, Rebecca Chamberlain, and Jennifer E. Merrill. 2008. "Beyond the 'Binge' Threshold: Heavy Drinking Patterns and Their Association with Alcohol Involvement Indices in College Students." *Addict. Behav.* 33(2):225–234.

Schorling, John B, Margaret Gutgesell, Paul Klas, Deborah Smith, and Adrienne Keller. 1994. "Tobacco, Alcohol, and Other Drug Use Among College Students." *Journal of Substance Abuse* 6(1):105-15.

Schulenberg, John E., Jennifer L. Maggs, and Klaus Hurrelmann. 1997. *Health Risks and Developmental Transitions during Adolescence.* New York, NY: Cambridge University Press.

Schulenberg, John E., Alison L. Bryant, and Patrick M. O'Malley. 2004. "Taking hold of some kind of life: How developmental tasks relate to trajectories of well-being during the transition to adulthood." *Development and Psychopathology* 16(4):1119–40.

Schulenberg, John E. and Nicole R. Zarrett. 2006. "Mental Health During Emerging Adulthood: Continuity and Discontinuity in Courses, Causes, and Functions." Pp. 135–72 in *Emerging Adults in America: Coming of Age in the 21st Century.* Washington, DC: American Psychological Association.

Sher, Kenneth J. and Patricia C. Rutledge. 2007. "Heavy drinking across the transition to college: Predicting first-semester heavy drinking from precollege variables." *Addictive Behaviors* 32(4):819–35.

Vander Ven, Thomas. 2011. *Getting wasted: Why college students drink too much and party so hard*. New York: NYU Press.

Vik, Peter W., Patrice Carrello, Susan R. Tate, and Clinton Field. 2000. "Progression of consequences among heavy-drinking college students." *Psychology of Addictive Behaviors* 14(2):91–101.

Wechsler, Henry, Andrea Davenport, George Dowdall, and Barbara Moeykens. 1994. "Health and behavioral consequences of binge drinking in college: A national survey of students at 140 campuses." *JAMA: Journal of the American Medical Association* 272(21):1672–77.

Wechsler, Henry and S. B. Austin. 1998. "Binge drinking: the five/four measure." *Journal of Studies on Alcohol* 59(1) 122.

Wechsler, Henry, Beth E. Molnar, Andrea E. Davenport, and John S. Baer. 1999. "College alcohol use: A full or empty glass?" *Journal of American College Health* 47(6):247–52.

Wechsler, Henry and Bernice Wuethrich. 2002. *Dying to Drink: Confronting Binge Drinking on College Campuses*. Emmaus, PA: Rodale.

White, Aaron M., Courtney L. Kraus, and Harry Swartzwelder. 2006. "Many College Freshmen Drink at Levels Far beyond the Binge Threshold." *Alcohol. Clin. Exp. Res.* 30(6):1006–1010.

White, Aaron and Ralph Hingson. 2013. "The Burden of Alcohol Use: Excessive Alcohol Consumption and Related Consequences among College Students." *Alcohol Res.* 35(2):201–218.

Young, Jock. 1971. *The Drug Takers: Social Meanings of Drug Use*. London: MacGibbon and Kee.

Chapter Two

Informal Social Control

Social control is a central concept in sociology and its role in social life and social theory is both fundamental and complex (Chriss 2007; Innes 2003; Janowitz 1975; Meier 1982). As a concept of study, it is intertwined to matters of social order, or how different people, cultures, and societies organize their existence together. *The study of social control - namely, all those mechanisms and resources by which members of society attempt to assure the norm-conforming behavior of others - is almost as old as the discipline of sociology itself* (Chriss 2013). Social controls are essential for understanding modern life. Social scientists have always been attentive to social controls and how social actors "both intentionally and unintentionally, on a personal level and when acting in groups, come to conform with the norms and rules so that the social world can be understood as ordered, rather than chaotic" (Innes 2003:2).

Although sociologists rarely agree upon a universal definition of social control, **social controls are the resources that a society uses to insure compliance with norms.** Social controls are the mechanisms and social processes that regulate the conduct of social actors; they are the actions and reactions intended to alter people's behavior, especially those who are viewed as deviant or criminal (Black 1976; Cohen 1985; Criss 2007; Innes 2003). As a broad sociological concept, social control is often used synonymously with *social order* and *socialization* when referring to the ongoing production and maintenance of coordination and harmony across society. For example, Horowitz (1990) stated that "social control merges out of and serves to maintain ways of life and social practices of groups" (5), while MacIver and Page (1949) proposed that "social control is the study of how society patterns and regulates individual behavior"(3).

These definitions, and others like them, allude to processes of socialization and matters of both social control and the social order. Although intimately associated, these concepts are distinguishable. **Socialization is a prerequisite to social control; it is the production of self-controlled individuals. Human beings *must* learn about the informal rules and guidelines, the formal laws and regulations, and the associated sanctions of their social order so that they *can* be controlled.** The social order is the organized arrangements of society. According to Innes (2003:6):

> The concept of social order refers to the conditions of existence of society, in that every society intrinsically has a degree of organization and this is a social order. A social order is not static, but is constantly in process, being produced and reproduced by the combined attitudes, values, practices, institutions, and actions of its members. Thus social order is composed of the diverse sets of ideas, actions, and interactions, which in some fashion contribute to the ongoing constitution of societal organization. The boundaries between social ordering practices and social controls are neither fixed nor stable, and over time, shift their balance.

The definitional boundaries between social control and social order are flexible and overlapping. Social order is never merely the product of social controls and social ordering practices often perform social control functions. The social order is a product of both social controls and socialization; we are socialized into, and controlled by, society's core arrangements, its knowledge, values, beliefs, norms, establishments, and institutions. The deployment of social control is intended to preserve and protect this social order. **As social phenomena, socialization, social order, and social control operate together in dynamic fashion to produce the social realities of human life.** For the purposes of this book, the concept of social control is central, as the sum of human mechanisms that preserve, produce, and reproduce the social order by sanctioning and socializing those who deviate from the normative arrangements of social life.

Informal Controls

The traditional view of social control is reactive. A person engages in criminal/deviant **behavior** (e.g., burglary, robbery, assault) and the police are called, a person expresses an offensive **attitude** (e.g., sexism, racism, white nationalism) and their friends shun them, or a person is born with a deviant **condition** (e.g., stuttering) and they are encouraged to enroll in speech therapy. Social controls are often referred to as **sanctions**, as they involve responses to norm violations. **Norms** are the behavioral codes or guidelines that direct people into certain behaviors, attitudes, or self-presentations that conform to societal acceptability. There are three types of norms: **folkways, mores, and laws** (Morris 1956; Sumner 1906). **Folkways** are basic everyday norms regarding custom, tradition or politeness. Violations of folkway norms do not produce serious consequences, but a person might consider the violator as weird, rude, or naïve. **Mores** are norms based on general social consensus and more transgressors can experience serious social criticism because abiding by these norms are viewed as critical to social harmony. Mores are seen to threaten the social order and people who violate them may be considered immoral or dangerous to society. **Laws** are norms that are supported by codified social sanctions. People who violate them are subject to fines, arrest, imprisonment, and sometimes death.

Although every member of a society rarely agrees upon all norms, there is typically a general consensus regarding normative guidelines for behavior. **Sanctions can be positive or negative** as they are socially constructed expressions of approval or disapproval (Adler and Adler 2011). Positive sanctions develop conformity and control by rewarding people for following norms, while negative sanctions encourage conforming behavior by reprimanding people for violating normative guidelines. They are important in relation to social control because they offer people incentives or punishments for certain forms of behavior. Sanctions often function to correct or reform deviant behavior and can be **assimilative** or **coercive**

(Gusfield 1963). Coercive reform involves law, force, or intimidation, while assimilative reform employs integrative strategies such as education, therapy, or rehabilitation. The nature and severity of sanctions depends heavily upon whether they derive from the formal or informal control systems (or both) that adjust and guide human activity and order the social world.

Informal Control Groups

The informal responses to certain **attitudes, behaviors,** or **conditions** are potent methods of controlling and coordinating society and human interaction. Informal controls occur through sanctions that are not codified into law or tied to legal intervention. They operate through the ongoing processes of social interaction, as people are socialized to what activities are acceptable and responsible, and what behaviors will elicit sanctions. These guiding prescriptions for behavior are inherently tied to the social order:

> When persons engage in regulated dealings with each other, they come to employ social routines or practices, namely, patterned adaptations to the rules—including conformances, by-passings, secret deviations, excusable infractions, flagrant violations, and the like. These variously motivated and variously functioning patterns of actual behavior, these routines associated with ground rules, together constitute what might be called a 'social order' (Goffman 1971:xi).

Informal controls are central to maintaining the social order. **One may even say that informal controls *are* the social order.** They occur in every day, ordinary life and document the ways by which people of a particular culture or society regulate, modify, and influence the behavior of their fellow citizens. Informal controls are grounded in the processes of socialization and would be ineffective without the social training experienced through the family, the community, peers, school, work, religion, and even the mass media.

Informal controls operate "below the State" (Innes 2003:52), or outside the realm of formal control apparatuses such as the police, courts, and prisons. Once again, Goffman (1983) draws attention to the role of informal controls outside of the State and formal law:

> The modern nation state, almost as a means of defining itself into existence, claims final authority for the control of hazard and threat to life, limb and property throughout its territorial jurisdiction. Always in theory, and often in practice, the State provides stand-in arrangements for stepping in when local mechanisms of social control fail to keep breakdowns of interaction order within limits. Particularly in public places but not restricted thereto. To be sure, the interaction order prevailing in most public places is not a creation of the apparatus of a State. Certainly most of this order comes into being and sustained as it were, in some cases in spite of overarching authority not because of (6).

According to Goffman, informal controls flow through social life and human interaction, with formal legal intervention occurring when these informal processes of control are no longer sufficient. Social actors are continuously controlling and being controlled through their daily interactions. However, to be a competent participant on the social order, one must be **socialized** into the shared cultural assumptions that guide social life.

The **socialization** process begins early in life and relies heavily on a person's social bonds within the context of **primary groups** (Cooley 1902). A primary group provides the most important setting for socialization. For children, primary groups typically involve family members, but this intimate socialization also occurs in the context of schools, peers, and neighborhoods (Andersen and Taylor 2007; Bates and Babchuk 1961; Giddens 2011). These initial interactions with primary group members typically involves emotional attachment, face-to-face and continuous contact, and small and familiar environments (Cooley 1955). It is in these settings that primary groups provide emotional support, socialization, and encourage either deviance or conformity (Bates and Babchuk 1961). In primary groups, children learn basic rules of conduct and the norms and laws of society. Parents and teachers educate children on what is right and wrong, provide positive and negative sanctions, and start teaching them the intricacies of the social order. Primary groups are an important controlling and organizing mechanism throughout a person's life (Harrington and Fine 2000). They consist of one's closest associates and confidants, provide social support, advice and guidance, act as authority figures and can significantly impact behavior. The behavior of primary groups is characterized as **expressive**, meaning that relationships are founded on bonds of loyalty, commitment, and friendship (Cooley 1955). Informal control is typically the most potent within these small group contexts that operate at the local level.

Secondary groups provide further socialization, but unlike primary groups, are larger in size, more impersonal, and goal oriented (Andersen and Taylor 2007). Secondary groups typically exist to accomplish a particular task and include interactions such as those between customers and clerks, employers and workers, or professors and students. Although secondary relationships can evolve into primary relationships they provide socializing interaction beyond those of close-knit, familiar primary groups (Giddens 2011). Secondary interactions are important as they provide people with learning experiences into the routine patterns of behavior and interactional ground rules that constitute the social order (Goffman 1971, 1983).

Reference Groups can include primary relationships (e.g., family, friends, and teachers), secondary relationships (e.g., social organizations, work groups, casual acquaintances), and include groups in which one does not belong (e.g., government leaders, actors, rock star).

Reference groups refer to those that an individual identifies with and typically subscribes to their beliefs, values, and norms (Eisenstadt 1954). Such groups influence behavior as one may emulate the behavior and ideas of a reference group and conform to the norms and beliefs of that group (Shibutani 1955). Reference groups do not need to be positive and observing the behavior of a set of people one dislikes can reinforce a preference for other beliefs, values, and ways of behaving.

Finally, **social networks** consist of the sum total of a person's relationships. Social networks include both primary and secondary groups and involve both weak and strong relationships and bonds (Andersen and Taylor 2007; Giddens 2011). These networks can include family members, work colleagues, and classmates, they tie us to countless people in the community and larger society. Social networks provide people several functions that impact behavior and foster control. They provide bonds that may reinforce conforming or deviant behavior, they allow for the diffusion of important and helpful information, and provide social support and guidance.

Primary groups, secondary groups, reference groups, and social networks are important because together they provide necessary socialization and constitute the social order. They also establish systems of formal and informal social controls in a person's life. These groups and networks provide interactional learning environments and the hierarchal and stratified social structure of society. The dynamic interplay of socialization, interaction, and structure operating within these groups and networks provide latent and manifest social control processes that preserve and maintain social life. The theoretical perspectives that follow exhibit how groups and networks come to promote conformity and social control or foster deviance and crime.

Symbolic Interaction

Symbolic interactionism examines social life from the perspective of people and how they perceive and react to the world around them (Blumer 1969; Goffman 1959; Mead 1934). Herbert Blumer (1969) specifies three basic principles of the framework: 1) **human beings act toward objects on the basis of the meanings those objects have for them**; 2) **these meanings arise through interaction**; and 3) **these meanings are modified by human beings through an interpretive and interactive process**. According to Symbolic Interaction, anything can be an object, a gesture (the middle-finger, sign of the cross), a symbol (a name-brand, road sign), a person (the president, a professor, or a college student). For example, marijuana as a substance would be considered an object. People hold a variety of beliefs and meanings toward marijuana (e.g., dangerous drug, medical marvel, safe recreationally). These meanings are not inherent or permanent to marijuana as an object, but arose as human beings interacted and passed on information and beliefs about the substance. Finally, meanings toward marijuana are subject to modification (as we have seen through medicalization and legalization), as people give new meanings to the object (marijuana) through interaction and information. Thus, social order is created and sustained through this form of interaction, as people give meaning to objects and behaviors, and work to find proper responses to their situation. Over time, people learn the normative and expected responses to objects in their lives that preserve the **interaction order** and reduce **informal** and **formal sanctions** (Goffman 1983). However, the meanings we apply to objects are always subject to change and modification.

The development of the **self** is a dynamic social process (Cooley 1902; James 1890), a product of **socialization** necessary for maintaining **self-control** and **social order** (Matsueda 1992; Mead 1934). From a sociological perspective, the self is a *somewhat* stable set of perceptions of who we are as individuals. The self is not fixed or permanent; it is in flux and changing over our lives; a social process in which we experience feelings about who we are, derived from how we see ourselves from the viewpoint of others. This process is known as **role-taking** or viewing and interpreting the self through the lens of people in our lives.

This processes of socialization and role-taking forms the biological being into a truly social being (Cast 2004; Matsueda 1992). While people often believe that the self (as well as personality) is genetically determined, sociologists understand the self to be a constant product of social interaction with others and wider society. From the reflexive process of role-taking, there emerges a sense or conception of the self as an "object" (Turner 1976:990). Role-taking and socialization give us a unique form of self-awareness; the ability to be both a subject (feelings and perceptions of who we are) and object (seeing ourselves as we think others do). These processes *are* the self.

Early in life, individuals take the role of **significant others** such as parents, teachers, or peers. As this socialization process evolves, they begin to take the role of larger groups, the community, and different facets of society. According to Mead (1934), this stage refers to taking the role of the **"generalized other,"** which "includes the norms, rules, and expectations, governing various positions and roles of a group, community, or society" (Matsueda 1992:1581). Basically, when we think about ourselves and actions, deliberate decisions, or recollect our past, the generalized other represents an internalized hidden audience, and is thus a powerful form of control that influences our behavior. We learn, through role-taking and the generalized other, to view ourselves and behave via a lens of wider society (primary groups, secondary groups, reference groups, social networks, and the norms and rules of our culture). The generalized other constitutes both self-control and social control as individuals internalize and behave in accordance to the rules, beliefs, and norms of their social groups, culture, and wider society.

Structural Symbolic Interaction

Structural symbolic interactionism focuses on the structure of society for the formation of self and social control. According to identity theory (Stryker 1968, 1980) the self is a set of internalized roles, or identities. Put another way, each facet of the self reflects an identity that is "composed of the meanings that a person attaches to the multiple roles they typically play in highly differentiated contemporary societies" (Stryker and Burke 2000:284). **Roles** are the behavioral expectations, attached to the **status positions**, that organize and structure society. **Identities**, as public facets of the **self**, are the internalized role obligations attached to the status positions occupied by people in their social networks. Identity is essentially the most public aspect of self. Our identity is often tied to the status positions (I am a student) and associated role obligations (I study, write papers, earn grades) we hold within the structure of society. Identity can be derived from our membership in social groups or the shared meanings between us and of those around us about "who we are" (e.g., I am a father, a student, a soccer player, a heavy drinker)." (Vander Ven: 2011). **Identity** refers to who or what one is, the various meanings attached to oneself by self and others, and the self-characterizations individuals make in terms of group memberships. Finally, **identities are a source of motivation for action** (Burke and Reitzes 1991; Foote 1951; Gecas 1982; Heise 1979) particularly those actions that confirm one's valued identities.

Stryker (1980), asserted that the self is multilayered and that a person's identities are organized along a hierarchy of **identity salience**, or "the probability that an identity will be invoked across a variety of situations, or alternatively across persons in a given situation" (Stryker and Burke 2000:286). A key determinant of identity salience is **commitment**, as it determines the hierarchal ordering of identities (Stryker 1980). Commitment to an identity has been formulated in numerous ways. Becker (1960) suggested commitment as "consistent lines of activity" over time and across situations (33). He argued that commitment is an outcome of

"side bets" (i.e., other interests or investments) that motivate an individual to follow a line of activity. The implication is that as a person attaches "side bets" to a particular identity, the investment to that identity is enhanced, and one will follow particular lines of behavior that support that identity. Stryker (1968) defined commitment by the number and depth of relationships one has by virtue of invoking a certain identity. Kanter (1972) defined commitment as the attachments that link individuals reciprocally to groups or communities, or the willingness of members to give their energy and loyalty to a community. McCall and Simmons (1966) argued identity commitment is increased when one benefits from material rewards such as money, goods, or prestige and Burke and Reitzes (1991) noted that the stronger the salience of an identity, the harder one will work to maintain it.

Overall, these conceptions of commitment involve an effort to maintain certain perceptions of self and identity (Burke and Reitzes 1991) that provides ties to certain activities, organizations, and people. Structural symbolic interactionism views the self as emerging in an organized society that exists *before* the appearance of new members. Social structure does referee the development of self, but people do not conform to positions or roles through external threats, legal sanctions, or formal controls (Becker 1960; Stryker 1980; Burke and Renzetti 1991). In contrast, people occupy status positions and perform the role behaviors that confirm their valued identities because they form "a stable and organized set of generalized others" (Matsueda 1992:269) within the differentiated groups, communities, and cultural norms society. The commitment to certain identities (i.e., status positions and role obligations) determines a person's social networks and the degree to which those networks or relationships will serve as a generalized other (Mead 1934). This has been termed **"differential organizational control"** or the process by which social control operates through the different groups in a person's life (Matsueda 1992).

Social Control, Differential Association, SSSL

According to **Social Control Theory** (Hirschi 1969), conformity is achieved through socialization and the formation of bonds between an individual and normative society. **The stronger the bonds to society, the less likely a person will commit deviance and crime.** These bonds consist of four central elements. *Attachment* refers to the emotional and psychological ties one has to significant others such as family and friends. These people typically represent conventional norms and values and compel the individual to act accordingly. *Commitment* represents an individual's accomplishments and goals (e.g., money, employment, education, status, social networks) that could be lost if one turns to crime and deviance. *Involvement* refers to the conventional activities in which a person participates. By engaging in these prosocial activities one has less opportunity to participate in deviance. Finally, there is the social bond of *belief*, or the degree to which one adheres to the values, beliefs, and laws that represent normative society. According to Hirschi (1969), these prosocial bonds operate both directly and indirectly. The bonds do not need to be continually present to control behavior as people internalize these conventional attitudes, commitments, and beliefs and act accordingly.

According to **Differential Association Theory** (Sutherland 1947), deviance and crime are learned behaviors. In contrast to social control theory which asserts that deviance is thwarted by strong bonds to conventional society, differential association posits that people need to learn how to be deviants. The theory states that 1) criminal behavior is learned 2) criminal behavior is learned in interaction with other persons in a process of communication 3) the learning of criminal behavior occurs within intimate personal groups 4) when criminal behavior is learned, the learning includes both techniques and rationalizations for the behavior. In this sense, people are conforming and law-abiding, but given their intimate social groups and their learning environments, they may be exposed to and taught how and why to be deviants and/or criminals.

According to **Social Structure—Social Learning (SSSL) Theory**, the culture and structure of society and the particular communities, groups, and other contexts of interaction, arrange different sets of learning environments and/or bonds to society. According to Akers (2009:323):

> Differences in the societal or group rates of criminal behavior are a function of the extent to which cultural traditions, norms, social organization, and social control systems provide socialization, learning environments, reinforcement schedules, opportunities, and immediate situations conducive to conformity or deviance.

Originally asserted by Sutherland (1947), a person's associations with other people, whether deviant or law-abiding, are determined by their place in larger society. He posited that communities are organized both for deviant (norm violations) and conforming behaviors (following the rules) and are reflections of "**differential social organization**" (Sutherland 1947:9). This viewpoint was later expounded by Cressey and Sutherland, who noted:

> A high crime rate in urban areas can be considered the end product of social conditions that lead to a situation in which relatively large proportions of persons are presented with an excess of criminal behavior patterns" (1960:55).

Continuing with the idea that social structure arranges different sets of learning environments, SSSL (Akers 2009) posits that characteristics of the social structure provides a context for social learning and social bonds. These structural variables include the ecological (i.e., relations of humans to one another and to their environment), community, and geographical distinctions across society (i.e., urban versus rural, population size and density, differences in ecological city areas), as well as the socioeconomic and sociodemographic characteristics of social groups (i.e., race/ethnicity, class, gender, age, occupation, education, marital status, religion, status). The SSSL model also draws on structural explanations that examine abstract conditions, such as **anomie** (Durkheim 1997) **conflict** (Quinney 1977) and **social disorganization** (Shaw and McKay 1942). These ideas view social order and stability as conducive to conformity, while disorder and conflict favor to crime and deviance.

The central point of SSSL is that these structural variables (i.e., ecology, geography, race/ethnicity, class, education, gender, conflict, anomie, and social disorganization), locate people in differential primary, secondary, and reference groups. The very groups and environments that provide socialization, learning, and social bonds and thus the opportunities that foster or discourage deviant or conforming behavior. Simply stated, social structure arranges distinctive sets of learning environments where differential associations produce and maintain behavior. These structural arrangements and learning environments can also dictate an individual's bonds to conformity.

Deviant Careers and Labeling

The study of a "career" as a sociological concept provides another useful framework to examine both deviant and conventional patterns of behavior. Since the 1960s, researchers have used this theoretical concept to understand deviant career patterns, especially drug-using and drug dealing trajectories (Adler and Adler 1983; Faupel 1991; Levy and Anderson 2005). Through **differential opportunity structures** (Cloward and Ohlin 1960) and **structurally arranged learning environments** (Akers 2009; Sutherland 1947) people come to occupy both deviant and legitimate careers. People generally inhabit several careers throughout their lives, and though these careers might complement or conflict with one another, they serve to organize and direct a person's life (Van Maanen 1977). Deviant careers are also fluid, meaning that individuals move in and out of deviance across time and place (Sharp and Hope 2001).

Sociological research on respectable or legitimate careers focuses on occupational pathways within legitimate formal organizations (Becker and Strauss 1956; Blankenship 1973; Hughes 1958) such as being a doctor, professor, or business executive, while research on deviant or criminal careers recognizes the unstable, illegitimate structure of deviant trajectories such as drug dealing, organized criminality, or gang membership. A central facet of both conventional and deviant professions is the training and socialization (Adler and Adler 2011) that teaches a person the requirements for entry, the management techniques, and the potential exiting strategies of their career. In the preliminary, or entry stage, a person must "assemble the knowledge, skills, motives, equipment, and contacts" needed for career success (Luckenbill and Best 1981:201). Thus, those with experience have an advantage over the neophyte (Becker and Strauss 1956). During the **entry phase**, a person carries out new activities and behaviors, sometimes in a tentative and experimental fashion, and after the initial foray into deviance, one must assess the new experience:

> The deviant may evaluate the risks involved in the career shift, the prospects for success, the quality of the potential reward, and so forth. The reactions of others, including deviant associates and social control agents, can help the deviant assess the shift...some deviants may not decide to pursue the shift, but others continue, entering the stage of *routine* (Luckenbill and Best 1981:202).

Once the deviant behavior becomes **routine**, the **training** and **socialization** process continues, as one learns to manage the deviant career. Unfolding in an unstructured context with few institutional supports, the deviant career continuously poses new challenges and demands that must be negotiated (Faupel 1991). Due to this, a deviant career is rarely a lifelong commitment (Adler and Adler 1983; Luckenbill and Best 1981) because the deviant grows wary of dealing with uncertain life experiences, social control agents, and undependable rewards (Allen, Heymann, and Kelly 1977; Carey 1968). Thus, a person may shift to forms of deviance that pose fewer risks and offer more dependable rewards. Such career shifts have been called "**status passages**" as they entail movement processes from one social context to another and may also involve identity transformation (Glaser and Strauss 1971; Goffman 1961; Hughes 1958). Similar to the entry phase, when a person **drifts** toward deviance (Matza 1964) testing the waters while maintaining conventional ties, **disengaging** from a deviant career is rarely an abrupt act (Adler and Adler 1983; Lieb and Olson 1976). The deviant typically faces numerous **phase-outs** and **re-entries** because breaking long-term career patterns, ties to deviant associates, and identity commitments can prove difficult. Ultimately, a deviant career is plagued with uncertainty. Both social control agents and deviant associates can present problems and risks and deviants lack the institutional support and stability of legitimate careers. Deviants must learn to evade formal control agents and adopt tactics to maintain access to resources (i.e., information, supplies, connections) while negotiating the stress, exhaustion, risk, aging, and irregular compensations that often accompany deviant careers.

Social scientists have also focused on the outcomes or processes that result from various modes of social control. A risk of the deviant career is for the individual to be **caught and identified** and face both **formal** and **informal sanctions**. Sociologists (Becker 1963; Goffman 1961; Lemert 1951; Tannenbaum 1938) have examined the consequences of this move from **primary** to **secondary deviance** and developed the **labeling theory** approach. **Primary deviance** is the initial act, the stage where the individual is not interacting with a deviant/criminal label. **Secondary deviance** is when the individual is caught and publicly identified by social control agents and labeled as a deviant/criminal. They posited that deviance does incite social controls, but social controls also invoke deviance. Basically, when a person is labeled as a deviant/criminal, they may continue to behave in a deviant/criminal manner as their identity is spoiled and they are treated differently by their social groups and wider society.

Labeling theorists also shift the focus to *how* and *why* certain activities and conduct come to be defined as deviant, especially by those with **social power**. To labeling theorists, social control and deviant behavior should be examined in unison with the definitions applied to certain activities by formal control institutions and powerful elites. Agents of social control, like the police, lawmakers, politicians, the courts, mental hospitals, and doctors, not only respond to deviance, but actively construct and define what behaviors are deviant *and* if they warrant formal intervention and regulation. For labeling theorists, there is nothing inherently wrong in the act. On the contrary, crime and deviance is **relative** and varies across to time, place, and cultures. Labeling theorists have argued that behaviors like drug use are viewed as deviant, and warranting social regulation, because of the power and political clout of elite members of society, rather than the collapse of social order or threat to public safety.

Notes and Discussion Questions:

References

Adler, Patrica A. and Peter Adler. 1983. "Shifts and oscillations in deviant careers: The case of upper-level drug dealers and smugglers." *Social Problems* 31(2):195–207.

Adler, Patricia A. and Peter Adler. 2011. *Constructions of Deviance: Social Power, Context, and Interaction*. Mason, OH: Cengage Learning.

Akers, Ronald L. 2009. *Social Learning and Social Structure: A General Theory of Crime and Deviance*. New Brunswick, N.J.: Transaction Publishers.

Allen, John, Phillip B. Heymann, and Diane Hall Kelly. 1977. *Assault With a Deadly Weapon*. McGraw Hill-International.

Andersen, Margaret L. and Howard Francis Taylor. 2007. *Sociology: Understanding a Diverse Society*. Cengage Learning.

Bates, Alan P. and Nicholas Babchuk. 1961. "The Primary Group: A Reappraisal." *The Sociological Quarterly* 2(3):181–92.

Becker, Howard S. 1960. "Notes on the Concept of Commitment." *American Journal of Sociology* 66(1):32–40.

Becker, Howard S., and Anselm L. Strauss. 1956. "Careers: Personality, and Adult Socialization." *American Journal of Sociology* 62(3):253–63.

Black, Donald. 1976. *The Behavior of Law*. United Kingdom: Emerald Publishing.

Blankenship, Ralph L. 1973. "Organizational Careers: An Interactionist Perspective." *The Sociological Quarterly* 14(1):88–98.

Blumer, Herbert. 1969. *Symbolic Interactionism: Perspective and Method.*: Englewood Cliffs, N.J.: Prentice-Hall, Inc.

Burke, Peter. J. and Donald C. Reitzes. 1991. "An Identity Theory Approach to Commitment." *Social Psychology Quarterly* 54(3):239–51.

Carey, James T. 1968. *The College Drug Scene.* Englewood Cliffs, N.J.: Prentice-Hall.

Cast, Alicia D. 2004. "Role-taking and interaction." *Social psychology quarterly* 67(3):296–309.

Chang, Johannes Han-Yin. 2004. "Mead's Theory of Emergence as a Framework for Multilevel Sociological Inquiry." *Symbolic Interaction* 27(3): 405–27.

Chriss, James J. 2007. *Social control: An Introduction.* United Kingdom: Polity Press.

Cloward, Richard. A., and Lloyd E. Ohlin. 1960. *Delinquency and Opportunity.* New York: Free Press.

Cohen, Stanley. 1985. *Visions of Social Control: Crime Punishments and Classification.* United Kingdom: Polity.

Cooley, Charles Horton. 1955. *Primary Groups.* New York: Alfred A. Knopf, Inc.

Cooley, Charles Horton. 1964 [1902]. "Human Nature and the Social." Piscataway, N.J.: Schockten Books.

Durkheim, Emile. 1997. *The Division of Labor in Society.* New York: Free Press.

Eisenstadt, Shmuel. N. 1954. "Reference Group Behavior and Social Integration: An Explorative Study." *American Sociological Review* 19(2):175–85.

Faupel, Charles E., Alan M. Horowitz, and Greg S. Weaver. 2010. *The Sociology of American Drug Use*. New York: Oxford University Press.

Foote, Nelson. N. 1951. "Identification as the Basis for a Theory of Motivation." *American Sociological Review* 16(1):14–21.

Gecas, Vicktor. 1982. "The Self-Concept." *Annual Review of Sociology* 8:1–33.

Giddens, Anthony, Mitchell Duneier, Robert Applebaum, and Debra Carr. 2011. "Introduction to Sociology." W.W. Norton International Publishing.

Glaser, Barney G., and Anslem L. Strauss. 1971. *Status Passage: A Formal Theory*. Mill Valley, CA: Sociology Press.

Goffman, Erving. 1959. *The Presentation of Self in Everyday Life*. New York, NY: Doubleday.

Goffman, Erving. 1961. *Asylums: Essays on the Social Situation of Mental Patients and Other Inmates*. New York: Anchor Books.

Goffman, Erving. 1963. *Stigma: Notes on the Management of a Spoiled Identity*. Englewood Cliffs, N.J.: Prentice Hall.

Goffman, Erving. 1983. "The Interaction Order: American Sociological Association, 1982 Presidential Address." *American Sociological Review* 48(1): 1–17.

Gusfield, Joseph R. 1963. *Symbolic Crusade: Status Politics and the American Temperance Movement*. Champaign, IL: University of Illinois Press.

Heise, David R. 1979. *Understanding Events: Affect and the Construction of Social Action*. United Kingdom: Cambridge University Press.

Hirschi, Travis. 1969. *Causes of Delinquency*. Berkeley, CA: University of California Press.

Horowitz, Allan V. 1990. *The Logic of Social Control*. New York: Plenum.

Hughes, Everett C. 1958. *Men and Their Work*. Glencoe, IL: Free Press.

Innes, Martin. 2003. *Understanding Social Control*. McGraw-Hill International.

James, William. 1890. *The Principals of Psychology*. New York: Holt.

Kanter, Rosabeth Moss. 1972. *Commitment and Community: Communes and Utopias in Sociological Perspective*. Boston, MA: Harvard University Press.

Lieb, John and Sheldon Olson. 1976. "Prestige, Paranoia and Profit: On Becoming a Dealer of Illicit Drugs in a University Community." *Journal of Drug Issues* 6(4):356-67.

Lemert, Edwin M. 1951. *Social Pathology: A Systematic Approach to the Theory of Sociopathic Behaviour*. New York: McGraw-Hill.

Levy, Judith. A. and Tammy Anderson. 2005. "The Drug Career of the Older Injector." *Addiction Research & Theory* 13(3):245–58.

Luckenbill, David F. and Joel Best. 1981. "Careers in Deviance and Respectability: The Analogy's Limitations." *Social Problems* 29(2):197–206.

McCall, George J. and Jerry Laird Simmons. 1966. *Identities and interactions: An Examination of Human Associations in Everyday Life.* New York: Free Press.

MacIver, Robert M. and Charles Page. 1949. *Society.* London: Macmillan.

Matsueda, R. L. 1992. "Reflected appraisals, Parental Labeling, and Delinquency: Specifying a Symbolic Interactionist Theory." *American Journal of Sociology* 97(6):1577–1611.

Matza, David. 1964. *Delinquency and Drift.* New Brunswick, N.J.: Transaction Publishers.

Mead, George Herbert.1934. *Mind, Self, and Society.* Chicago, IL: University of Chicago Press.

Morris, Richard T. 1956. "A Typology of Norms." *American Sociological Review* 21(5):610–13.

Quinney, Richard. 1977. *Class, State and Crime: On the Theory and Practice of Criminal Justice.* United Kingdom: David McKay Company.

Shaw, Clifford R. and Henry D. McKay. 1942. *Juvenile Delinquency and Urban Areas.* Chicago, IL: University of Chicago Press.

Sharp, Susan F. and Trina L. Hope. 2001. "The Professional Ex-Revisited Cessation or Continuation of a Deviant Career?" *Journal of contemporary ethnography* 30(6):678–703.

Shibutani, Tamotsu. 1955. "Reference Groups as Perspectives." *American Journal of Sociology* 60:562-69.

Stryker, Sheldon. 1968. "Identity Salience and Role Performance: The Relevance of Symbolic Interaction Theory for Family Research." *Journal of Marriage and the Family* 30(4):558–64.

Stryker, Sheldon. 1980. *Symbolic Interactionism: A Social Structural Version.* Menlo Park, CA: Benjamin/Cummings Publishing Company.

Stryker, Sheldon. 2008. "From Mead to a Structural Symbolic Interactionism and Beyond." *Annual Review of Sociology* 34:15–31.

Stryker, Sheldon and Peter J. Burke. 2000. "The Past, Present, and Future of an Identity Theory." *Social Psychology Quarterly* 63(4):284–97.

Sumner, William. G. 1906. *Folkways: A Study of the Social Importance of Usages, Manners, Customs, Mores, and Morals.* Boston, MA: Ginn and Company.

Sutherland, Edwin H. 1947. *Principles of Criminology.* Philadelphia, PA: Lippincot.

Tannenbaum, Frank. 1938. *Crime and the Community.* New York: Columbia University Press.

Turner, Ralph H. 1976. "The Real Self: From Institution to Impulse." *American Journal of Sociology* 81(5):989–1016.

Van Maanen, John. 1977. *Organizational Careers: Some New Perspectives.* New York: Wiley.

Vander Ven, Thomas. 2011. *Getting wasted: Why college students drink too much and party so hard.* New York: NYU Press.

Chapter Three

Formal Social Control

Social control is a central concept in sociology and its role in social life and social theory is both fundamental and complex (Chriss 2007; Innes 2003; Janowitz 1975; Meier 1982). As a concept of study, it is intertwined to matters of social order, or how different people, cultures, and societies organize their existence together. *The study of social control - namely, all those mechanisms and resources by which members of society attempt to assure the norm-conforming behavior of others - is almost as old as the discipline of sociology itself* (Chriss 2007). Social controls are essential for understanding modern life. Social scientists have always been attentive to social controls and how social actors "both intentionally and unintentionally, on a personal level and when acting in groups, come to conform with the norms and rules so that the social world can be understood as ordered, rather than chaotic" (Innes 2003:2).

Although sociologists rarely agree upon a universal definition of social control, **I understand social controls to be the resources that a society uses to insure compliance with norms.** Social controls are the mechanisms and social processes that regulate the conduct of social actors; they are the actions and reactions intended to alter people's behavior, especially those who are viewed as deviant or criminal (Black 1976; Cohen 1985; Criss 2007; Innes 2003). As a broad sociological concept, social control is often used synonymously with *social order* and *socialization* when referring to the ongoing production and maintenance of coordination and harmony across society. For example, Horowitz (1990) stated that "social control merges out of and serves to maintain ways of life and social practices of groups" (5), while MacIver and Page (1949) proposed that "social control is the study of how society patterns and regulates individual behavior"(3).

These definitions, and others like them, allude to processes of socialization and matters of both social control and the social order. Although intimately associated, these concepts are distinguishable. **Socialization is a prerequisite to social control; it is the production of self-controlled individuals. Human beings** *must* **learn about the informal rules and guidelines, the formal laws and regulations, and the associated sanctions of their social order so that they** *can* **be controlled.** The social order is the organized arrangements of society. According to Innes (2003:6):

The concept of social order refers to the conditions of existence of society, in that every society intrinsically has a degree of organization and this is a social order. A social order is not static, but is constantly in process, being produced and reproduced by the combined attitudes, values, practices, institutions, and actions of its members. Thus social order is composed of the diverse sets of ideas, actions, and interactions, which in some fashion contribute to the ongoing constitution of societal organization. The boundaries between social ordering practices and social controls are neither fixed nor stable, and over time, shift their balance.

The definitional boundaries between social control and social order are flexible and overlapping. Social order is never merely the product of social controls and social ordering practices often perform social control functions. The social order is a product of both social controls and socialization; we are socialized into, and controlled by, society's core arrangements, its knowledge, values, beliefs, norms, establishments, and institutions. The deployment of social control is intended to preserve and protect this social order. **As social phenomena, socialization, social order, and social control operate together in dynamic fashion to produce the social realities of human life.** For the purposes of this book, the concept of social control is central, as the sum of human mechanisms that preserve, produce, and reproduce the social order by sanctioning and socializing those who deviate from the normative arrangements of social life.

Policing

The law comprises a central route through which social control is authorized and enacted. Traditionally, it is a form of governmental control, or the regulations and processes that the state uses to intervene in social conflicts between individuals and organizations (Black 1976). Handled principally by state and government agencies that constitute the criminal justice system (i.e., the police, the courts, the prison system), formal regulation is expansive, expensive, and the form of social control that dominates the attention of the public.

The face of formal social control are the **police**. The police are the gatekeepers into the criminal justice system, the layer of control that can introduce an individual into the adjudication and punishment processes of formal law. As such, "police decisions in terms of when, why, and how and against whom to enforce the law are especially consequential in determining which deviant acts are defined as criminal and thus subject to social control" (Innes 2003:64). The police are the central instrument through which the state intervenes into peoples' lives and maintains order and control. The traditional functions of the police are crime management (i.e., detecting and stopping crime), order management (i.e., resolving low-level conflicts and maintaining social order), and security management (i.e., maintaining a continuous and omnipresent demonstration of state power and authority) (Innes 2003).

The central philosophy of **community policing** is that policing involves more than traditional crime fighting, and police focus should include maintaining social order, providing public service, and generally assisting the community (Cordner and Biebel 2005; Sklansky 2008). Community policing allows citizens' voices in the formation and implementation of policies and caters to needs, norms, and values of particular neighborhoods and communities. This **problem-oriented** style of policing minimizes random car patrols, response times, and intensive investigations and emphasizes foot patrols, door-to-door policing, and other community oriented strategies that stress police-citizen interaction (Sklansky 2008). This style of police work encourages proactive rather than reactive crime fighting methods, as police interact with citizens on a routine basis and provide problem-solving techniques and conflict mediation. Community policing is important because it provides one example of changes in social control, as the civil sphere, citizens, and the community become a central mechanism in the delivering and enhancing of formal control.

The idea of **zero-tolerance policing** originated with the "Broken Windows" theory of crime purported by James Q. Wilson and George Kelling (1982). In their article, they contended that an atmosphere of uncontrolled petty crime rates creates the impression that "no one is in control" and that more serious crime can be committed with impunity. Stated differently, unimpeded disorder and incivility in a particular place sends an implicit invitation to more dangerous criminals. Supporters of the zero-tolerance approach argue that enforcing less serious types of crimes and public disorder (i.e., loitering, begging, public drunkenness, and nuisance behaviors) or 'quality of life offenses' will reduce more serious problems in society (Burke 1998; Punch 2007). This mentality redefines acts typically considered annoying and aesthetically degrading to social problems requiring swift and assertive police enforcement (Harcourt 2001; Innes 1999).

Power and Normalization

Understanding the current landscape of formal social control in the United States cannot be restricted to the shifts and adaptations only within the police, the courts, and the prisons. Scholars such as Foucault (1977, 1979) and Cohen (1985) examine the extension of power and control of both non-state/non-governmental entities (e.g., doctors, psychologists, universities and colleges, religious organizations) and quasi-state agencies (e.g., welfare, education, and community corrections).

For Foucault (1977), social control, once centralized and identifiable through the police, the courts, and the prisons, has been diffused, leaving power and control fragmented and opaque. Foucault identified the architectural design of the **panopticon** as the central constitution of modern "disciplinary" power and control (Gutting 2005). The panopticon (i.e., "all-seeing") refers to an architectural prison design in which the prisoner never sees the correction officer who conducts surveillance from a privileged, hidden, and radial position. The fundamental function of the panopticon design is that the inmates feel the gaze of authority and power at every moment, they internalize the panoptic tower, and become agents in their own discipline and control:

> [T]he major effect of the Panopticon: to induce in the inmate a state of conscious and permanent visibility that assures the automatic functioning of power. So arranging things that the surveillance is permanent in its effects, even if it is discontinuous in its action; that the perfection of power should tend to render its actual exercise unnecessary; that this architectural apparatus should be a machine for creating and sustaining a power relation independent of the person who exercises it; in short, that the inmates should be caught up in a power situation of which they are themselves the bearers (Foucault 1977:201).

This panoptic prison model metastasized throughout modern society, its disciplinary regime operating within other socializing institutions such as the school, the hospital, the corporation, and the mental asylum as a potent mode of power and control over citizens. The control functions of the psychologist, the social worker, the health clinician, and educator are less discernible and visible than criminal justice personnel. This disciplinary power and control is derived from three distinctly modern means: **hierarchal observation, normalizing judgment, and examination.**

Hierarchal observation entails the omnipresent feeling of surveillance that is based on the panopticon prison model. However, direct observation under a single gaze is impractical in modern society; thus, there are "relays" of observers, heirarchally ordered to "supervise the supervisors" (Foucault 1977, 1997). This modern method of surveillance can be seen in the military, business, and manufacturing. Hierarchal observation operates through supervision, reporting, and accountability and serves to keep people in-check and hold the organization together (Rabinow 1991).

Normalization judgment, which basically serves as a corrective function, is concerned with what people have not done, or their failure to meet required expectations or abide by society's standards (Gutting 2005). Normalization involves the construction of ideal forms of behavior and action and operates by rewarding or punishing individuals for conforming or deviating from the ideal (Dreyfus and Rabinow 1982). Once identified, these abnormal or deviant transgressions generally involve a punitive response, and thus are potent forms of power and control. Foucault (1977, 1979) saw projects of normalization in countless social institutions, founded on bodies of knowledge (e.g., sociology, criminology, and psychology) that enabled classification and definition of diverse forms of deviance. Thus, normalization operates through standards applied to our social world:

> This idea of normalization is pervasive in our society. On the official level, we set national standards for educational programs, for medical practice, for industrial processes and products; less formally, we have an obsession with lists that rank-order everything from tourist sites, to our body weights, to levels of sexual activity...normalizing judgment is a peculiarly pervasive means of control. There is no escaping it because, for virtually any level of achievement, the scale shows that there is an even higher level possible (Gutting 2005:84).

Examination is a powerful method of control, a confluence of observation and normalizing judgment, which constitutes the final component of disciplinary power (Foucault 1977; Rabinow 1991). For those who undergo examination (i.e., students being tested, patients being observed, employees being assessed), it elicits truth about their knowledge, health, or qualifications and allows for social control by directing them to study, improve, or seek treatment. The examination also allows for a "field of documentation" through the results of exams, reviews, and assessments that provide detailed information that turns the individuals into a "case" and an opportunity to control (Foucault 1977).

> The examination, surrounded by all its documentary techniques, makes each individual a 'case': at which at the same time constitutes an object for a branch of knowledge and a hold for a branch of power. [The case] is the individual as he may be described, judged, measured, compared with others in his very individuality; and it is also the individual who has to be trained or corrected, classified, normalized, excluded, etc. (Foucault 1977:191).

These techniques of disciplinary power and control culminate into what Foucault (1997) refers to as **governmentality**, or the "techniques and procedures for directing human behavior" (Foucault 1997:82). These governmentalties direct children, governments, households, the state, and oneself. Government, as he summarizes, is "an activity that undertakes to conduct individuals throughout their lives by placing them under the authority of a guide responsible for what they do and for what happens to them" (Foucault 1997:68). It is the modern exercises of observation, normalization, and examination that allow for modes of power and control over individuals. Rather than locating social control and power in a single entity such as the state (i.e., police, courts, and prisons), governmentaility recognizes that a wide variety of authorities govern in diverse sites, in relation to different goals (Rose et al. 2006). The state is now connected with different groups and paradigms of knowledge that administer and control peoples' lives in the pursuit of specific objectives (Garland 1997). Fundamental to these strategies is that power and control would not only derive from "the great technologies such as the panopticon but would turn to mundane, little governmental techniques and tools, such as interviews, case records, diaries, brochures, and manuals" (Rose et al. 2006:89).

Community Corrections

Drawing on Foucault's ideas, Stanley Cohen (1985) identifies the "community corrections" reformation as evidence of the dispersal of power, control, and discipline away from the prison and into the community. As community corrections alternatives such as half-way houses, juvenile detention centers, probation, and parole expand, so does the judicial and punitive power of the probation officer, the social worker, the health practitioner, and the psychiatrist. According to (Cohen 1979b), the diversion of people from traditional courts and corrections simply moves social control from within prison walls and effectively embeds control functions into the community. These community treatments and controls expand official intervention and increase the number of people becoming involved in the criminal justice system. Community alternatives to the traditional criminal justice system lead to an expansion and intensification of the system "a dispersal of its mechanisms from more closed to more open sites and a consequent increase in the invisibility of social control and the degree of its penetration into the social body" (Cohen 1985:83). Cohen (1979a, 1985) identifies three central shifts in social control as a consequence of the expansion of community corrections.

First, is the process of **widening the net and thinning the mesh** (Cohen 1979b). These concepts point to the irony that community corrections, as alternatives to incarceration, result in an increase, rather than a decrease, of offenders who come in contact with the criminal justice system. The net is widened because a larger population is subject to social controls, and the mesh is thinned because individuals become ensnared in these new systems rather than simply being screened out. Cohen explains (1979b):

> Where the police used to have two options—screen right out (the route for by far the majority of encounters) or process formally—they now have the third option of diversion into a program. Diversion can then be used as an alternative to screening and not an alternative to processing...the new movement—in the case of crime and delinquency at least—has led to a more voracious processing of deviant populations, albeit in new settings and by professionals with different names. The machine might in some respects be getting softer, but it is not getting smaller (349-350).

A second consequence of community corrections is **blurring the boundaries** or the increasing invisibility of the social control machine (Cohen 1979b). Previously, prisons and other institutions of control had clear spatial boundaries to separate the deviant from conventional society. According to Cohen (1979b):

> These spatial boundaries were reinforced by ceremonies of social exclusion. Those outside could wonder what went on behind the walls, those inside could think about the "outside world." Inside/outside, guilty/innocent, freedom/captivity, imprisoned/released—these were meaningful distinctions (344).

Today, these symbolic and physical markers of social control are no longer distinct. It has become increasingly difficult to determine where the prison ends and the community begins. The control of deviant behavior is no longer the responsibility of a distinct isolated system, but engages the community, the family, the schools, and the neighborhood in discipline, normalization, and control.

Finally, there is the consequence of **masking and disguising** and presenting these community corrections alternatives as softer than they really are (Cohen 1979b). By employing social work rather than legal methods of diversion, these alternatives can hide their most coercive intentions and strategies. It is not always self evident that community corrections are more humane and less stigmatizing. Although they exist in the community, they are often a source of unchecked detention and coercion that proliferate in a bureaucracy of diversion and alternatives (Cohen 1979b). Community agencies, operating outside of the traditional criminal justice system and under the guise of a social work rationale, operate with decreasing legal justification. The community corrections process often ignores procedural safeguards and due process as adjudication, assessment, and program placement unfold outside the codified procedures of the criminal justice system. A deviant may be referred to a residential treatment or juvenile detention facility not simply because a rule has been broken, a requirement within the criminal just system, but because that individual might "benefit" from services offered in a particular program. This absence of legal safeguards prior to and post admission to the program raises a concern as to the lack of visibility and accountability of such processes (Griffin 2012). As Cohen (1985) notes:

> "[T]he generation of new treatment criteria and the pervasiveness of the social welfare and preventative rhetorics, often ensure an erosion of traditional rights and liberties. In a system of low visibility and accountability, where a high degree of discretion is given to administrative and professional bodies (in the name of 'flexibility') there is often less room for such niceties as due process and legal rights. Police diversion programs are the most notable examples here: juveniles usually proceed through various filters on the assumption or admission of guilt. As one critic of such programs comments: 'to force a youngster to participate in a diversion program under the threat of adjudication, has most of the elements of the formal justice system save due process (70).

Both Foucault (1977, 1979) and Cohen (1979a, 1985) examine the gradual refinement and expansion of mechanisms of control and discipline in modern society. Under the guise of **observation, normalization** and **examination** (Foucault 1977) or **community corrections** (Cohen 1979b), they explicate the ways that the government in unison with other agencies have acquired increasingly potent and invasive formal control over people's private lives. This diffusion of social control is clearly demonstrated in the therapeutic ethos of Western Societies as medical social control has ascended to dominance, competing with the law for power and authority in the realm of formal control (Chriss 2007).

Medical Social Control

Throughout the twentieth century, numerous behaviors and conditions previously considered deviant have been reconstituted as diseases, a process referred to as the medicalization of deviance (Conrad and Schneider 1980; Conrad 1979, 2007). **Medicalization** occurs when a problem is "defined in medical terms, described using medical language, understood through the adoption of a medical framework, or 'treated' with medical intervention" (Conrad 2007:5). Medicalization is a potent form of social control as "medicine functions (wittingly and unwittingly) to secure adherence to social norms (Conrad 1979:1). From "homosexuality, shoplifting, mental illness, gambling, drug abuse, and sexual dysfunction, the increasing medicalization of society allegedly destigmatizes a variety of human and social problems (Zola 1972). As treatment rather than punishment become preferred sanctions for deviance, medical practitioners increasingly function as agents of social control (Conrad 1992) by constructing and enforcing medical norms and disseminating medical counsel and intervention. **Medical social control uses medical means to minimize, eliminate, or normalize deviant behavior** (Conrad 1979).

According to Conrad (1979), during the process of medicalization a medical perspective becomes the dominant definition of certain phenomena and diminishes competing definitions. The medical perspective becomes dominant over others and medical norms come to regulate and control behavior. Such norms serve a normalizing (Foucault 1977) and corrective function as certain behaviors are chastised and people are informed about the healthy, desirable, and functional ways of being and living:

> Medical social control also includes medical advice, counsel, and information that is part of the general stock of knowledge; eat a well-balanced diet, cigarette smoking causes cancer, being overweight increases health risks, exercising regularly is healthy, teeth should be brushed twice daily, etc. Such aphorisms, even when unheeded, serve as road signs for desirable behavior (Conrad 1979:2).

As certain forms of deviance become medicalized, medicine increasingly functions as an independent, direct, and physical agent of social control through medical technology (e.g., behavior modification, psychotherapy, psychosurgery, and prescription medicine). Medicalization also involves medical collaboration with other authorities and agencies of control (Conrad 1979). Doctors, nurses, and clinicians work directly and indirectly with schools, welfare agencies, treatment centers, prisons, and corporations providing services, guidelines, and examinations. Medical practitioners become information providers, gatekeepers, and institutional agents as medical intervention and control increasingly becomes interwoven into the fabric of society:

> The medical profession's status as official designator of the 'sick role', which imbues the physician with authority to define particular kinds of deviance as illness and exempt the patient from certain role obligations, is a general gatekeeping and social control task (Conrad 1979:5).

Along with these direct medical control functions is the formation of *medical ideology* as deviant behaviors and conditions are located within a medical framework. This form of social control includes the adoption of medical or quasi-medical imagery and vocabulary, and further imbues medical authority over the situation. Medical ideology is often supported because it diminishes blame and forms a shield that protects deviant individuals from condemnation (Conrad 1979). In contrast to medical technology and medical collaboration, medical ideology can exist independently, without the involvement of medical professionals:

> The medical profession claims, but has no ownership of, medical rhetoric and vocabulary. It can be used by other organizations independently of the medical profession. Physicians may disown or challenge a particular use of medical vocabulary, but they must challenge it through the media, courts, the legislature or in some other public arena (Conrad 1979:7).

Non-medical groups may significantly impact medical ideology because the medicalization of deviance or alleged "social problems" can support social interests, political agendas, and economic institutions, as illness designations are often socio-political in nature.

According to scholars such as Foucault, Cohen, and Conrad, formal methods of social control are no longer determined explicitly by the state and the criminal justice system. Social rules, regulations, and guidelines have become increasingly relegated to medical practitioners, welfare agencies, private security firms, community corrections, and the civil sphere as boundaries between formal and informal controls become increasingly blurred in modern society.

Notes and Discussion Questions:

References

Black, Donald. 1976. *The Behavior of Law*. United Kingdom: Emerald Publishing.

Burke, Roger Hopkins. 1998. *Zero Tolerance Policing*. Ann Arbor, Michigan: Perpetuity Press.

Chriss, James J. 2007. *Social control: An Introduction*. United Kingdom: Polity Press.

Cohen, Stanley. 1979a. "Community control: a new Utopia." *New Society* 15(79):8.

Cohen, Stanley. 1979b. "The Punitive City: Notes on the Dispersal of Social Control." *Crime, Law and Social Change* 3(4):339–63.

Cohen, Stanley. 1985. *Visions of Social Control: Crime Punishments and Classification*. United Kingdom: Polity Press.

Conrad, Peter. 1979. "Types of Medical Social Control." *Sociology of Health and Illness* 1(1):1–11.

Conrad, Peter. 1992. "Medicalization and Social Control." *Annual Review of Sociology* 18:209–32.

Conrad, Peter. 2007. *The Medicalization of Society: On the Transformation of Human Conditions into Treatable Disorders*. Baltimore: Johns Hopkins University Press.

Conrad, Peter and Joseph W. Schneider. 1980. *Deviance and Medicalization, from Badness to Sickness*. St. Louis, MO: Mosby Press.

Cordner, Gary and Elizabeth Perkins Biebel. 2005. "Problem-Oriented Policing in Practice." *Criminology & Public Policy* 4(2):155–80.

Dreyfus, Herbert L. and Paul Rabinow. 1982. *Michel Foucault: Beyond Structuralism and Hermeneutics*. Chicago, IL: University of Chicago Press.

Foucault, Michel. 1977. *Discipline and punishment*. New York: Pantheon.

Foucault, Michel. 1979. *History of sexuality volume 1: An introduction*. New York: Random House.

Foucault, Michel. 1997. *The Essential Works, 1954-1984, vol. 1: Ethics, Subjectivity and Truth*. New York: The New Press.

Garland, David. 1997. "'Governmentality'and the Problem of Crime: Foucault, Criminology, Sociology." *Theoretical criminology* 1(2):173–214.

Griffin, Diarmud. 2012. "Restorative Justice, Diversion and Social Control: Potential problems." *Diversion and Social Control: Potential Problems* (March 9, 2012).

Gutting, Gary. 2005: *Foucault: A Very Brief Introduction*. United Kingdom: Oxford University Press.

Harcourt, Bernard E. 2001. *Illusion of Order: The False Promise of Broken Windows Policing*. Boston, MA: Harvard University Press.

Horowitz, Allan V. 1990. *The Logic of Social Control*. New York: Plenum.

Innes, Martin. 1999. "'An Iron Fist in an Iron Glove'The Zero Tolerance Policing Debate." *The Howard Journal of Criminal Justice* 38(4):397–410.

Innes, Martin. 2003. *Understanding Social Control*. McGraw-Hill International.

Janowitz, Morris. 1975. "Sociological Theory and Social Control." *American Journal of Sociology* 81(1):82-108.

MacIver, Robert M. and Charles Page. 1949. *Society*. London: Macmillan.

Meier, Robert F. 1982. "Perspectives on the Concept of Social Control." *Annual Review of Sociology* 8:35-55.

Punch, Maurice. 2007. *Zero Tolerance Policing*. United Kingdom: Policy Press.

Rabinow, Paul. 1991. *The Foucault Reader*. United Kingdom: Penguin.

Rose, Nikolas, Pat O'Malley, and Marianna Valverde. 2006. "Governmentality." *Annual Review of Law and Social Sciences* 2:83–104.

Sklansky, David A. 2008. *Democracy and the Police*. Stanford, CA: Stanford University Press.

Wilson, James Q. and George Kelling. 1982. "The police and neighborhood safety: Broken windows." *Atlantic Monthly* 127:29–38.

Zola, Irving Kenneth. 1972. "Medicine as an Institution of Social Control." *The Sociological Review* 20(4):487–504.

Chapter Four

Research Methods

The inception of this research project began at West Green University, a public residential university with roughly 17,000 undergraduate students located in the Midwestern United States. A competitive regional institution, West Green University primarily enrolls White, middle-class students hailing from metropolitan and rural in-state locations. As an undergraduate at West Green University, I majored in sociology and criminology, played rugby, worked at the student center, and was a regular "college partier." West Green University has a national reputation for its collegiate drinking and consistently ranks as a "Top Ten Party School" in the Princeton Review. With a plethora of bars, pubs, weekend block parties, and rowdy student neighborhoods, the college and the surrounding community foster a cultural environment where alcohol use is a normative pastime.

During my senior year at West Green, I was hired at Zippy's Pub, a popular college bar located on Central Street, the rustic brick thoroughfare that constituted the downtown district of West Green University. I started working "the door" and my primary responsibilities were checking patrons identification and date-of-birth, scrutinizing each ID for forgery or misrepresentation, managing crowd control, and removing unruly clientele. Zippy's Bar was lively and consistently crowded with both college students and locals from the surrounding community. On weekend nights it was typically a shoulder-to-shoulder crowd, with loud music, televised sporting events, billiards, and drunken revelry. I spent countless evening hours talking with students, dealing with intoxicated patrons, resolving conflicts, and watching the nights of the West Green party scene unfold.

In 2004, I graduated with a bachelor's degree in "Criminal Psychology" and was admitted to the Master's program in the Department of Sociology at West Green University. During my first year as a graduate student I also started bartending at Zippy's Pub, serving cocktails, shots, and beers to the student population. My evolving employment continued to offer me a fresh vantage point from which to view and analyze the college party scene. I was able to step outside the intoxicated effervescence of undergraduate social life and observe student drinking behaviors, interactions, and indiscretions from a unique position of relative sobriety. My student affiliation and status position as a bartender established me as a **complete-member researcher** (Adler and Adler 1987) in the West Green party scene and I was able to have countless conversations about alcohol and drug use with students, community members, and fellow employees. It was during this time that I became involved in an ethnographic research project on undergraduate drinking (Vander Ven 2011). With the guidance of my adviser, I began assisting in data collection and analysis. I got my first lessons on the rigorous steps of qualitative methodology and conducted fieldwork, one-on-one interviews, and data analysis.

Equipped with my burgeoning sociological lens, my knowledge of drugs and alcohol, and my position as a bartender, I developed a master's thesis about college drinking. I analyzed how students used alcohol to facilitate certain behaviors or conceptions of self, the problems they encountered with intoxication, and the techniques of neutralization they utilized to justify or excuse their intoxicated transgressions. This phenomenon was interesting to me as patrons regularly became over intoxicated and would later apologize to me or other bartenders for their drunken behavior. In contrast, I was also interested in the students who rarely cared about their drunkenness and used alcohol as an excuse to justify any untoward activities. With these themes in mind, I jotted field notes after work and recruited interview participants through bartending, house parties, and classrooms. I worked at Zippy's Pub for nearly three years while I taught sociology classes at West Green University, developed my investigation into undergraduate drug and alcohol use, and completed my Master's thesis.

In 2006, I graduated from West Green University and was accepted into a doctoral program at Campus University, a public research university located in the western United States. A residential flagship university with approximately 29,000 undergraduate students, Campus University is a "destination" school, boasting an advantageous geographic location that supplements the in-state population with a smaller number of upper-middle to upper class out-of-state students. As a large, Research I institution, Campus University represents a modest national presence in athletics, scholarship, and departmental rankings. Similar to West Green, Campus University is also composed primarily of White students of traditional college age and has been historically identified as a "party school."

As a first-year doctoral student, I was again interested in undergraduate drug and alcohol use and Campus University provided me with a campus and community where partying behaviors were normative. On any given weekend student neighborhoods were alive with large keg parties, private house gatherings, and outdoor drinking festivities as students wandered from house to house with the grins and laughter of youthful intoxication. Music blared onto front lawns, audible over the shouts and screams of beer pong games, drunken debates, and the occasional altercation. Continuous police patrols attempted to contain the collegiate revelry and flashing red and blue lights, minor-in-possession tickets, and underage arrests were nothing unusual. On Thursday, Friday, and Saturday nights, the streets and sidewalks of the Campus University community were unfailingly crowded with lines of students wrapped around the popular club-style bars. Greek life flourished, football games and tailgating were a popular pastime, and the university had a thriving drug culture, boasting the largest "420" celebration in the United States. It was against the backdrop of this thriving college party scene that, in 2006, I again started researching undergraduate drinking and drug use. My project developed as I pinned down what I wanted to know about undergraduate drug and alcohol use and how I could gather such data. Although my project evolved over my seven years of graduate work, I started my investigation with a fundamental, yet malleable research agenda.

Research Approach

I sought to approach this project with a **beginner's mind** and I questioned the traditional viewpoint that college partying is a widespread **social problem**. This approach labels student drinking and drug use as an inherently negative activity (Wechsler and Wuethrich 2002; Wechsler et al. 1999, 2000) and neglects any benefits students may derive from this form of social interaction (Dworkin 2005; Ravert 2009; Vander Ven 2011). From my past research and personal history I understood that students who participate in the college party scene sometimes encounter serious consequences as a result of their drinking and drug use, but the majority do not, and they regard the problems they do encounter as learning experiences and/or customary outcomes of partying. In starting my research, I disregarded Henry Wechsler's claim that "binge drinking" is the foremost public health hazard facing college students. Although I understood that problems and consequences associated with undergraduate partying do occur, I wanted to analyze these issues through my fieldwork and listen to the perspectives and experiences of students. I did not want to define the situation as *prima facie* problematic.

Furthermore, I was not just interested in alcohol. Studies that focus on the college party scene typically address alcohol consumption only and tend to ignore students' experimental and recreational use of other drugs. Although alcohol is certainly their primary choice for intoxication, they interweave illicit drug use into their experimentation with conscious-altering substances, a trend common to **emerging adulthood** and the university years (Arnett 1991). Finally, from my own years of maturing through college and watching friends progress from their first years in the dorms to graduating seniors ready for the "adult world," I was interested in students' development of **self-control** and their experiences with varying forms of **social control**. The vast majority of students who participate in the college party scene graduate, albeit with varying degrees of success, and move on with emerging adult lives; they learn to mediate the responsibilities of school with their participation in the college party scene. I wanted to explore the social controls that guide students through their college years.

Thus, I was interested in *what* the norms and informal rules of the party scene were, *why* students' partying behaviors shifted throughout their college careers, and *how* they managed academics and thriving social lives rife with late nights, drugs, and heavy drinking. Due to my burgeoning research ideas, I understood that **qualitative methods** best suited my project because I wanted to analyze the college party scene *through* the experiences of the students who lived it. Qualitative methods collects data that cannot be quantified and provides in-depth knowledge of the social scene being studied. In my opinion, **quantitative research** treats the college party scene as an external and foreign world. They quantify student drug experiences for tabulation and measurement and they claim to operate as objective observers finding fundamental truths about university social life (Wechsler and Weuthrich 2002). Quantitative researchers are generally interested in causal explanations, patterns, rates, and predictions about a peripheral social world (Glesne 2006). I was not interested in quantifying student drug experiences for the purposes of tabulation and regression and I was less concerned with objectivity and statistical generalizability (Kvale 1996). While quantitative studies are valuable for knowing, for example, if heavy drinkers have lower grades than moderate drinkers, how many students are past month marijuana users, or if men drink more than women, it often neglects the environment in which these behaviors occur.

I wanted to focus on **emic**, or insider perspectives of undergraduate students and investigate the norms, interactions, and forms of social control that govern university social life. As Rubin and Rubin note (1997:34), "social research is not about categorizing and classifying, but figuring out what events mean, how people adapt, and how they view what has happened to them and around them." Even in the infancy of this project, I knew that a qualitative approach suited my research objectives. According to Page and Singer (2010:17) "the prime directive in the **ethnographic study of drug use** is to achieve an understanding of how and why the behaviors of interest take place in a given natural habitat and what forms these behaviors take." **Ethnographic research** entails studying people in their own environment, to understand their lives, and provides a rich understanding of how and why people think, behave, and interact in a given environment. Thus, I took an **inductive** (Charmaz 2006), or **abductive** (Adler and Adler 2009) approach to analyzing undergraduate drinking and drug use. I did not use a **deductive** approach, which starts with a specific hypothesis and tests whether the hypothesis is supported by the evidence or data. In contrast, I used an **inductive** approach, starting with data collection and developing concepts, theories and identifying larger patterns. **Abductive** research is a combination of the two. The researcher is not completely new and unfamiliar with the social setting being studied. Thus, the researcher may have some concepts, questions, or theories to be explored (deductive), but still builds their research from the "ground up," collecting data to identify new or emerging concepts and theories. Using this approach, I spoke with students directly, and analyzed my data to identify conceptual themes that emerged within the culture of undergraduate life. I intended to accentuate the complexity and fluidity of my setting and concentrate on the meaning and context of the college party scene.

Getting In

Access into the scene I wished to study was not an issue for me. Harrington (2003) has noted that ethnographers gain access to research information to the degree they share a valued social identity with participants. Similarly, Denzin (1974) has stated that a sociological research method is most effective when those being studied closely resemble the sociologist. **Evaluating for access** is very important for an ethnographer and is the initial process where the researcher figures out if they can actually infiltrate the group they hope to study. The ethnographer asks: Can I, as the researcher, access this setting? Will people speak with me? Allow me to be involved in their lives and activities? Thus, access is also the process by which an ethnographer starts to gain entry into the setting. I am confident that undergraduate students identified me as an equal or an insider, rather than an outsider, and this granted me access to my population of interest. Students identified with me in three central ways. First, I shared personal characteristics with the majority of CU undergraduates I studied: I am white, resembled a college age student, and was a registered student at the University of Colorado. Second, I was only a few years older than most students, and was attentive enough to recognize and understand the sociocultural pulse of undergraduate life. These personal attributes provided an essential basis from which students could relate to me in a demographic sense, at least providing a framework to form an initial connection. Third, my personality and sociability provided me further rapport with students. **Rapport** involves a positive relationship between the ethnographer and those being studied, often characterized by mutual trust, participation, and effort. I looked the part and talked the part. I was not relegated to the periphery within this university social scene, but could be invited and included in students' social activities. I could do all this without appearing out of place. I understood that interactions between researcher and participant significantly influence the ethnographic data-gathering process, and I knew that my insider status was an asset that enhanced my subject recruitment and data collection.

Participant Observation

Using my similarities with undergraduates, my personal history with the college party scene, and my role as a Campus University instructor, I was able to employ an **opportunistic research strategy** (Lofland et al. 2006; Riemer 1977). Opportunistic research involves two components. First, a research opportunity that presents itself to the researcher. Second, using the personal characteristics and/or biographical experiences of the ethnographer as a springboard for study. I began speaking with students to develop my empirical ideas and build upon my existing knowledge. I talked with students from my Deviance and Drugs in U.S. Society courses and also utilized my **participant-as-observer** role (Adler and Adler 1987) in the setting and interacted with participants in some aspects of the party scene within the Campus University community. As a participant-as-observer, the researcher both observes and becomes a member of the setting. Though I was no longer an undergraduate and found potential **cultural clash and ethical issues** a barrier to attend house parties, running into students at bars, restaurants, and concerts in the Campus University community was virtually unavoidable for me, but provided me with contacts and data. Thus, I was not a **complete-member researcher** which often entails full membership in the group, covert research, and walking a tightrope between the role of researcher and role as a group member. In the **covert role** the researcher is secretive, concealing their researcher status, and participants do not know they are being studied, it is often considered unethical and even dangerous. In the **overt role**, the researcher is open about their status and participation, even if they do not divulge everything about their research goals. However, I was more than just a wallflower within these nightlife settings and I could interact with undergraduates as a **co-participant**. Although my role as a university instructor sometimes placed me in an **"outsider" status** (Horowitz 1986), the courses I taught (i.e., Drugs and Deviance) facilitated countless colorful discussions with students about drug trends and party life. My outsider status permitted me to see patterns that might be more complicated for those completely immersed in the scene to observe (Naples 1996), while my **insider status** allowed me the ability to communicate and to gain **"confessional rapport"** (Warren 1988). Confessional rapport involves not only a positive relationship between the ethnographer and those being studied but also involves those being studied feeling comfortable "confessing" or giving information to the researcher.

Although I discuss participant observations and interviews separately, during my fieldwork the two were often intertwined, as "doing participant observation in another culture, as well as one's own, involves a great deal of **informant interviewing**" (Lofland et al. 2006:18). Whenever I conducted **participant observation**, I was always listening, analyzing, and asking questions in locations where undergraduate drinking took place. In these settings I was mindful of the activities of those around me such as students' alcohol and drug consumption, how they behaved under the influence, and their interactions among one another. I was often introduced as and/or recognized by those present as a "drugs professor" or "drugs researcher" and engaged in a wide variety of conversations with students and their friends. I attended 21-and-over establishments and consumed small amounts of alcohol to fit into the scene, but was always careful to maintain a clear head for my research purposes. I generally jotted notes when I returned home for the evening.

Furthermore, I explored **emerging concepts** through lively class discussions. I always reserved a full class period and dedicated that time to one of my main research themes, such as the career of college partying, gender norms, or formal and informal social controls operating within the party scene. In these class periods I presented my empirical research ideas and emerging conceptual themes and discussed them openly and in-depth with my students. The atmosphere of large group discussions, fostered by the comfortable and open atmosphere of my classroom, generated new ideas and directions for my research.

The data I recorded from my participant observations were included in my empirical field notes. Throughout this process I used three sets of field note strategies as suggested by Lofland et al. (2006). My **empirical field notes** consisted of descriptions of events, people, conversations, and of the social setting itself. These field notes were derived from my participant observation. My **analytical field notes** reflected my conceptual ideas that I discerned from my data. I recorded patterns, occurrences, and themes directly from all of my data sources. My **methodological field notes** were composed of methodological concerns, problems and issues encountered in the field, and the continuous progression of my role as a researcher.

From my participant observation in my classes and the social scenes at Campus University, I developed my empirical research design (Maxwell 2005). First, I became interested in how women accomplished femininity within the male dominated college party scene. I recognized that the drinking norms at Campus University were associated with masculinity and was curious how women balanced their desired presentations of femininity with the heavy alcohol use of college life. I also wanted to explore students' transitions into university life in relation to their substance use and social control. Although students still partied their senior year of college, I observed patterns of change as they matured through their university career. With these empirical ideas guiding my fieldwork, I began recruiting for in-depth qualitative interviews.

Sampling

Through my participant observation, classroom discussions, and complete member research role, I implemented a variety of selection strategies. I chose informants through **opportunistic sampling** (Riemer 1977) or sampling from the immediate surroundings and recruited participants from classrooms and fieldwork conversations. I chose former students involved in the party scene and recruited students from a variety of undergraduate classes. Early in my research process I also used **strategic sampling,** or choosing participants that meet certain requirements, and I decided to primarily interview junior and senior students to capture their collegiate life histories. I utilized **snowball sampling** (Berg 2001; Biernacki and Waldorf 1981) and was introduced to participants through social networks and friends-of-friend as students offered me a chain of referrals and helped me locate participants through peer networks.

Ultimately, I implemented a **theoretical sampling** method (Charmaz 2006; Strauss and Corbin 1990; Strauss 1987), moving back and forth between my conceptual developments and my empirical investigation, sampling continually to refine my analysis. Theoretical sampling involves recruiting participants who can help the researcher strengthen their concepts and theories. Given my knowledge of the social environment I studied, my past research experience, and my ongoing data collection, theoretical sampling was the primary strategy that guided my study. Developed by Glaser and Strauss (1967), theoretical sampling assists in the development of conceptual categories until no new properties emerge. For example, I sampled undergraduate budtenders to strengthen my marijuana medicalization categories and sampled senior women to build my data on how students learn gender norms throughout college. I saturated my emerging conceptual outlines with data, constantly sorting and diagraming them to integrate emerging theory. Thus, I interviewed and observed, jotted field notes and transcribed, developed conceptual categories and themes, and followed emerging theoretical underpinnings. I continued my interviewing and analysis until I was confident I had reached a point of **theoretical saturation**, a point when "gathering fresh data no longer sparks new theoretical insights, nor reveals new properties of core theoretical categories" (Charmaz 2006:113). Once theoretical saturation is reached, the researcher stops collecting data. Through my theoretical sampling method, I constructed a **meaningful sample** with the purpose of moving from local truths to general visions (Geertz 1973). I did not seek generalizations in the statistical sense, but worked to construct a sample characteristic of my subject matter (i.e., college drug use and social control) with a final goal to develop valid theoretical ideas about social control (Strauss and Corbin 1990).

Interviews

Through my theoretical sampling process, I collected a significant bulk of data from in-depth interviewing. I decided that **qualitative interviews** were optimal because they allowed me in-depth access to students' feelings and thoughts about their social environment and permitted me "to understand experiences and reconstruct events in which I did not participate" (Rubin and Rubin 1997:7). In sociological research, **interviews** are considered conversations with a purpose. I strove to treat my interviewees as partners in the research rather than subjects. I discussed my personal history and my current fieldwork to help my participants feel comfortable revealing their own experiences. The interviews could take a casual tone. I laughed, shared stories, and reminisced over memorable college times with my participants. However, these interviews also took a serious tone when students discussed troubling times regarding their substance use.

My interviews were **retrospective**, focusing on the socialization and learning processes of students. These **life history interviews** (Rubin and Rubin 1997) provided me with students' experiences as they passed through different stages of their collegiate careers and provided me with their narratives and stories that I interpreted to make the college party scene understandable (Watson and Watson-Franke 1985). In my interviews I focused on students' interpretation of their life experiences and elicited reflections concerning drug use in ways that students might never contemplate to such an extent in their everyday thoughts. I tried, through the interview process, to make sense of *how* students' lives unfolded within the college party scene and *why* these patterns existed. As themes and concepts developed in my interviews, I continued interviewing, classroom discussions, **content analysis**, and fieldwork to **cross check** (Douglas 1976) my data against my own knowledge and initial interviews. Cross-checking involves testing information against common sense and general knowledge and hard facts such as news reports and other research studies. Cross-checking is a method to ensure accuracy. Content analysis is a sociological research method that analyzes social life through the words and images of documents such as newspapers, magazines, and other forms of media.

I conducted interviews in a quiet, private office. The interviews lasted an average of 1.5 hours and I completed 100 interviews in all for this entire project. Since students differed in their partying behaviors and experiences, I conducted my interviews in an **open, semi-structured** (I avoided closed or leading questions) manner that resembled a casual and comfortable conversation (Fontana and Frey 1994; Holstein and Gubrium 1995). Asking all students the exact same questions made little sense to me, as I was interested in their life experiences within the college party scene. Although there were main themes I wanted to discuss, such as gender norms, freshman naivety, or senior maturity, I let the conversation carry the interview as each student had different stories to tell me. This interview approach provided me with novel information and informative stories and further served to promote a relaxed environment.

Medical Marijuana

In 2009, during my fieldwork and interviews, I noticed that an increasing number of my students, research subjects, and their friends were obtaining a medical marijuana license. Students were talking about the growth of the medical marijuana industry during classroom discussion and interviews, talking about friends who had seen a doctor and procured a medical license, and admitting they were now legal cannabis users. At the same time, the numbers of marijuana dispensaries in the Campus University Community were increasing and the local and regional newspapers were printing countless articles on the booming medical marijuana industry.

In 2000, Colorado voters had passed amendment 20, which lawfully authorized patients with a physician's recommendation and a valid registry card to use marijuana for medicinal purposes. The law allowed licensed cardholders no more than six personal plants and two ounces of marijuana or permitted them to designate a primary caregiver to cultivate and provide them with cannabis. In the State of Colorado a primary caregiver was a person, other than the patient or physician, who was responsible for managing the well-being of a patient. The caregiver could legally grow, possess, and distribute marijuana for the patient.

In 2009, the medical marijuana industry exploded in Denver and Boulder. First, the Colorado Board of Health opted not to require a limit on the number of patients to whom a primary caregiver could provide marijuana. This allowed medical cannabis dispensaries to operate and provide cannabis products to unlimited customers. Second, the U.S. Department of justice announced it would no longer expend federal resources to arrest and prosecute those who operated legally under state medical marijuana laws (Mikos 2011). Dispensaries in Colorado reached an estimated high of 1,100 in 2009, with the majority located in Denver, Colorado Springs, and Boulder (Weinstein 2010). In 2011, 119 medical marijuana dispensaries filed for registration in Boulder and 102,592 Colorado residents possessed valid registry ID cards (CDPHE 2011).

It was during this massive policy shift in Colorado that my research on undergraduate drug use took a new direction. Luckily, my years of research on the college party scene allowed me, once again, to approach this emerging phenomenon with an **opportunistic research strategy** (Lofland et al. 2006; Reimer 1977). I was already familiar with the illicit marijuana market (with how illicit closed-door drug markets operated) and immersed in the Campus University party scene as a **participant-as-observer** (Adler and Adler 1987). I revisited **IRB** for approval. An **Institutional Review Board (IRB)** is a group of scholars within a university who review and approve research proposals. The purpose of an IRB is to protect human subjects, as well as the researcher, from potential danger, ethical issues, or violations of the law. Furthermore, in 2009 I saw a local physician, obtained my medical license, and began frequenting the cannabis shops in the Campus University community, speaking with owners, managers, employees, and cardholders. I engaged customers and employees in marijuana-related discussions, introducing myself and asking questions about their experiences within the medical marijuana community. I scheduled interviews on site and handed out my business cards to expand my contacts. I also collected data on the presentation of the dispensaries I visited, taking careful notice of how the dispensary marketed marijuana, how employees and customers related to one another, and what marijuana products (e.g., smokables, tinctures, edibles) and additional amenities (e.g., massage, acupuncture, and oxygen) were available to customers. Although the medical license provided me entry into the dispensaries, my **status position** as the "Drugs in U.S. Society" professor at Campus University provided me added credibility with those in the industry. Furthermore, the medical card was crucial to my research as it allowed me to **penetrate fronts** (Douglas 1976) and to experience the scene *with* my informants. I jotted notes and memos after leaving dispensaries and wrote notes-on-notes (Klienman and Copp 1993) to develop emerging themes.

Through my participant-observation I developed analytical questions, sharpened them in my informal conversations, and gathered more focused data through my in-depth interviews. My direct access into dispensaries and the numerous contacts I developed from past research allowed me a variety of selection strategies. For my student interviews, I implemented **strategic methods** of sampling, consciously recruiting undergraduate cardholders to discuss and analyze their motivations for obtaining a medical license and their shifting interpretations of marijuana. This **strategic sampling** (Lofland et al. 2006; Zelditch 1962) allowed me to recruit people valuable to the study, such as student cardholders who were also caretakers, growers, dispensary employees, or **"budtenders."** Budtenders were the dispensary employees who offered product information, recommendations, and guidance to licensed customers. I **snowball sampled** to interview contacts outside the student networks I had developed through my participant-observation and my classes. Finally, I followed the evolution of the medical marijuana industry through the media (i.e., content analysis). I collected and analyzed newspaper and magazine articles and watched local and national television news reports that covered the Colorado medical marijuana "boom." Given the constant changes in medical marijuana policies, laws, and community relations, these news reports served as an invaluable resource for current information and as a way to **cross-check** (Douglas 1976) my interview and observational data.

Once again, I used a **theoretical sampling** method (Charmaz 2006; Strauss 1987), moving back and forth between my conceptual developments, empirical investigation, and sampling strategies to continually refine my analysis. I conducted all the interviews in a quiet, private office. The interviews lasted an average of one-and-a-half hours. I completed 40 interviews with undergraduate cardholders, focusing on their reasons for applying for a medical license, their previous experiences in the illicit drug market, and their shifting perceptions and understandings of marijuana.

Data Analysis

As I conducted interviews and fieldwork I simultaneously analyzed my data. **Data analysis** involves the identification of emerging **concepts** (Coffey and Atkinson 1996). The identification of concepts is crucial to inductive qualitative research. **Concepts** are logically developed ideas about the social setting or experience being studied. Concepts are the building blocks of theory and can vary in their level of abstraction. Some concepts are very straightforward, familiar, and simple to define (e.g., height, education, age, income). Other concepts are more abstract, diffuse, harder to define and often blurry (e.g., racism, political power, happiness). In my analysis, I used a **focused coding** approach (Charmaz 2006; Lofland et al. 2006), coding conceptually by identifying themes and patterns and interweaving my data and field knowledge. Focused coding suited my purposes and allowed me the freedom to move "across interviews and observations and compare people's experiences, actions, and interpretations" (Charmaz 2006:59). Basically, I moved back and forth between my data collection and analysis, developing theory through a constant **comparative method** (Glaser and Strauss 1967). Through this dynamic process, I created an analytic framework that guided my analysis as I identified themes/concepts that transcended my specific social context and offered a theoretical contribution.

My analysis process was abductive and resembled my theoretical sampling method. This **abductive** approach (Adler and Adler 2009) required me to continually move back and forth between my empirical observations, participant interactions, and conceptual themes. This continuous and dynamic interaction between the empirical world and my analysis served to strengthen the legitimacy and validity of my conceptual themes and theoretical contributions. In this process my participants' voices were heard through my conceptual (**emic**) categories and I presented my inductive interpretations through my theoretical (**etic**) categories.

Problems and Issues

Throughout this research I faced a number of isolated methodological issues. First, I sometimes encountered students who were hesitant to speak with me about their illegal drug use, even with assurances of confidentiality. Although this was rare, it was a problem I knew I would encounter among a few students. For participants I had recruited from my previous classes, this was never an issue as I had built trust/rapport through classroom discussion and subject material about drugs. For students I recruited through participant observation or snowball sampling I started interviews with general questions on the college party scene and student drug use, allowing me to share snippets of my personal history and experiences to develop **rapport** and be accepted as **"wise"** (Goffman 1963). I gradually worked in questions regarding their personal alcohol consumption and then questioned students on their experiences with illicit drugs. With continued IRB approval, I was granted permission to gain **"verbal consent"** from student participants. This was most helpful in alleviating student fears of discussing illegal behavior, as many were hesitant to sign their name on a consent form.

Second, although recruiting undergraduate medical marijuana cardholders from classes, dispensaries, and my emerging student network was never a problem, gaining interviews with growers and owners proved more difficult. For me to gain access to this population I needed a legitimate Colorado medical marijuana license, and this process required me to bend the truth. I was not completely honest with the doctor concerning my motivations to acquire a medical license (Adler 1985; Carey 1972; Douglas 1976). Once I had access to dispensaries, my status as a drugs professor, my personal knowledge of the marijuana subculture, and the evolving medical industry offered me immediate rapport with budtenders, but the owners and growers, often positioned behind the scenes, were more difficult to interview. Owners and growers were often extremely busy with the management, paperwork, and constantly evolving laws of the medical marijuana industry. Furthermore, they were understandably hesitant of interviews as their trade remained highly illegal under federal regulation. Finally, the dispensary industry experienced a national and local media frenzy in the first years of the medical marijuana boom, and many owners/growers were inundated with reporters, television stations, and interview requests. Luckily, through students who worked at dispensaries and my participant observation, I was able to gain rapport with three dispensaries, interviewing and hanging out with their owners and growers. This fieldwork provided me with invaluable information into the medical cannabis scene and deepened my understanding of the medicalization process.

Third, I quickly grew tired of fieldwork on the **periphery** of the college party scene. Although the new university environment and thriving social scene had initially been exciting, alluring, and provided me with passion and energy for my fieldwork, I eventually reached data saturation on direct observation around intoxicated students. The bars and restaurants surrounding Campus University were typically staffed by undergraduates and frequented by student partiers on any given weekend. For professors and graduate instructors, student sightings within the Campus University community on evenings out were common and routine. Although run-ins with students were rarely contentious or awkward, and typically friendly and entertaining, I no longer felt comfortable bumping into students every time I went to dinner or out for drinks. I gradually phased out my fieldwork in bars and later that year moved to a larger city away from Campus University where I could separate my research life from my social life.

Finally, I understood the potential influence of my **positionality** as the researcher. I acknowledged that I was writing from a position of privilege. As a white, heterosexual male, I fit a traditional "college" demographic and understood that I had experienced the college party scene differently than students with divergent characteristics and personal histories. I recognized this possible research effect and constantly stepped outside my privileged position and analyzed this social scene through a different lens. I also understood that I was studying the privileged strata of society. My informants embodied the demographics typical to participation in college partying: they were heterosexual, at least middle class, White, American-born, unmarried, childless, of traditional college age, and interested in drinking. I acknowledged that I could only speak to the experiences of White, young, heterosexual, middle-to-upper-class students, although this demographic constitutes the majority of participants within the college party scene.

Notes and Discussion Questions:

References

Adler, Patricia A. 1985. *Wheeling and Dealing: An Ethnography of an Upper-Level Drug Dealing and Smuggling Community*. New York: Columbia University Press.

Adler, Patricia A. and Peter Adler. 1987. *Membership roles in field research*. Thousand Oaks, CA: Sage.

Adler, Patricia A. and Peter Adler. 2009. "Using a Gestalt Approach to Analyze Children's Worlds." Pp. 225–37 in *Ethnographies Revisited: Constructing Theory in the Field*, edited by A.J. Puddephatt, W. Shaffir, and S.W. Kleinknecht. New York, NY: Routledge.

Arnett, Jeffrey. 1991. "Still Crazy After All These Years: Reckless Behavior Among Young Adults Aged 23-27." *Personality and Individual Differences* 12(12):1305–13.

Berg, Bruce. 2001. *Qualitative Research Methods for the Social Sciences*. Needham Heights, MA: Allyn and Bacon.

Biernacki, Patrick and Dan Waldorf. 1981. "Snowball Sampling: Problems and Techniques of Chain Referral Sampling." *Sociological Methods and Research* 10(2):141–63.

Charmaz, Kathy. 2006. *Constructing Grounded Theory: A Practical Guide Through Qualitatve Analysis*. Thousand Oaks, CA: Sage.

Coffey, Amanda J., and Paul A. Atkinson. 1996. *Making Sense of Qualitative Data: Complentary Research Strategies*. Thousand Oaks, CA: Sage.

Colorado Department of Public Health and Environment. 2011. "The Colorado Medical Marijuana Registry: Statistics." Retrieved November 16, 2011.

Denzin, Norman K. 1974. "The Methodological Implications of Symbolic Interactionism for the Study of Deviance." *The British Journal of Sociology* 25(3):269-82.

Douglas, Jack D. 1976. *Investigative Social Research: Individual and Team Field Research*. Beverly Hills, CA: Sage.

Dworkin, Jodi. 2005. "Risk Taking as Developmentally Appropriate Experimentation for College Students." *Journal of Adolescent Research* 20(2): 219–41.

Fontana, Andrea and Frey, James H. 1994. "Interviewing: The Art of Science." in *Handbook of Qualitative Research*, edited by Norman Denzin and Yvonna S. Lincoln. Thousand Oaks, CA: Sage.

Glaser, Barney G. and Anselm L. Strauss. 1967. *The Discovery of Grounded Theory: Strategies for Qualitative Research*.

Glesne, Corrine. 2006. *Becoming Qualitative Researchers: An Introduction*. Boston, MA: Allyn and Bacon.

Geertz, Clifford. 1973. *The Interpretation of Culture*. New York: Basic Books.

Goffman, Erving. 1963. *Stigma: Notes on the Management of a Spoiled Identity*. Englewood Cliffs, N.J.: Prentice Hall.

Harrington, Brooke. 2003. "The Social Psychology of Access in Ethnographic Research." *Journal of Contemporary Ethnography* 32(5):592–625.

Holstein, James and Jaber Gubrium. 1995. *The Active Interview*. Thousand Oaks, CA: Sage.

Horowitz, Ruth. 1986. "Remaining an Outsider: Membership as a Threat to Research Rapport." *Urban Life* 14(4):409–30.

Kleinman, Sherryl, and Martha Copp. 1983. *Emotions and Fieldwork*. Thousand Oaks, CA: Sage.

Lofland, John, David Snow, Leon Anderson, and Lofland, Lyn H. 2006. *Analyzing Social Settings 4th ed*. Belmont, CA: Wadsworth Thomson.

Maxwell, Joseph A. 2005. *Qualitative Research Design: An Interactive Approach*. Thousand Oaks, CA: Sage.

Mikos, Robert A. 2011. "A Critical Appraisal of the Department of Justice's New Approach to Medical Marijuana." *Stanford Law and Policy Review* 22:633-99.

Page, Bryan J. and Merrill Singer. 2010. *Comprehending Drug Use: Ethnographic Research at the Social Margins*. Piscataway, NJ: Rutgers University Press.

Ravert, Russell D. 2009. "'You're Only Young Once' Things College Students Report Doing Now Before It Is Too Late." *Journal of Adolescent Research* 24(3):376–96.

Riemer, Jeffrey W. 1977. "Varieties of Opportunistic Research." *Urban Life* 5(4):467–77.

Rubin, Herbert J. and Irene S. Rubin. 1997. *Qualitative Interviewing: The Art of Hearing Data*. Thousand Oaks, CA: Sage.

Strauss, Anslem L. 1987. *Qualitative Analysis for Social Scientists*. New York: Cambridge University Press.

Strauss, Anslem L. and Juliet Corbin. 1990. *Basics of Qualitative Research*. London: Sage.

Vander Ven, Thomas. 2011. *Getting wasted: Why college students drink too much and party so hard*. New York: NYU Press.

Warren, Carol A. B. 1988. *Gender Issues in Field Research*. Nebury Park, CA: Sage.

Watson, Lawrence C. and Maria-Barbara Watson-Franke. 1985. *Interpreting Life Histories: An Anthropological Inquiry*. New Brunswick, NJ: Rutgers University Press.

Wechsler, Henry, Beth E. Molnar, Andrea E. Davenport, and John S. Baer. 1999. "College alcohol use: A full or empty glass?" *Journal of American College Health* 47(6):247–52.

Wechsler, Henry and Bernice Wuethrich. 2002. *Dying to Drink: Confronting Binge Drinking on College Campuses*. Emmaus, PA: Rodale.

Weinstein, Jack. 2010. "Growing Pains: Entrepreneurs Cash in on Medical Marijuana." Retrieved April 21, 2011 (http://www.boulderkindcare.org/INTHENEWS/tabid/96/articleType/ArticleVie /articleId/27/Growing-Pains-Entrepreneurs-cash-in-on medical-marijuana-By Jack Weinstein.aspx).

Zelditch, Morris, Jr. 1962. "Some Methodological Problems of Field Studies." *American Journal of Sociology* 67(5):566-76.

Chapter Five

Entering the Party Scene

Leaving home for college is perhaps the most highly anticipated, yet greatly feared, transitional change for economically able young adults in the U.S. (Karp, Holmstrom, and Gray 1998; McBroom, Fife, and Nelson 2008). Students are elated to be free and independent of parental rules, yet this significant life transition can produce anxiety and trepidation as they adjust to structural changes in their living arrangements, academic circumstances, and social networks (Karp et al. 1998). For students, the college years are a crucial coming-of-age-experience where they can rehearse adult roles, experiment, take risks, and navigate adult responsibilities (Becker 1960; Dworkin 2005; Karp et al. 1998; Ravert 2009).

Incoming Freshmen

Students did not enter college as blank slates, but reported being bombarded with imagery about university life through the news media, Hollywood movies, network television, and collegiate recruiting strategies prior to their arrival on campus (Fallows 2003; Keup 2007; Kuh 1991). The cultural messages from these sources shaped the ideas, perceptions, and expectations incoming freshmen had about their post-secondary education. Often, these cultural messages fostered unrealistic expectations or romanticized ideals among college bound students that did not accurately reflect the realities of university life (Keup 2007). Students' personal expectations about how their university career would unfold often clashed with cultural ideals and their first-year experiences. Students anticipated a career building education, but had to choose an appropriate major of study; they foresaw lively and fulfilling social experiences, but had to build friendships among strangers in a new environment; and they expected to party, but had to gain the social capital to do so. For students, accomplishing these collegiate goals was often difficult and frustrating. Marc, a 21-year-old senior and physiology major, discussed his struggle to find his footing freshman year:

> I think freshman year, or those first couple of years of college, it's about playing different roles. And college is really about sorting yourself out. I mean it really is exciting, you are away from high school friends, your parents, and that environment that coddled you into being, and for the first time you have to ask yourself, "What am I like?" Am I happy here?" "Am I not happy here?" You know, these very self-identifying questions. And it's hard. When I was in high school, growing up, I never thought I might go to college and not be happy, or not be able to meet people I could really bond with, or go to college and have second thoughts, and I did. And in those first years everyone plays with different roles because everyone is just figuring it all out. You are in this big new place, your safety net of friends is gone, and that can be difficult to deal with in a lot of ways. You've got to declare a major, but have fun, meet some girls, you know. And I think that's where all the partying comes in, because it's not really time to figure it all out and you need to meet people and try new things and figure out what you like. Honestly, everything about those first years of college makes you want to be a part of something new and I think that's what fuels all the partying.

Like Marc, countless participants reported a sense of confusion regarding the behavioral expectations of their collegiate **status position** (Stryker 1980). Although they held preconceived notions about *what* the **roles** of an American college student involved (i.e., declare a major, study, attend class, meet friends, socialize, party, date, hook-up), *how* to go about being a first-year student and accomplishing these behaviors was a much more complicated issue.

A Social Major with an Academic Minor

For first-year students, initial forays into substance use were fostered by a detachment from academics and a desire for social experiences. A primary college expectation was to find a career, and many students arrived at Campus University with an open or undeclared major and intended to explore their scholarly options. Their high school education had prepared them in the basics of English, math, history, social studies, and science, and they anticipated developing more specific academic interests in their first year of college. They generally enrolled in the introductory 101 courses for various disciplines or the remedial writing and math classes required by the university. Students had mixed feelings about their first-year courses; many compared them to the monotony of their high school curriculum or found certain areas of study uninteresting and unfulfilling. Much of their freshman year curriculum was not part of a declared major or formalized academic career plan and students did not see how these courses fit into their overall education. Even for students who found their first and second-year classes stimulating and rewarding, they expressed difficulty in pinning down a specific major or academic direction. John, a 22-year-old environmental geography major, noted his academic confusion freshman year:

> I guess some people have a specific focus, but when I was a freshman, I had no idea. I was in some engineering classes because I did well in math and science in high school, but I hated it. I liked some of my other electives, but I couldn't stand my engineering classes and it just didn't work for me. It's not easy to figure out what you want to be, what you're really going to declare.

John's discussion illustrated an initial disconnect with school that was echoed by numerous respondents. Some entered Campus University burnt out after thirteen years of compulsory education. Others were simply following an expected trajectory of college attendance, or as Kristen, a 21-year-old senior and biology major, stated, "it's not *if* you are going to college, but *where* you are going to college." Located within new **structural arrangements** (Akers 2009) of higher education, freshman students initially lacked strong **bonds** to their education (Hirschi 1969). Without a specific major or academic direction, students reported an initial lack of *commitment* to their studies. Furthermore, the structure and culture of first-year academics fostered minimal *attachment* to educators and irregular *involvement* in scholarly activities. In contrast to high school, their professors did not typically know their names or hold them directly accountable for assignments, attendance, and participation in classroom activities. The **primary group** relationships in high school between students and their teachers, fostered by intimate classroom settings and continuous interaction and supervision, had largely shifted to a **secondary group** dynamic. In large introductory classes, students and professors related to one another in a more distant and instrumental basis. As opposed to daily obligations indicative of high school classes, freshmen were assigned long-term projects or semester term papers that did not require their immediate attention. They were no longer committed to a full slate of daily, back-to-back classes, with extracurricular after-school activities, mandatory detentions, study halls, or bus schedules. Their courses occurred periodically throughout the day, often with long breaks between classes or mornings completely absent of class commitments.

Although students entered collegiate academics in search of a scholarly purpose, their education often took a backseat to the more pressing matters of *being* social. They were excited about the potential for discovering new academic paths and novel intellectual challenges, but they found the social aspects of university life initially more important. John later stated, "Looking back on my first years of college I took all these random classes I barely remembered. But I do remember all the people I met and the friends

I made. That was the first thing I really wanted to do." Even for those students who declared a major area of study as incoming freshmen and held a strong bond to their education, their social concerns trumped their academic obligations. Many noted that "graduation was a long way off" and that "there was plenty of time to figure it all out." Students did not completely disregard their studies because they understood the importance of maintaining grades, learning about different schools of thought, and progressing towards graduation, but during freshman year their academics were typically secondary. Ethan, a 21-year-old engineering major, recounted his academic and social issues freshman year:

> Basically, the first semester of my freshman year I never had time to do anything, but all my buddies were going out. I gave myself this huge workload because I had declared an aerospace engineering major and I was miserable. I actually failed one of my classes, so I cut back on my workload and for the first time I could party. And things got so much better. I got to socialize and double the people I knew, I got to get outside my normal range of friends and drink. I knew academically it was impacting my studies; I could see that I could be performing better, but I was happier. I had this new social experience, but I was also working towards my goals at my pace. It really matured me.

Ethan's story illustrated how students started locating their educational goals in relation to their social pursuits. Their secondary education had mandatory regimes of classes, sports, and extracurricular activities that could not be as easily neglected for social activities such as partying. Students began to realize that in college, they had the academic agency to develop a more pragmatic, working relationship between their education and their social interests. Mary, a 21-year-old junior from Maryland, expressed her first year negotiations with schoolwork and socializing:

A: Well, when I first came to college, my success was defined as getting good grades. I got a 3.8 my first semester, and I was an integrative physiology major, so I knew I couldn't keep a 3.8 GPA and have any life. I really cared about school, but I decided then that I would never drop below a 3.0 because I'm not looking for a career that will consume my life so I didn't want school to consume my entire life. I felt like if I didn't go out and party I was missing something, I wanted to meet people. But it's hard to sometimes to do both, they don't teach you that.

Q: What do they not teach you?

A: How to go to college and party.

Mary's discussion illustrated the tug-of-war students realized would be a central feature of university life. Fulfilling their expectations for academic success and their desire for a flourishing social life would require a delicate balance they had not needed to learn in high school. It took time and effort to rebuild their social lives. Students reported that missing a class, cramming for an exam, or "half-assing" a term paper was largely unimportant freshmen year, as they had not committed to an academic major that would define their career. Some simply couldn't care less about certain classes while others did not know how to manage a taxing social life and college academics.

Students found themselves with a **foot in both the academic world and the social world** (Matza 1964), but they initially lacked **commitment** (Becker 1960; Burke and Reitzes 1991; Kanter 1972) to the academic role of their collegiate **status position** (Stryker 1968, 1980). The personal, social, and cultural expectations of having a vibrant social life, along with their naivety in balancing academics and socializing, fostered students to **drift** toward their developing social scene. They found their new world of social pursuits more exciting and the development of friendship networks more pressing. Although some students reported unshakeable academic dedication during their freshman year, even **rate-busting** (Heckert and Heckert 2002) overachievers made sacrifices to pursue a social life. Students' initial disconnect from educational goals, combined with the structural and cultural differences of university academics, allowed freshman the opportunity to detach from academics and build a new social life.

A Social Scene with Freshmen Struggles

Students' first-year academic disconnect and focus on developing a social life was primarily fueled by their desire to learn about their university environment and the new people in it. For incoming students, Campus University was initially overwhelming. Arriving at a large, residential campus of nearly 30,000 undergraduate students, they found themselves in a **"world of strangers"** (Lofland 1973). Students' primary friendship groups were dismantled during the move from high school to college and they entered university life lacking the emotional bonds, social support, and familiarity of their once close confidants. Faced with personal and cultural expectations to meet new and different peers, make friends, and create long-lasting personal bonds, students' first task of their transitioning social life was to develop a primary social network. Researchers note that exploring and establishing peer relationships and friendship networks are primary developmental missions of emerging adulthood (Havighurst 1972; Schulenberg, Bryant, and O'Malley 2004). In the past, their friends were furnished almost automatically through family connections, neighborhood proximity, or school affiliation (Becker 1960), but in this new social environment students were left to make these connections on their own. Although some students eventually rushed fraternities or sororities, explored campus groups, or joined intramural sports teams, they initially bonded with those in their residence hall. However, this social process did not occur in a vacuum and students noted that they typically gathered around alcohol and drugs to foster this occasionally awkward and disconcerting "what's your name?" social process. Molly, a 21-year-old junior and advertising major, recalled her dorm days of drinking and partying with friends:

> When I came to Campus University, I didn't know anyone. And freshmen year, you're basically partying and taking shots in the dorms because you don't know anybody and need some liquid courage. Everyone is just trying to make friends in a sea of new faces. My girlfriends and I used to smoke and watch movies every Sunday; those were some of the best times in my life. We bought some weed from this guy in our dorm, did our best to hide it, and maybe drank some wine if we could. It was just a great way to laugh and hang with people.

Their social scene started in the dorms, as did their initial collegiate experiences with drugs and alcohol. They smuggled beer and liquor into their rooms that they procured through resourceful peers, older siblings, or a fake ID. First-year students crowded in their dorm rooms to smoke marijuana purchased through the local "dorm room dealer" (Mohamed and Fritsvold 2010) or from classmates with a medical marijuana license (O'Brien 2013). They challenged each other to drinking games, played video games, listened to music, watched movies, laughed and shared stories, and started to build new primary relationships. A central tenet of sociology is that drug use, even when deliberately used alone, produces bonds among people (Faupel 1991). This is not surprising, given that researchers have found substance use facilitates peers relationships and that adolescents who experiment with drugs and alcohol exhibit enhanced levels of peer acceptance and involvement (Maggs, Almeida, and Galambos 1995; Maggs and Hurrelmann 1998). Students, like countless others through the history of human life, found that recreational drug use could reduce social tensions and foster the bonds of camaraderie and friendship they sought. Dave, a 21-year-old junior and business major, discussed his feelings about his drinking and drug use during freshman year:

Having some drinks, doing some drugs, it helps you meet people. It's just, you know alcohol is a social thing, it helps ease your anxiety, your mind, and it's easier to meet people when you're more confident and open. And then there is the social function, whatever drugs you do, whether it's marijuana, ecstasy, or acid, you're hanging out with people and having these new experiences. It's all just part of the process.

This "process" described by Dave functioned to bridge the divide between strangers. Meeting peers was not an always relaxing task as students were often nervous, restrained, or shy, as they hesitantly made the social rounds in their residence hall. As Miller, a 22-year-old senior and physics major recalled, "drinks just get everything off the ground." But meeting their peers in the dorm was only the first stage of building friendships. Partying also offered students the chance to **penetrate fronts** (Douglas 1976) and gather information about their potential friends or future roommates. Jill, a 22-year-old senior with a double major in sociology and dance, recounted her socializing process freshmen year:

I certainly drank more freshmen and sophomore years. You're in the dorms and really don't know anybody and partying just brings everyone together around something. And freshman year especially, you're like going out with different people all the time. One night it was people from this floor, then kids from that floor, and then three of their friends I'd never met. And you're partying with people you don't know, which is a whole different thing. Because you realize that there are people you like to hang with, and there are people who are a liability, and people who get weird, and so it's all this big new experience with all these new people.

Penetrating fronts was important because students wanted to figure out the people they felt comfortable getting drunk with, those they had fun with, and those they did not. With their primary friendship groups broken, students desired fellow partiers who would watch out for them, support them in times of crisis, and who they could trust if they were overly intoxicated. The recreational use of drugs and alcohol also introduced an exciting dynamic into burgeoning relationships or routine interactions that would not have occurred while sober. Although students certainly forged friendships while sober and made long-lasting social ties through studying and other recreational activities, substance use was a novel coming-of-age vehicle towards this end, an activity around which these young adults could gather.

These primary relationships would be the foundation for entrée into a larger party scene students saw outside the residence halls. Students' first friendship groups operated as the initial springboard for experimentation with drugs and alcohol and fostered their exploration of the Campus University nightlife. Partying in the dorms and forging new friendships and relationships was ultimately a **backstage** (Goffman 1959) exercise for students to prepare for the party scene.

The Party Scene

Although students used drugs in the dorms, the "real" party scene existed off-campus in the bars and student neighborhoods surrounding Campus University. This scene was the **reference group** (Eisenstadt 1954; Shibutani 1955) for students' internalization of party norms and beliefs. With their newfound freedom and independence, students wanted to fulfill a central college expectation: partying. In their collegiate status position, freshmen anticipated managing their own time and space, dictating their own whereabouts, and making independent and self-directed decisions. For the first time in their lives, they were distanced from the watchful eyes of parents, teachers, and other authority figures who mandated their daily routines and activities. With this new freedom and a detachment from academic obligations, a personal and cultural expectation was to party with their new friends. Kelly, a 21-year-old, sociology and history major, recalled her party fervor freshmen year:

> A: For the first time you don't have the risk of your mom and dad calling or something, or wondering where you are. You have no curfew; no one is going to come in your room and yell at you. You're in college, like in the dorms for the first time, being able to go wherever. It's the time to party and do all that stuff we couldn't do.
>
> Q: Was that expected with everyone?
>
> A: Oh yeah, it's just the time to get everything out of your system. You're really limited at home and I think everyone gets here with this idea that we're going to drink some drinks and do some drugs.
>
> Q: And is that pretty common?
>
> A: All my friends did, it's what we're told we're supposed to do!

For students, a primary college expectation was experimenting with drugs and alcohol. They understood the college years to be a time for active self-exploration (Dworkin 2005) and a place to "obtain a wide range of experiences before settling down into roles and responsibilities of adult life" (Arnett 2000:475). Because students anticipated losing these opportunities as adults (Ravert 2009), the college social scene was considered the optimal time and location for recreational substance use. Nathan, a 22-year-old senior and pre-med major, discussed his drive toward partying his freshman year:

A: You come to this new place and you're free, so it seems. And now you are supposed to be on your own, making the decisions. And at least in my context, having my parents constantly on top of me was gone, there really isn't the same people telling you, "don't do that," and I think that plays a huge role. You're on your own in that way, and so we're like, "it's time to party."

Q: And party hard?

A: Well I guess, I mean I had some pretty drunk nights, but I never did anything bad, like hurt anyone or myself. I think it's just different, the size of it all.

Q: But you got in trouble?

A: Yeah, it's like we all do, all over again.

The expectation to party was central to the college experience and the party scene was a social phenomenon that attracted the attention of first-year students. It was natural for these young adults to want to venture out of their tiny, cramped living quarters and experience new and different social scenes. However, other factors played a central role in pushing students into the party scene as they realized that socializing and drinking in the dorms was risky business.

New Authority

Students quickly learned that they had traded the authority of their parents for the surveillance and punitive policies of Campus University. Although they no longer had the curfews, chores, and punishments from their former home lives, their expectations for alcohol or drug use in the residence hall were swiftly suppressed. Luke, a 21-year-old, senior and finance major, elaborated:

> You come in freshman year, and it's like everything and everyone in your whole life has given you the notion that college is a time to party. You've got to study, but it's time to try some drugs and do some drinking. You see it in the movies, you hear people like your brothers and sisters, even your parents tell stories and it's just what happens in college. But you get here and your dorm is like a minimum-security prison. You have the R.A. watching you, then you have the CSOs [Campus Safety Officers), and the police patrol your hall. They always patrol, all of them, knocking on your door and asking you questions.

Students reported that the **formal control agents** of the university structure were extremely invasive and told stories of room searches, hallway frisks, and routine arrests and citations. The dormitories operated as a form of constant supervision as students felt an omnipresent feeling of **surveillance** through "relays" of observers, hierarchically ordered to **"supervise the supervisors"** (Foucault 1977, 1997). Resident Assistants, who were fellow students and lived in the dormitories conducting rounds and room checks, were monitored by the hall directors, who filed infractions, citations, and arrest reports to Campus University and Dining Hall Services. These "in-house" control agents were aided by CSOs, criminal justice oriented undergraduates who were hired by Campus University Police to patrol campus grounds, buildings, and dormitories and notify dispatch of any alcohol or drug use on campus. The final layer of this hierarchal control was the campus police who patrolled and searched dorms rooms and the city police who primarily arrested students off-campus.

This hierarchal system of observation and control subjected them to multiple forms of **policing** (Cordner and Scarborough 2010; Crawford et al. 2005; Innes 1999; Jones and Newburn 1998; Ratcliffe 2012), which operated simultaneously to create a hostile environment towards any form of partying, no matter how mundane. Resident Assistants and campus safety officers aided the campus police, and though these campus security forces were not private security *per se*, they operated as such, and notified campus police officers of substance use violations, questioned students, searched rooms, and filed reports. The campus police also used a **community style of policing**, proactively patrolling the dorms, listening for sounds of partying and speaking with students to detect intoxication. Campus security agencies implemented **intelligence-led policing**, targeting certain dorms and students with previous infractions and citations whose information was located in comprehensive database. Finally, the policies regarding substance use in the residence halls were strictly **zero-tolerance** and even the most benign and harmless party behaviors were swiftly enforced by campus security forces. Although students managed some new freedoms by being away from home, university officials were often stricter than their parents. Liz, a 20-year-old Junior and psychology major, noted:

> My parents were cool with me drinking. They knew I was going to do it, so long as I was responsible and would never drive, puke, black-out and all that stuff. If I was mature about it, they never really got pissed at me. Plus, my dad always said if I ever needed a ride home or I was drunk somewhere and didn't feel safe, he would come get me, no questions asked. But in the dorms it was like zero-tolerance, no matter how responsible you were, and empty beer can or some weed and you get an MIP [Minor in Possession] or even arrested.

Students were very critical of the strict laws that operated in their residence halls and they were confused about the substance-free and zero-tolerance atmosphere the university was trying to achieve. They learned it was difficult and dangerous to socialize and drink in the dorms as formal university sanctions could place them in both legal and academic trouble.

Students who were caught by city police, campus police, campus safety officers, or resident assistants for their drug and alcohol use faced an array of community sanction, fines, and treatments (Cohen 1985) to examine and normalize their deviant and criminal behavior (Foucault 1977). They often faced penalties from Campus University and the city that included fines, community service, restorative justice, treatment classes, drug education classes, drug testing, probation, suspension, and expulsion. Unsurprisingly, the students who found their names and information logged into this system of sanctions experienced increased attention from the formal control agents of hierarchal observation.

Party Capital

If the situation experienced in the residence hall was any indicator, students learned they lacked **social power** and **"party capital"** in their new university environment. Viewing the party scene as a culture stratified by networks, resources, and social ties, first-year students found they were the lower class. Similar to Bourdieu's (1984) conception of **social capital,** **"party capital"** comprised students' social ties to each other and the sum of resources available because of those ties. As freshmen, the cultural and social resources available to them were minimal as they occupied a lower status in relation to their upperclassmen. The party scene at Campus University was a social hierarchy, and students with valued resources and commodities (i.e., a house, a car, alcohol, a cannabis license, a fake ID, or drug connections) held higher positions in that hierarchy. Older and more experienced seniors and juniors had party capital while freshmen did not.

An Uncharted World

For entering students, their lack of **party capital** initially stemmed from being unaccustomed to their new environment. Although their high school once felt like a populated, fast-paced place, the size of Campus University created initial perceptions of a vast and uncharted world. Navigating the campus and the surrounding city for a party scene (i.e., big parties, booze, drugs, single men or single women) was important for incoming freshmen. They used their new primary group relationships, developed in the dorms, to venture out and explore campus neighborhoods and meander through downtown. They passed the lively bars and the wild parties of their vast new social scene. Jake, a 21-year-old senior majoring in biology, recalled his first impressions of the party scene at Campus University:

> When I was a freshman, there were like a hundred parties here on the weekends, and it felt like a thousand. And you try and get a feel for it all because you're isolated, and it's weird being a freshman. You're bombarded with this huge campus, this town, and all these parties and you want to go out and experience it, but it can be overwhelming at first. You definitely don't feel like you're part of it.

Students' initial experiences in their new environment prompted feelings of segregation from a very visible party scene. They felt as if their knowledge, connections, and housing situation located them across a **sociocultural border** (Sellin 1938) and they felt distanced from a proximate social world. In high school, they attended parties thrown by their friends at homes of unsuspecting parents, but trolling student neighborhoods for access to parties was a strange new phenomenon. They entered college with high expectations of being involved in a thriving social scene, but encountered a vast new environment where they felt like outsiders. Although Campus University sponsored first year initiation events, these were substance free and entirely unpopular among new undergraduates. Students could continually view a college social scene such as they had imagined as high school seniors, but they had minimal access to it. Jen, a 22-year-old senior, economics major, noted:

> You feel like such a little fish and you really want to find your social group, to have fun, and that's why you want to go out and experience it

all, but it's not easy at first. Going out and being social involves alcohol a lot of times, and you're really restricted as a freshman. Plus, you're in this giant place and you're with all these new people and you want to see what everyone else is doing. And when you see what everyone else is doing, it's going out to the bars, to parties, tailgating before football games and all that stuff.

Navigating entrée was often difficult for college freshmen. Sometimes their new friends had older siblings or upper-class friends who invited them to house parties or snuck them into bars; other times older peers in their classes extended an invitation to a party or two. Typically however, they lacked the social capital to legitimately enter bars and parties, so students worked together to navigate the seemingly inaccessible party scene. They trolled in groups searching for parties, they procured fake IDs, or they snuck booze into social events. And while entrée was crucial, learning the normative expectations of drinking, drug use, and sociability was also vital. Although 13 years of compulsory education may have prepared students for college academics, their experiences with substance use and their drug and alcohol education had had not prepared them for the intensity of college partying. They had to learn that men threw most of the parties and that women were much more welcome at these events, that alcohol was often scarce for nameless freshmen, and that keg lines often favored house seniority and close friends. Students had to learn about their personal limits and drug safety with beer and hard liquor, marijuana and MDMA, or LSD and cocaine. They had to navigate how to get home safely and avoid cops and Resident Assistants, how to help sick friends, and generally how to party without getting into trouble.

The Age of No Access

Although dorm life and a lack of social ties reduced first-years students' party capital, their age constituted the primary factor reducing their agency. Being under the age of 21 and unable to legally purchase or consume alcohol further segregated first-year students from the university party scene. Although they could generally procure alcohol from upper-class students, through a fake ID, or from older siblings, this process was certainly not on their own terms and they lacked control over their own substance use. Alcohol purchased in this fashion included cases of cheap beer to be chugged swiftly or bottles of low-grade liquor for discreet and undetected shots. Furthermore, they could not legally attend bars, drink at parties or concerts, or tailgate before football games. They held minimal control over where and how they could drink and socialize. Students drank heavily and quietly in their dorm rooms before they ventured out in the party scene because their access to alcohol was very limited. Although alcohol was blatantly present at all college parties, for freshmen (especially men) having access to an alcohol supply was never a guarantee. Mitch, a 22-year-old senior and marketing major, noted:

> Let's say, for example when I was a freshman, and you go out to parties. You have to wait in keg lines or know someone who has the beer. If you want something to drink, you can't bring your own because you'll have a better chance of getting an MIP. So you get some cheap shit and get hammered before you go anywhere. If you get your hands on some beer, and then you keep getting drunk, if you don't, at least you have a buzz.

Students reported drinking or getting high in their cars to avoid trouble in their residence halls. Jen, a 21-year-old senior and psychology major, referred to this as a "car-bar" and recalled her pre-partying experiences freshmen year: "And we would just drink and drink as much as we could, double-shots of vodka and stuff like that. It was large quantities of cheap alcohol, stuff you could drink quick, stuff that you could hide."

Sorry for Partying

Although an absence of party capital impeded students' agency and control in the university party scene, they also lacked personal experience with drugs and alcohol. Although numerous respondents had experimented in high school, the size and intensity of the party scene at Campus University was often overwhelming. Matt, a 21-year-old senior and economics major, elaborated:

> I had no idea until I started going out my freshmen year. You really can't understand, you just can't, until you walk into one of those crazy huge parties, how big it is. In high school, and I know it depends on where you went, but you probably didn't have more than 50 kids at a party. I never did. But when I walked into my first big house party, people were doing coke in the bathroom and these people in the kitchen had really dilated eyes and there were people that were just hammered. People were just packed in. It was a really big shock, like going from the minors to the majors.

In contrast to the dormitory environment, the party scene off-campus was a different animal. Although students' curiosity and desire to party drew them to off-campus parties and local bars, they reported an initial naivety about these more intense scenes. Not only were parties overwhelming, but as students broadened their social networks, they began to realize that a multitude of drugs were available through certain peers. The intensity of the party scene and the availability of drugs shocked even the more seasoned high school partiers. Amanda, a 21-year-old political science and studio art major, stated:

> I came here thinking since I did other drugs in high school, that everybody here at Campus University had drunk as much as me or had done the same drugs. But I was wrong. First, there were more drugs around than I was used to. There were these guys I knew who sold coke and molly, another girl who would trade or sell her Xanex, and these guys I knew I

could get LSD from. I was also shocked some people had never tried anything but alcohol; some people had never even gotten drunk before. If it was a culture shock for, me I wonder what it was like for them?

First-year students lacked experience and knowledge regarding the norms and rules of alcohol and drug use. As Jen, a 21-year-old senior and political science major, stated, "I drank in high school, so I knew what to expect from alcohol, and that was about it." Similarly, Matt, the 21-year-old junior and economics major, noted, "I had partied in high school, gotten drunk, and done some molly, but partying at Campus University was a whole different experience." Basically, first-year students were rookies, and their reflective stories about freshman year, especially regarding alcohol, reflected immature and reckless partying, a lack of personal control and reasonable limits. Freshman year was the year of excess. Kristin, a 21-year-old senior and history major, reminisced about her partying freshman year, and like numerous informants she did not have a definitive explanation, but noted, "freshman year was about how drunk you could get, don't ask me why, but you're supposed to be drunk or on something." Similarly, Molly, the 21-year-old advertising major, noted, "freshman year was disgusting, I don't know how we did it, and I don't know how we lived it." And Jane, a 21-year-old senior and sociology major, noted, "I mean freshmen year was like drink and drink and drink, if it was there, you drank it."

Although alcohol consumption was certainly the most widely used substance by college students, experimentation or recreational use of other illicit drugs was also a central theme. Students consistently reported trying new drugs like marijuana, ecstasy, cocaine, LSD, psilocybin, and various prescription medications. Although marijuana was the most widely used illicit substance by students at Campus University, ecstasy was a particularly popular drug of choice during my research. Jeff, a 22-year-old senior and marketing major, stated:

A: I still like molly, and I'll probably always use it on certain occasions.
The first time I did it was freshman year, this guy was selling at this party,
so we took some. I felt great, but we took it way too late, we were up all
night kept pounding beers, and didn't drink enough water. I felt like shit
the next day.

Q: And you would have done that differently?

A: Hell yeah, now I would have a show to go to, you know, drop it at the
right time and definitely not drink as much. You just figure out how it
works best for you and what you want.

Students' stories regarding drug use reflected a lack of knowledge of the
cultural recipes and **rituals** (Zinberg 1986) of consumption (Maloff et al.
1979). They often reported taking too much, at the wrong place, at the
wrong time, and with the wrong people, or neglecting the safety guidelines
for certain substances. Jessica, a 22-year-old senior and business major,
elaborated:

> Looking back now we were just oblivious half the time, and as we went
> through it all, we messed up, but learned and that's how we got our drugs
> 101. It wasn't like it was always a bad thing, but we definitely learned from
> each other. Everything I know now about drinking and drug use has been
> through my friends. I mean, you don't learn anything from the stuff they
> teach you in high school or coming into freshmen year. I was always
> fighting with my high school health teacher and I guess I see where they
> are coming from. They don't want to teach the lighter side because all of
> the sudden they are the teachers promoting drug use. I mean it's a joke,
> our eyes just glazed over when they taught it. I don't want some health
> teacher who's never done it telling me how bad it all is. Even a kid I know
> telling me about his experiences with drugs is better than someone lying to

me. And that's what college is, especially those first years, all this trial and error. That's what you get. It's not something like economics and you can say here are the stats and the formulas; you just can't do that with drugs.

Students understood, upon reflection, their naivety and inexperience with substance use. They discussed that freshman year involved "learning the hard way" about drugs, social life, and academics. They discussed stories of arrests, MIPs, probation, suspension, failing grades, and GPAs still recovering from those first party years. However, while some expressed disappointment, the vast majority were not regretful for partying, but only wished they had understood both the informal/safety rules and norms of drug consumption, practical and responsible mechanisms of self-control, and the university regulations and laws. Thomas, a 21-year-old sociology and journalism major from Michigan, noted:

> Freshman year was a lot of experimenting. You really didn't know what you were doing. What did I learn? I learned that seven shots of vodka will sneak up on you in a bad way, coke freaks me out, that pot is totally safe, and that I like taking ecstasy at shows. It's just a weird onslaught of lots of drinking and not really knowing, just being stupid. I wasn't really trying to be a dumbass back then, I just didn't know any better half the time.

When I asked Kelly, the 21-year-old senior, how she would sum up her freshman year partying experiences, with two MIPs, a couple of blackouts, and a trip to detox, she laughed, shrugged, and told me: "sorry for partying." Although the expression "sorry for partying" was popular during my research, the mentality of the term was prevalent throughout my college career and all my years of fieldwork. The phrase basically means that you partied hard, maybe too hard, but you had an awesome time and you were not sorry for it. Students used the expression after an especially drunken or crazy night partying, when they had done something immature, embarrassing, or irresponsible, or all of the above. A student's use of the phrase "sorry for partying" acknowledges his or her potentially untoward or inappropriate behavior, but excuses the evening/incident as a product of the party culture. However, the saying does not necessarily denote bad behavior, especially in the context of the college party scene. As Jack, a 19-year-old sophomore, explained:

> It basically means you had an awesome time. Maybe you got outta hand, but you rocked out the night. I think it's really about never apologizing for partying hard. You're supposed to get it done, so when your friends say "Oh, man you were lit last night." You say, "sorry for partying." When they say, "Dude, you I can't believe you ran from the cops at that party, it's sorry for partying." It basically fits every scenario.

"Sorry for partying" could be used for almost any occasion. Even when not verbally stated, it was an understood mindset of college partying, especially during those first years when students were adjusting to their newfound independence and testing and learning their limits with drugs and alcohol.

Conclusion

The initial transition from high school to university life resulted in a breakdown of familiar and reliable structures for ordering students' lives (Karp, Holstrom, and Gray 1998). The move to college constituted a structural and cultural shift that located them in a transitional status position (i.e., college student). Similar to the notion of **"liminality,"** during their move from home to college, students experienced a period of time when they were in between old and new statuses. This structural shift meant that they would leave behind their past role behaviors of high school to navigate the responsibilities, activities, and risks of being an independent and self-directed college student. Learning university life involved negotiating unfamiliar academic terrain, developing intimate and depth primary friendships, and experimenting with drugs and alcohol within a thriving and intense college party scene.

As students became accustomed to their new freedoms of college life, they experienced the punitive, zero tolerance policies of Campus University. Students were unable to party, even moderately and quietly in their dorm rooms without incurring harsh formal sanctions. Even though students managed strategies and techniques to hide their drug and alcohol use in the residence halls, for many, the risk was overwhelming, especially for those who had already been cited. The punitive policies at Campus University reflected the "law and order" stance of the War on Drugs. The rules students experienced relied heavily on **deterrence** as undergraduates were controlled primarily through identification, arrest, and disciplinary penalties. These sanctions served an **expressive** (Garland 2001) rather than **rehabilitative** function, as Campus University attempted to correct students' deviant behavior by making an example out of their unlucky peers.

At the *structural* level, the strict prohibition of alcohol and drug use produced a strain on the student population by denying lawful and appropriate ways to party. Students drank and used drugs in secrecy, away from any manner of oversight or control. Similar to the "**iron law of prohibition**" (Gray 2011) (i.e., the more heavily a drug and its users are enforced, the more dangerous the drug and its use becomes), students often consumed the strongest of liquors in a rushed manner to be discreet and quick in their intoxication. The opportunities to develop moderate and controlled drinking were scarce because students could not drink casually in their own rooms, pick out liquor that struck their fancy, or bring their own six-pack to a party. Furthermore, their lack of **party capital** (i.e., safe location, age, friendship networks) criminalized their consumption of alcohol and forced them to drink heavily before parties, sporting events, or other social functions. For students, breaking the law by procuring alcohol illegally or entering bars underage was standard through fake IDs or older peers. They wandered campus neighborhoods searching for non-hostile party environments, drank whatever liquor was available, and drank excessively as they had minimal outlets to do otherwise.

At the *cultural* level, these heavy drinking practices were sustained by subcultural norms and values about partying. As the punitive zero-tolerance policies pushed partying behaviors behind closed doors, students were thrust into a **deviant subculture** where they learned distinct ideologies and norms regarding alcohol use. Students existed in a culture of surveillance and were monitored by peers (i.e., Campus Safety Officers and Resident Assistants), private citizens (i.e., bouncers, bartenders, athletic security, and private firms), and the police. This intense enforcement created **subcultural boundaries** between students and conventional society as they devised subculturally specific ways to obtain alcohol and drink secretly and discreetly. For students, generating channels into the party scene was important because the pressure to drink at parties and bars was rife and students who did not conform to this norm were stigmatized. Furthermore, failing to notify Resident Assistants of overdose or other problems for fear of sanctions produced a culture of fear, distrust, and excess. Students were effectively distanced from **conventional norms** and behaviors surrounding alcohol use and learned ideas and beliefs of **normality** (Goffman 1983) within a **deviant organization** of their neophyte peers (Best and Luckenbill 1980). Students experienced a **cultural border** (Sellin 1938) in which they were culturally separated from normative drinking practices by punitive strategies aimed at curbing the party scene at Campus University.

At the *interactional* level, these punitive policies also impacted students' burgeoning social networks. Upon an arrest or citation, students faced sanctions ranging from community service, fines, jail time, drug testing, suspension, or expulsion. Once students were caught in this wide net of sanctions, they were emotionally and socially distanced from their burgeoning social life as those students who faced even the most minimal formal sanctions often became afraid to hang out with peers (e.g., guilty by association) for fear of further troubles with the city or the university. Furthermore, students who found themselves doing community service, working extra shifts to pay fines, or using time and money toward drug testing regimes, were distanced from their academic obligations. Once students were in the Campus University conduct system, any further trouble was cumulatively added to their previous transgressions, even if they had completed their service, suspension, fines, or drug testing mandates. These conditions impacted students' peer interactions, social outlets, and emotional states and produced social anxieties and further concealment of substance use.

Similar to alcohol, students were strictly prohibited from using marijuana, and if caught by formal control agents were subject to medical interventions that reflected modern modes of normalization (Foucault 1977) and community corrections (Cohen 1985).

For students, their exposure to medical control proliferated through a process of *medical collaboration* (Conrad 1979) with the formal control agents of Campus University. As there is rarely one dominant designation (i.e., legal or medical) over deviant behaviors, many acts of deviance are subject to both criminalized and medicalized definitions and sanctions (Conrad 1979). While students found themselves subject to the coercive (Gusfield 1963) controls of campus and city police, Campus Safety Officers, and Resident Assistants, Campus University policies concerning substance abuse also had an "assimilative" medical component. Not only were students subject to more punitive-style (i.e., suspension, community service, drug-testing, or jail) sanctions, their underage drinking or illicit drug use was further subjected to medicalized governmentalites (Foucault 1997; Rose, O'Malley, and Valverde 2006). This medical control was intertwined with formal university controls and operated in students' lives in three central ways.

First, students caught and identified by formal control agents were examined by other people such as doctors, psychologists, health clinicians, psychiatrists, and drug treatment specialists. Just as students were subject to hierarchal observations (Foucault 1977) and surveillance through campus police, Resident Assistants, and Campus Security Officers, their substance use behavior was subject to medical *examination* and they were turned into a "case" by the Campus University health system (Foucault 1977). Students underwent psychological testing, drug abuse assessments, and psychiatric evaluation. They were scored on their level of risk taking and substance abuse, and the results of their evaluations, interviews, and assessments were documented and filed, and would be a guideline for mandated treatment. Students were notified, based on these medical tests and evaluations, that they were failing to meet university expectations, societal standards of drinking or drug use, or told they had a substance abuse problem. This medical control process was intended to perform a normalizing or corrective function by informing students that they were not meeting proper standards of conduct, personal health standards, or university expectations in relation to their peers and campus policy.

Second, the intertwined relationship of formal control and medical control within the university party scene served to increase the number of students subject to university regulations and interventions. The activity of college partying was dealt with as a legal problem (i.e., underage drinking and illicit drug use) and a medical problem (i.e., the greatest health hazard facing college students today), subjecting students to a wide range of interventions. These medical controls *widened the net* and *thinned the mesh* (Cohen 1985) as students who would normally complete legal sanctions were subjected to further monitoring through the medicalization of college partying. Whereas the police could process students formally or screen them out, upon notification to university officials, students were subjected to a wider set of medical interventions such as mandated health and substance abuse classes, Alcoholic Anonymous groups, psychological counseling, harm reduction courses, and drug testing.

Third, the medicalization of students' drinking and drug use also *presented* these medical controls as softer than formal controls (Cohen 1985) when they were often just as harsh. Subjecting students to an array of medical examinations and psychological evaluations, labeling them as alcoholics or drug abusers, charging them large sums of money for compulsory treatment, and contacting their parents with such information may be no more humane and effective than fines, suspension, and community service. Furthermore, while the police typically operated under due process and the codified procedures of the criminal justice system, medical controls unfolded outside the legal system and the university was not required to abide by such procedural safeguards. Students might be referred to a Campus University health program, treatment service, or psychological counselor not because they violated a particular rule, but because *someone* (i.e., a conduct officer) decided they might benefit from services offered by that program. While students were sanctioned on evidence in a courtroom for violations brought to the city, Campus University did not need to follow such niceties as due process and legal rights when sanctioning students to medicalized interventions. Furthermore, if students did not complete their medical evaluations and treatments, they were once again subjected to increased drug testing, fines, community service, and risk of suspension.

Notes and Discussion Questions:

References

Akers, Ronald L. 2009. *Social Learning and Social Structure: A General Theory of Crime and Deviance*. New Brunswick, N.J.: Transaction Publishers.

Becker, Howard S. 1960. "Notes on the Concept of Commitment." *American Journal of Sociology* 66(1):32–40.

Arnett, Jeffrey Jensen. 2000. "Emerging Adulthood: A Theory of Development from the Late Teens Through the Twenties." *American Psychologist* 55(5):469–80.

Best, Joel and David F. Luckenbill. 1980. "The Social Organization of Deviants." *Social Problems* 28(1):14-31.

Bourdieu, Pierre. 1984. *Distinction: A Social Critique of the Judgement of Taste*. Cambridge: Harvard University Press.

Burke, Peter. J. and Donald C. Reitzes. 1991. "An Identity Theory Approach to Commitment." *Social Psychology Quarterly* 54(3):239–51.

Cohen, Stanley. 1985. *Visions of Social Control: Crime Punishments and Classification*. United Kingdom: Polity Press.

Conrad, Peter. 1979. "Types of Medical Social Control." *Sociology of Health and Illness* 1(1):1–11.

Cordner, Gary W. and Kathryn E. Scarborough. 2010. *Police Administration*. New Providence, N.J.: Matthew Bender and Company.

Crawford, Adam, Stuart Lister, Sarah Blackburn, and Jonathan Burnett. 2005. *Plural Policing: the Mixed Economy of Visible Security Patrols*. United Kingdom: Polity Press.

Douglas, Jack D. 1976. *Investigative Social Research: Individual and Team Field Research*. Beverly Hills, CA: Sage.

Dworkin, Jodi. 2005. "Risk Taking as Developmentally Appropriate Experimentation for College Students." *Journal of Adolescent Research* 20(2): 219–41.

Eisenstadt, Shmuel. N. 1954. "Reference Group Behavior and Social Integration: An Explorative Study." *American Sociological Review* 19(2):175–85.

Fallows, James. 2003. " The New College Chaos." *The Atlantic Monthly* 292(4): 106-14.

Faupel, Charles E. 1991. *Shooting Dope: Career Patterns of Hard-Core Heroin Users*. Gainesville, FL: University Press of Florida.

Foucault, Michel. 1979. *History of sexuality volume 1: An introduction*. New York: Random House.

Foucault, Michel. 1997. *The Essential Works, 1954-1984, vol. 1: Ethics, Subjectivity and Truth*. New York: The New Press.

Garland, David. 2001. *The Culture of Control: Crime and Social Order in Contemporary Society*. Chicago, IL: University Of Chicago Press.

Goffman, Erving. 1983. "The Interaction Order: American Sociological Association, 1982 Presidential Address." *American Sociological Review* 48(1): 1–17.

Goffman, Erving. 1959. *The Presentation of Self in Everyday Life*. New York, NY: Doubleday.

Gray, James P. 2011. *Why Our Drug Laws Have Failed and What We Can Do About It: A Judicial Indictment of the War on Drugs*. Philadelphia, PA: Temple University Press.

Gusfield, Joseph R. 1963. *Symbolic Crusade: Status Politics and the American Temperance Movement*. Champaign, IL: University of Illinois Press.

Havighurst, Robert J. 1972. *Developmental Tasks and Education*. New York, NY: David McKay.

Heckert, Alex and Druann Maria Heckert. 2002. "A New Typology of Deviance: Integrating Normative and Reactivist Definitions of Deviance." *Deviant Behavior* 23(5):449–79.

Hirschi, Travis. 1969. *Causes of Delinquency*. Berkeley, CA: University of California Press.

Innes, Martin. 1999. "'An Iron Fist in an Iron Glove'The Zero Tolerance Policing Debate." *The Howard Journal of Criminal Justice* 38(4):397–410.

Jones, Trevor and Timothy Newburn. 1998. *Private Security and Public Policing*. New York: Oxford University Press.

Kanter, Rosabeth Moss. 1972. *Commitment and Community: Communes and Utopias in Sociological Perspective*. Boston, MA: Harvard University Press.

Karp, David A., Lynda Lytle Holstrom, and Paul S. Gray. 1998. "Leaving Home for College: Expectations for Selective Reconstruction of Self." *Symbolic Interaction* 21(3):253–76.

Keup, Jennifer R. 2007. "Great Expectations and the Ultimate Reality Check: Voices of Students During the Transition from High School to College." Journal of Student Affairs Research and Practice 44(1):3-31.

Kuh, George D. 1991. "The Role of Admissions and Orientation in Creating Appropriate Expectations for College Life." *College and University* 66(2): 75-82.

Lofland, Lyn H. 1973. *A World of Strangers: Order and Action in Urban Public Space.* New York: Basic Books.

Maggs, Jennifer L., David M. Almeida, and Nancy L. Galambos. 1995. "Risky Business: The Paradoxical Meaning of Problem Behavior for Young Adolescents." *Journal of Early Adolescence* 15(3):344–62.

Maggs, Jennifer L. and Klaus Hurrelmann. 1998. "Do Substance Use and Delinquency Have Differential Associations with Adolescents' Peer Relations?" *International Journal of Behavioral Development* 22(2):367–88.

Maloff, Deborah, Howard S. Becker, Arlene Fonaroff, and Judith Rodin. 1979. "Informal Social Controls and their Influence on Substance Use." *Journal of Drug Issues* 9:161–84.

Matza, David. 1964. *Delinquency and Drift.* New Brunswick, N.J.: Transaction Publishers.

McBroom, Elizabeth M., Eric M. Fife, C. Leigh Nelson. 2008. "'Risky Business': The College Transition, Loneliness, and Alcohol Consumption. *The Journal of First-Year Experience and Students in Transition* 20(2):45-63.

Mohamed, Rafik A. and Erik D. Fritsvold. 2010. *Dorm Room Dealers: Drugs and the Privelees of Race and Class.* Boulder, CO: Lynne Rienner.

O'Brien, Patrick K. 2013. "Medical Marijuana and Social Control: Escaping Criminalization and   Embracing Medicalization." *Deviant Behavior* 34(6): 423-43.

Ratcliffe, Jerry. 2012. *Intelligence-Led Policing*. United Kingdom: Willan Publishing.

Ravert, Russell D. 2009. "'You're Only Young Once' Things College Students Report Doing Now Before It Is Too Late." *Journal of Adolescent Research* 24(3):376–96.

Rose, Nikolas, Pat O'Malley, and Marianna Valverde. 2006. "Governmentality." *Annual Review of Law and Social Sciences* 2:83–104.

Schulenberg, John E., Alison L. Bryant, and Patrick M. O'Malley. 2004. "Taking hold of some kind of life: How developmental tasks relate to trajectories of well-being during the transition to adulthood." *Development and Psychopathology* 16(4):1119–40.

Sellin, Thorsten. 1938. *Culture and Conflict in Crime*. New York: Social Science Research Council.

Shibutani, Tamotsu. 1955. "Reference Groups as Perspectives." *American Journal of Sociology* 60:562-69.

Stryker, Sheldon. 1968. "Identity Salience and Role Performance: The Relevance of Symbolic Interaction Theory for Family Research." *Journal of Marriage and the Family* 30(4):558–64.

Stryker, Sheldon. 1980. *Symbolic Interactionism: A Social Structural Version*. Menlo Park, CA: Benjamin / Cummings Publishing Company.

Zinberg, Norman E. 1986. *Drug, Set, and Setting: The Basics for Controlled Intoxicant Use*. New Haven, CT: Yale University Press.

Chapter Six

The Dual Career

A period of both youthfulness and maturation, the university years are marked by educational pursuit, identity development, self-exploration, risk-taking, and drug and alcohol use. Researchers have posited that some level of substance use throughout the college years of **emerging adulthood** is expected and normative (Schulenberg and Zarrett 2006; Schulenberg, Maggs, and Hurrelmann 1997). These party behaviors result not only from youthful proclivities for experimentation and risk-taking, but from students' anticipation of "losing such opportunities as adults" (Ravert 2009:377). It seems that students are right. Substance use among young adults reaches its peak during the early twenties (Chen and Kandel 1995; Jackson et al. 2005; Johnston, O'Malley, and Bachman 2003), there is limited initiation of use after age 25 (Chen and Kandel 1995; Hser, Longshore, and Anglin 2007), and patterns of use tend to decrease rapidly as people age into middle and late adulthood (SAMSHA 2003, Schulenberg et al. 2004). Shulenberg and Zarrett (2006) argue that the majority of college students replace substance use and other associated behaviors with adult roles and maturing out of substance use is often a function of achieving adult responsibilities such as employment and marriage.

In this chapter, we are introduced to the *dual career*, or the intertwined paths of school and partying that constituted university life. As students' transitioned into their final years of college, they understood that their university success was contingent on a reciprocal balance between their academic responsibilities and their social lives. I focus on the structural, cultural, and interpersonal shifts in students' academic careers and social lives that impacted their substance use. I also examine how their drug and alcohol use came to fit into the social order of their lives during this period of emerging adulthood.

From Academic Life to the Economic Life

As students progressed through their college career, they started to see their academic and scholarly pursuits as important steps toward an adult career and economic independence. In contrast to the detachment they sometimes felt from their studies freshman year, as students became more involved in their major, they became more invested in their classes, assignments, and grades. Students started to envision how their college training would lead to internships, graduate school, or entry-level career positions. The future was closer, and the anticipation of economic independence and adult roles replaced their freshmen year excitement of freedom and liberation from parents. Not only did students locate their education as the primary vehicle toward a future career, they also developed personal definitions of success, or what *they* wanted out of their collegiate years.

Academic Significance

Entering into their junior and senior years, my informants noted the changing structure of college academics that increased their **social bonds** (Hirschi 1969) to their education. In contrast to large classes where they felt like nameless faces or numbers in a grade book, students discussed both a qualitative and quantitative change in how they experienced their coursework. John, the 22-year-old junior and environmental major, who, during his first-year at Campus University struggled to find his academic niche, noted:

> As you get older, I think you have more classes that you really like. Those classes that you tell people about and that's kind of what keeps me going to classes, like the professors that know me and teach me things that apply to my major. It's like you're in a place where you want to learn and you start to see some end goal in sight.

This personalization of academic pursuits and the meanings they applied to being a student at Campus University served to enhance their attachment to the institution of education. Intensification in the pride of graduating also emerged as students sought the admiration and esteem of parents and **significant others**. Jill, the 22-year-old senior with a double major in sociology and dance, who had recalled her heavy partying freshmen year, discussed her change in outlook and behavior with regard to graduation:

> For me it was getting closer to graduating college, I never really realized how big of a celebration it really is because there aren't a lot of people who graduate college and it's a pretty big thing. I've put myself more in perspective with the rest of the world because now I realize how much I've learned. I realize how lucky I am that I'm able to be in school and have had my parents' help and stuff.

As students' **attachments** to their education increased, so too did their **commitment** to their declared major and their **involvement** in coursework. As they registered for their upper-division classes with reduced class sizes, personalized professor feedback, and demanding projects and assignments, they had to place more time and energy into their schoolwork to realize success. These **bonds** emerged not only to enhance academic pursuits but also to quell the heavier partying they reported freshman year. Nathan, the 22-year-old premed major, noted:

> I just find school more important, more demanding. I'm in the core of my major classes. So, I have to wake up in the morning, I wish I could party all night and not have a hangover (laughing), but I can't. I've had it happen

too many times. And I'm really pissed if I sleep all day. I get really mad. We didn't have a problem with it when we were younger, but we do now.

Students reported that in their latter years of college, the reality of graduation and finding employment was more pronounced. Students were in specific and discrete stage of **emerging adulthood** (Arnett 2000, 2004) where they would be required to experiment with adult roles such as economic independence and career development. Not only was the task of finding adult employment on the horizon, but students discussed gaining part-time work, internships, or volunteer opportunities during their latter years at Campus University. Many of these new endeavors centered on networking, resume building, or practical experience outside of their academics as students developed **commitment** (Becker 1960; Burke and Reitzes 1991; McCall and Simmons 1966) to their academic career. Kristin, the 21-year-old senior and sociology major, noted:

> I wish I was a freshman and sophomore again, it was so much more new and carefree. But now, I think for me and other seniors it has to do with jobs. People start getting part-time jobs and want to establish their own money. The commitment to school is definitely related to having to graduate and find a real job. I use to not care, or need to care, because I didn't have that idea about the future. That whole future thing starts looming junior and senior year. And then it's like, "all right, it's time to grow up." And that really changed my feelings on partying, it's almost like you have to earn it.

Kristin's comment, that students have to "earn" their partying, developed from the time and energy required of students' intimate class settings, professor interaction, core class requirements, approaching graduation deadlines, and expectations for future employment. Students reported a greater belief and investment in their educational career. They began to better understand the value of their education and internalized the attitude that these college years would provide them with the skills necessary for success in this stage of emerging adulthood. These burgeoning beliefs placed new meaning on substance use. Jane, a 21-year-old senior and sociology major, stated:

> And this year, senior year, I'm finally 21 and I've become more cautious about drinking. I only go out 2-3 nights a week and I'm not really trying to party hard or all night. Sometimes I only go out once a week, or I don't go out at all. You have to realize that if you want to be successful, you can't continue partying like freshman year. If you don't really need to be in school, if your family has a lot of money and you're in college just to do the college thing, then you can drink your way to graduation. But me and my friends, we are in school because we want to be. We want to do something, and so drinking and partying just becomes a different thing.

Although students began placing increased time and energy into their academics, they still partied, and they still found time to party hard. As they progressed through their college years, they learned to balance both partying and studying. This idea of a *dual career* required students to learn to balance their desire to party and socialize with the demands and rewards of a successful education. As the structural and cultural environment of students' academics changed, and the day of graduation neared, they began to organize their education and their partying differently. Students discussed how their educational career and their party career could complement or conflict with one another (Van Maanen 1977), and how they learned to balance the fluidity of these two careers and acquire the techniques, skills, and strategies to move back and forth, from one to the other (Sharp and Hope 2001). Kelly, the 21-year-old sociology and history major, elaborated:

And I mean, I still go out and drink, maybe like two nights a week, maybe three. But I always know what work I have to do. I know I need to get my work done, I mean, I never find myself at the expense of work, but I won't go out and party and then never get my work done. Sure, of course, I'll have a ton of stuff to do and I'll go out and party, but that's because I realize I can get my work done. I've learned to set aside my time and keep it low key on certain nights. If there is a paper due and there is a party, I'll just say no, I'm not going to party. And we've all made that choice to party and not get the paper done, but you learn that's just not how you do well in life.

This balance of the dual career was a negotiated process that students did deliberately as they learned various management techniques that worked for them. Socializing and partying or finding times to relax with friends and get high was still an important quality of life factor for my respondents, yet these social scenes needed to be accomplished in relation to academics. Mary, a 21-year-old junior from Maryland, who, as a physiology major decided academics would not rule her life, stated:

I just tell myself that if I sit down and do this, then I can go out tonight. I'll be like, "ok, I am going to the library for three hours, and if I get all of my shit done, then I can go out. So it's an incentive, I never really did that before. And if I don't go out, I've done it all before, and I know I'm not like missing anything.

Mary expressed her contrasting views from freshman year to senior year. In her first-year, she felt that "If I didn't go out and party, I was missing something," while senior year, she noted, "I know I'm not missing anything." Countless respondents echoed Mary's sentiments about the party scene as more commonplace or routine than freshmen year, yet the party scene itself had not changed. The social scene that had once pulled them from their academics was waning in importance. Even those students with "senioritis" who claimed to be getting their last days of heavy partying in before entering the "real world," mandated time and effort into their final papers and exams. Ben, a 21-year-old psychology major and intern at a local health clinic, noted:

> I mean, I get the senioritis thing, we all do, even my friends who really value school. We get to that point where we're like, "pshh, I don't care. I'm this close, I'm going out to party." But then there are the nights where we're like, "holy shit, I have so much to do!" And you freak out a little bit and get your work done, you know, start hanging out in Starbuck's and skip the bars for a while.

For students, the confusion surrounding their **status position** and associated **role behaviors** as college freshman subsided as they assembled the knowledge, skills, motives, and contacts necessary for academic career success. They understood that college was a time for experimentation with drugs and alcohol (Dworkin 2005; Ravert 2009), but that maturity, responsibility, and dedication was required of them to achieve success balancing their dual career.

Defining Success

A key facet for maintaining the dual career of academics and partying was students' pragmatic definitions of college success. These beliefs about their college experience involved combining goals of experimentation and partying *and* goals of academic achievement. They understood that their partying might hinder their schoolwork and factored this into their college lives. Students' dual career unfolded in response to these personal definitions of appropriate levels of schoolwork and substance use. These designations of success, though specific to each student, echoed ones general desire to accomplish both social and educational goals throughout their university career. To do this, they distanced themselves from goals that depended *only* on grades and GPAs and extended their collegiate goals to activities that they valued such as drugs and alcohol. Ben, the 21-year-old junior and psychology major, explained:

> I would say getting good grades, expanding my knowledge of the world. And college, I feel like, should be a setting to set me up for the next step in my life. And if it doesn't, then I don't see the point in being here. And it's not just grades, part of my success is going out, trying new things, partying, taking some acid and hiking around, you know, just living my life how I see fit.

These definitions of success reflected an emerging self-control as students accounted for their personal academic pursuits (i.e., grades, GPA, graduation), but included their own emerging adult goals of drinking, drug use, and partying. Students consciously and deliberately designated a reciprocal relationship between their partying and their schoolwork. They readily admitted that their partying had, at times, impeded their academics, but for many it was a part of *their* college experience. Marc, a 21-year-old senior and physiology major, noted:

> Partying has hurt my schoolwork at times; it does that every now and again. But that's what college is all about. You can't tell me that adults, throughout life, don't have shitty days at work or space out on a meeting because of going out. I haven't made it to class a few times and I've half-assed a paper or two because I wanted to go out, but in the big scheme of life, it just doesn't matter that much to me. I'll also go weekends without drinking because I have work to do. For me it was figuring out the give and take and I know I've had great college experiences through partying.

Marc's definitions of success accounted for his prediction and later experiences that sometimes, partying would impact his studies. Even for students who claimed that partying never hindered their schoolwork, they explicitly set aside time for drug and alcohol use and strove to minimize any impact on their academic pursuits. Students learned to manage because their desire to socialize and party during these precious college years was immense. Jill, the 22-year-old sociology and dance major, stated:

> In terms of schoolwork, partying hasn't had a major impact. I mean it may be easier to do my schoolwork if I wasn't hungover on Fridays, but it really has not had an extreme influence, especially since I have gotten older. I am really happy about the way I have learned to manage, and the way I have been doing in school. I don't think partying would be worth it if it got in the way of school. It is a balancing act, I really work hard and want to be successful, graduate with honors and in four years, but I also don't want to miss anything. And it's hard for me to stay in on Thursday night when I hear people outside partying, so I hate feeling like I'm missing out. So I know that when I go out a lot, that I need to make up for it equally by working extra hard, because for me, and my friends, it's really important to get those experiences, to not miss out and to have the best time I possibly could have, but also get good grades and a diploma.

Overall, respondents reported that their emerging values and beliefs about their university experience differed from conventional conceptions of what it means to be attending college. Although parents and school officials might not consider partying and socializing as critical to the collegiate years as studying, grades, and GPAs, students did. As seniors, students had learned the appropriate role behaviors for a college student (e.g., study, attend class, take good notes, schedule time effectively, prioritize classwork), but included their own personal conceptions about what being a college student was about for them. Matt, the 21-year-old junior and economics major, noted:

I mean you can't ignore certain factors like the amount of money you are putting into your education or the importance of a degree. I think everyone's definition of success is different, but now people are pretty successful partying and getting grades to graduate. I'm not always one of those people. I mean, I get really good grades, but I'm not always getting A's because I like to go out. I think college success for me is doing what you want. You have to take advantage of what is around you in college. I mean the whole partying and intramural sports, that has shaped me just as much as my education. You just have to find that even keel. You want to learn how to interact with people, you want to try new things, make friends and all those connections. You need the education, but you don't need an A in every class every time.

Finding balance for these dual careers, or as Matt noted, "an even keel," was not a simple task, but required trial and error, experience, learning, and a connection to academic life. For students, both academic changes and the proximity of the conventional social order (e.g., employment, early mornings, nine to five, and economic independence) operated as a normative social control to manage a dual career. Students still partied in their later years of college, but changes in their associations, reinforcements, and agency fostered a different manner of drug and alcohol use.

From Party Life to Social Life

As students progressed through college and toward graduation, they gained symbolic and tangible **party capital** that was structurally and culturally unavailable the first years of university life. They no longer felt like outsiders from the thriving social life of parties and bars. On the contrary, they were able to participate in the party scene whenever and however they pleased. The surrounding community of Campus University no longer seemed like a vast and uncharted world, and they had settled into primary networks of friends. Students lived on their own, away from the dormitory police patrols and the prying eyes, ears, and noses of Resident Assistants and Campus Safety Officers. With more adult forms of independence and freedom, students continued to drink, use drugs, and party, but their substance use was influenced by new modes self-control and social control fostered by structural, cultural, and interactional dynamics unknown to them freshman year.

Newfound Agency

A central factor that contributed to students' ability to learn self-control, especially with regard to alcohol use, was turning twenty-one. Although the 21st birthday typically involved a night of excessive drinking, and open access to bars meant a brief spike in consumption, students reported that being of legal drinking age significantly changed their drinking patterns. Mary, a 21-year-old senior and integrative physiology major, stated:

> Well, you turn 21 and it's cool for like a month and then you're just over the heavy stuff. Because all of the sudden you're allowed to do it. And before it's, "oh, I can drink!" So, it's just that you think about it differently. And it's also how your friends begin to think about it. And my friends and I are all older; I don't have a single friend under 21 anymore that I hang out with on a regular basis. And you're just able to drink on a more mature level. You just don't have that option before you're legally allowed to do it.

With more access to alcohol, students reported a reduction in their heaviest drinking. They were no longer forced to smuggle illegally acquired liquor into their residence hall, drinking quickly before parties or football games. They had direct entrée into the party scene they once worked so hard to access. They could attend a casual happy hour before walking to a party with a six-pack of their favorite beer. If they wanted to tailgate before football games they no longer feared police intervention or an underage citation. This structural change placed a large group of college students in a social position where they did not *have* to drink as heavily, sporadically, and dangerously. Ben, the 21-year-old junior and psychology major, elaborated:

> I feel like if I ever was a binge drinker, I do it less. Before you had to call someone to get you alcohol and sneak it everywhere. You had to have a reliable source, but now you can just go whenever and wherever. And this really calms it down for everyone, definitely for me and my friends. So, instead of like, "I need to drink this and get fucked up cause this is all I have," type of thing, now I can drink in bars and at restaurants, legally on my porch. And it can really slow things down because you have more options. It doesn't slow you down just because you hit this magic number (being 21), but you can just be your own boss and go places and get drinks. Me and my friends used to sneak around and would pour whiskey, or whatever we could get, into a bottle and carry it around, like crazy nasty mixtures. I would never drink that now. You just stop partying that way. I still get drunk, but it's not drinking just to get really drunk, like not just to get fucked up, it's more social I guess.

This structural change that allowed students agency and power, also shifted the cultural setting of the college party scene. Similar to the changing definitions attached to marijuana (see Chapter 9) that students experienced with conventional access through dispensaries, the meanings attached to alcohol evolved and shifted considerably. Similar to marijuana, alcohol became increasingly conventional and routine and lost its allure as a deviant activity. Just as students garnered control over their marijuana experience through different cannabis strains and edible options; they gained choices over alcohol intoxication that fit their mood, the setting, or their desired effect. Students acquired specific tastes for beer or wine, viewed drinking as an increasingly casual social endeavor, and saw themselves as more responsible adult drinkers, now distanced from the immature debauchery of freshman year. Although heavy drinking was still a facet of senior drinking, substance use began to take a different form as students were structurally placed in **different learning environments with new reinforcements** (Akers 2009; Sutherland 1947) for behavior. Kristin, the 21-year-old sociology major, stated:

> It's funny, I would try and go to the bars more freshman and sophomore year because of the fact I couldn't. Same with drinking. I just had to go as much as I could when I knew I could get in, I had to take advantage when it was there. I turned twenty-one and now I'm having wine with dinner and I actually appreciate and respect alcohol a lot more. When me and my friends all started turning 21 our junior year, alcohol became more of a background thing because it was there to be had. It's like you can go out and get a glass of wine, get your favorite beer, and if you go somewhere, you don't need to get all drunk beforehand because you'll get served. I can go places and drink what I choose. I don't have to drink what's there at some party or what someone else has for me. It just changes. You start to learn the tastes of alcohol and start to enjoy it for other things aside from getting drunk.

Students now frequented establishments such as restaurants and bars where they interacted with drinkers of all ages and began to view moderate and controlled drinking as the norm rather than the exception. Socializing in conventional establishments contributed to an environmental change where the heaviest drinking or drug use was less tolerated. Although the informal norms and rules of intoxication depended on the venue, at house parties, for example, there were no rules. Students reported that although their peers certainly had too much to drink in bars or became too "fucked up," the controls in bars such as bartenders, bouncers, concerned patrons, and normative boundaries of intoxication often discouraged the heaviest drinking. Students were increasingly expected to proctor their own alcohol use, and that of their friends, as social control subtly shifted from the police and Campus University officials to intimate peer groups.

The Changing Audience

As students matured through the college years they developed a closer, primary group of friends with people around whom they felt comfortable. Researchers note that university students typically move from superficial secondary networks to more intimate primary relationships, and the quality of these networks are associated with positive outcomes (Hays and Oxley 1986). As their friendship bonds developed, their friends served as safer interactional environments to use drugs, to drink, and to get drunk. Students had developed a trustworthy and dependable primary network. Jane, a 21-year-old senior and sociology major, stated:

> I really trust my friends, my circle of really good friends. In the past when I would get drunk, maybe too drunk, I wasn't with anyone who was close to me, I didn't have those close friends. I didn't know if I could rely on them much.

With a more trustworthy group of friends students reported having a comfortable group to have the occasional drunk night, experiment with drugs, or have more experienced friends show them the ropes when using certain substances. Although their friends allowed a few hedonistic evenings, these well bonded social networks were ultimately a tool toward control and moderation. These intimate groups provided "**drunk support**" when students encountered a "**drinking crisis**" (Vander Ven 2011) or other drug crisis. If students drank to a slovenly point or consumed greater amounts of drugs than they intended, their **primary group** members would help them regain control (e.g., walking them home, calming them down, providing them with water) or simply shield them from the troubles and disputes associated with over-intoxication (e.g., fights, police, injury, campus officials, bouncers). These primary groups were not automatically established; students developed these intimate support networks during their first years partying at Campus University.

Primary friendship groups also established boundaries of intoxication. Similar to the **subcultural norms** discussed by Faupel (1991), being involved with a primary network of friends meant abiding by the norms and rules of the group. As students moved into junior and senior year with these people, they all developed informal guidelines regarding drug and alcohol use that served as a form of informal control. In the past, the norms had revolved around hard partying, and while that was still a facet of the senior experience, accountability to ones friends dominated those later college years. Jen, a senior political science major with a minor in economics, noted:

> When I was younger I hung out with, you know, people I didn't know that well, this heavy party crowd. But of course, everyone was partying. I found that to be exciting when I got to college. I found that to be cool. And now, I had this conversation the other day with one of my really close friends, I'm glad I found groups of friends that don't really condone getting shitfaced every night. Every now and again, okay. But, maybe just go on a hike instead or other things like that. And it's weird how I never figured that out until now, I just knew that wasn't where I was anymore, and if it was, my friends I have now would sit me down because I'm surrounded with people who know me better.

Close friends, and a more stable social network helped keep students in line. Deep and developed social bonds provided students with honest, upfront, and even displeasing information about their substance use and behavior. The **positive or negative sanctions** (Heckert and Heckert 2002) experienced through friends were potent informal control mechanisms.

With a solid group of friends the context and audience of the college party scene changed and students' conceptions of partying shifted. No longer were they using drugs in what seemed to be a world of strangers. In the **anomic** and **normless** conditions of freshman year, students scrambled to meet peers and form friendships, but having maturing friends helped reduce the immense pressure to party that exists in contemporary university campuses (Herman-Kinney and Kinney 2013). Within their primary circles, the pressure to party was gradually reduced.

> It used to be more social pressure. Even when I go out now, if I'm not drinking people are like, "you want to drink?" "Why aren't you drinking?" But now I feel I can say, especially to my friends, I'm not going to drink tonight and they're cool about it. It's just not cool to give someone a ton of shit for not drinking anymore. We've all been there. Get over it. And so there is still the pressure to drink, but it's less now and I have the confidence to say, "not tonight."

This interactional decrease in the peer-to-peer pressure to party was just one example of how primary groups began to informally control and mediate drinking and drug using behaviors. These primary friendship groups served as a stable set of **generalized others**, operating as a source of students' **values, beliefs, perspectives, and self-comparisons** (Matsueda 1992; Mead 1934). Students learned from their friends, internalized past alcohol and drug experiences and applied them to their current patterns and thoughts on substance use. They based their behavior from the standpoint of their close-knit friend groups and reflected appraisals from primary groups members. Their friends provided a foundation for a regulated **"Me"** that informed an impulsive **"I"** that could easily be swept up in the wild and crazy effervescence of the college party scene. This **role-taking process**, or the continuous rehearsal between the "I" and the "Me," produced and reproduced informal guidelines and rules for students to follow. They started to develop a reflexive **"party consciousness"** through the norms of their primary group relationships. Dave, a 21-year-old, senior and finance major, discussed the norms and standards of his circle of friends that served as informal control:

> Compared to freshman year alcohol stops working as an excuse. My friends will call you out, or just rip on you. Back then if we were wasted and blacked out nobody apologized or needed excuses for their behavior, it was so accepted and so common. I really think it's *your* friends, I think it makes partying so different depending on who you have to answer to for your behavior.

The **anomic audience** of freshman year gave way to a tighter and bonded group where norms, beliefs, and values about drinking and drug use were established. Students appreciated these friendships, or as Amanda, a 21-year-old political science and studio art major, noted, "I just value my friendships more now that I know these are my good friends." Not only were friendship groups serving as a stable set of generalized others, as the most potent informal sanction, students often feared losing or alienating close friends for excessive or inappropriate partying. Kelly, a 21-year-old sociology and history major, elaborated:

> You just learn how to do it all better. I mean for me, it took making mistakes and feeling bad about myself. I never really alienated my friends. But it was always the fear of alienating them and making them mad or feel bad and not making them want to be my friends anymore. That was enough for me. I had developed this good group of friends and I wanted to enjoy my drinking experiences in general, which made me be like, "alright, c'mon, figure it out." And it's screwing up that makes people learn. It's really an increased respect for your friends. Because freshman year, like you really weren't sure who your friends were gonna be. There

were plenty of people you went out with, but you were trying to figure out who your real friends are. I just didn't care as much back then.

Through their primary friendship groups students experienced support, safety, advice, sanctions, and boundaries in relation to their partying behaviors. However, they also gained **party capital,** and they all began enjoying drugs and alcohol in a different manner. Together, they explored different bars and restaurants, tried different wines and alcohol, experimented with LSD, or took MDMA and went to shows. However, alcohol was still the most widely used drug in the college party scene and it was a pivotal change when students could incorporate drinking into conventional activities they enjoyed like hiking, skiing, trivia, tailgating, dinners, and happy hours. This cultural shift further changed students' patterns of substance use and the **meanings they applied to intoxication.**

Sorry for Partying (Not As Hard)

Students fully experienced the party scene by their senior year. And while each student's trajectory through the college party scene was distinct, general patterns of change were apparent in their drug and alcohol use. Students started to learn their limits, and though they still violated their desired levels of intoxication on various occasions, their partying was gradually evolving. With shifts in agency and audience, academic constraints, and approaching graduation, students reported developing a different style of partying as they moved through their junior and senior years of college. Students' gradually shifting party behaviors were mediated by **normative social controls** fostered through **social learning** and their emerging beliefs concerning intoxication. They began to apply new meaning to *why* they used drugs and alcohol. Jane, the 21-year-old senior and sociology major, elaborated:

Everybody still drinks, and sometimes just to get drunk. But we're doing it differently. To drink and act like you did as a freshman is deviant, in the bad sense, not the fun sense. You're supposed to get that kind of behavior out of your system. So, when I say deviant here, I'm using it in terms of something strange, I use it a lot to say something is abnormal. And you still have those crazy nights, but based off of me and my friends, they become crazy nights for a reason, like a party, or a celebration, or a birthday. They're not crazy just because you want to get wasted, that's getting old. It's like now you need more of a reason and if you're still drinking like you were freshman year, you're just looked at differently.

Students' drug and alcohol use became part of an occasion or a social event rather than simply the substance *being* the occasion or the event. Students did not always need a reason to drink, as almost any occasion sometimes sufficed (Vander Ven 2011), but the act of getting drunk, just to get drunk, started to lose its appeal. These shifting motivations were not learned or internalized in a vacuum, but were directly related to primary group norms and academic accountability.

Students also reported that certain levels of intoxication were increasingly seen as immature, irresponsible, annoying, and even dangerous. A person who abused alcohol and drugs, became regularly over intoxicated, or used at improper times at inappropriate locations, was increasingly stigmatized, as his or her behavior was something to be avoided. Students became more aware about *how* intoxicated they were becoming and *where* this behavior was occurring during their college career. Doug, a 22-year-old, sociology and history major, explained:

I think when we were younger, we defined ourselves by how much we could drink and party. And I think people my age are more respected if they don't necessarily abuse things. It's a total shift in the idea of what was once cool and acceptable. You just don't want to be that really fucked up person, it just loses its sense. You know? Now it's like, what are you doing with your life? And it used to be how many beers you can chug and how much fun you have, but that doesn't really tell people who you are anymore. As the real world gets closer, people start to define themselves differently. It's time to wake up from being drunk and make real decisions.

With these increasing concerns regarding intoxication, students reported a change in both their alcohol and drug use and noted that they had developed more responsible and mature substance use behaviors. They reported continuing to enjoy the use of alcohol and other drugs, but stories of **limiting** and **self-control** began to dominate as they discussed their latter years of partying. Someone without limits or boundaries regarding their substance use was potentially stigmatized and could attract a negative label (e.g., "stoner," "drunk," "liability," "druggie" or "shitshow"). At this point, such designations were unattractive and undesired. For students, their limits concerning alcohol and drugs were both symbolic and pragmatic and reflected *who* they were in life and *where* they were going with their future. Limits operated as an **informal control** and reflected maturity and moving forward in life. Students reported that substance use would be a continuous facet of adult life, but accomplished in a manner they viewed as appropriate for adulthood and reflective of their burgeoning "real-world" identity (i.e., new status positions and associated role behaviors). They reported that partying reflected different life stages and that the final phase of college involved a fundamental shift away from the heaviest partying behaviors. Molly, the 21-year-old junior and advertising major, discussed:

And it's not like I don't do drugs or drink anymore, because I do. I just did coke the other night and I still like to take ecstasy when I go to shows. But you have to learn to limit yourself, maybe do it once a month and have a good time with it, you know, don't do too much and stay in control. I know I'll always drink and always dabble in some drugs for special occasions. I mean clearly there are some mistakes I could live without, you know? Like maybe I didn't learn from my first mistake, but made the same mistake again, like I probably should have learned. But I mean, I would not have figured it all out if I hadn't fucked up a bunch of times. And when I was fucking up, all my friends were too and now we know and we don't party like that anymore. If you still party so hard that you're always over the line, it just looks bad. People start to wonder if you have a problem or any direction in your life. Like, what is the deal with so and so, is he ever going to get his shit together?

For students, these gradual changes in partying behaviors were not just derived from academic involvement and primary group norms, but from their **social learning of appropriate rituals** (Zinberg 1986) and *cultural recipes* (Maloff et al. 1979). These informal controls unfolded through students' past experiences and within their intimate friendship groups as students learned the subcultural norms and rules of drug use that fit into conventional lifestyles. As potent informal social controls, **cultural recipes** describe which substances to use, why, and in what amount to achieve desired effects; they identify when, where, and with whom to use certain drugs; they denote the positive and negative sanctions that reinforce or discourage different forms of substance use; and explain the social relations that make it convenient or inconvenient to use drugs in certain ways (Glassner and Berg 1980). Participants had to learn the cultural recipes that supported a productive and successful dual career by reducing negative consequences and sanctions. These cultural recipes were in their infancy upon students entrance into university life and only through trial and error, mistakes, information diffusion, and social learning, could students begin to incorporate cultural recipes into their lives. Jeff, a 22-year-old senior and marketing major, explained:

And the problem right now with college campuses is that most people don't know their limits, especially freshman and even sophomores. How would you know any of this until you do it? And so people are just partying past their limits, and that's the problem, especially with the underage drinking. They have never had a chance to learn any limits. And limits vary, which makes it hard for administrators, the government, whoever is trying to deal with this college binge drinking. Kids need to learn limits, but also what they want out of partying. And they just have few responsible learning experiences. I really think the drinking age should be 18. I think that right now alcohol is very accessible to underage people, especially on college campuses. And people are inclined to drink more because it's illegal and taboo, they're not supposed to do it. I mean it's fun, you're doing something illegal, you get high, you get drunk, and you don't have your parents looking over your shoulder. But now you have the cops, administrators, RAs telling you don't do this. Don't do what every other kid on campus across the U.S. is doing. It just doesn't make any sense to me.

Students were critical of the formal methods of control associated with campus police and the university conduct office that they experienced primarily during their time in the dorms. They attributed their shifting beliefs and behaviors regarding substance use to their social learning experiences and the lessons they learned from positive and negative sanctions through their primary friendship networks. Their informal control methods were not automatically activated upon entering the vast and uncharted college party scene, but required the proper structural, cultural, and interactional elements to materialize and evolve.

Conclusion

The transition to university life fosters experimentation as students experience greater independence and freedom from parental constraints. Furthermore, the collegiate culture encourages risky behavior as students report all-night parties, promiscuous sex, and drug use. In this context, college students are susceptible to cross the unclear boundaries between healthy experimentation and hazardous risk taking behavior (Dworkin 2005). It is important to note that college students can experience both positive benefits and negative consequences as a result of their drug and alcohol use. For emerging adults, testing limits, partaking in risky activities, and finding the streams of consciousness they value is important to their identity development and adult maturation. But the line between beneficial and dangerous is often blurred (Jessor and Jessor 1977; Jessor 1991; Lightfoot 1997). As Dworkin (2005:221) states: "Experimentation behaviors are not inherently dangerous or problematic, rather, negative outcomes occur under certain conditions. It is unlikely that a behavior will be either entirely problematic or conventional. It is possible to engage in both behaviors simultaneously."

Students dealt with learning **informal control** within this college environment (i.e., medical and formal controls) of Campus University. Students' informal controls were underdeveloped as they entered university life and they experienced a period of **anomie** or **normlessness** with regard to partying. They found themselves in a vast social network of independent and self-directed peers, a group of near strangers who held personal and cultural expectations to congregate, socialize, drink, and do drugs. The collegiate structure arranged students into an environment where their primary sources of learning and internalizing party norms were derived from one another or from reference groups of upperclassmen who were already involved in the party scene. Although students did work together to develop what they considered subculturally appropriate techniques and motivations for substance use, their party behaviors reflected youthful naivety and underdeveloped boundaries. Those who had high school experience with drugs and alcohol had an advantage over complete neophytes, but with nearly 6,000 in each freshmen class, the lack of norms, limits, and appropriate others from whom to learn from left a large group of emerging adults with little guidance. This learning environment produced and reproduced norms of excess and irresponsibility as this cycle continued over unbroken years.

The cycle of excessive partying gradually became mediated by **informal controls**. Students experienced the potency of informal regulation through academic and peer group norms that together, contributed to shifts in informal control mechanisms at the structural, cultural, and interactional level. At the *structural* **level**, a substantial portion of the student population formed a stronger commitment toward their studies and developed a sense that their education would impact their future opportunities. They anticipated that their academic pursuits would lead to adult employment and economic independence. Junior and senior level students constituted a group of **emerging adults** increasingly committed to their education, internships, and goals for future careers and status. At the *cultural* **level**, students' norms and beliefs concerning partying reflected these burgeoning academic and career goals and increasingly pushed students toward moderation rather than excess. For maturing undergraduates, patterns of consuming alcohol and drugs, and ways of behaving while intoxicated, started to align with conventional ideologies.

However, these structural and cultural shifts were only realized and possible through the *interactional* **level**, or within students' peer networks, which progressively held them accountable to academic obligations and normative patterns of substance use. Students experienced the burgeoning reality of adult roles and responsibilities and formed cultural boundaries and rules for substance use *through* their primary peer networks. Although every student's primary network was distinct and peers could certainly exert a counterproductive influence, generally close friends formed potent modes of informal control. Similar to Harrington and Fine's (2000) work on small group dynamics, students' **peer networks** constituted stable and trustworthy primary networks that offered emotional rapport, informal sanctions, and academic encouragement in times of need. These informal groups also created a dynamic learning environment where students could develop the appropriate **cultural recipes** (i.e., norms, rituals, and precautions) of drug and alcohol use that reflected maturing social contexts rather than the naivety and irresponsibility of freshmen year. Furthermore, friendship groups were an impetus for social change to the extent that students' friends challenged the prevailing collegiate cultural standards of partying and questioned previous motivations for using drugs and alcohol. These intimate groups were effective modes of control and regulation because they provided students with strong ties and relationships that were deep and enduring. In contrast to the sometimes fleeting and superficial relationships of students' first years of college life, their primary network constituted relationships that they valued and did not want to lose.

The confluence of academics and peer networks fostered evolving informal cultural norms that mediated students' drug and alcohol use patterns. These emerging social dynamics fostered social capital in students' lives. The potency of informal controls operated *through* this emerging social capital as students, as social actors, secured benefits by virtue of membership in their social networks and other social structures such as a collegiate education. Students' behavior was most effectively controlled by their peers because the intimate networks that provided them with social capital were deep and enduring and were not connections students wanted to fracture or lose. They felt a sanctioning gaze from their friends over the course of their college careers as status within their peer groups shifted away from heavy partying and towards attaining academic accomplishments, adult roles, and employment opportunities. For students, both direct and indirect evaluations from their primary friendship groups struck close to home as their friends provided them with a reflexive gaze through which they evaluated themselves.

Notes and Discussion Questions:

References

Akers, Ronald L. 2009. *Social Learning and Social Structure: A General Theory of Crime and Deviance*. New Brunswick, N.J.: Transaction Publishers.

Arnett, Jeffrey. 1991. "Still Crazy After All These Years: Reckless Behavior Among Young Adults Aged 23-27." *Personality and Individual Differences* 12(12):1305–13.

Arnett, Jeffrey Jensen. 2000. "Emerging Adulthood: A Theory of Development from the Late Teens Through the Twenties." *American Psychologist* 55(5):469–80.

Arnett, Jeffrey Jensen. 2004. "Emerging Adulthood: The Winding Road from the Late Teens Through the Twenties." New York: Oxford University Press.

Arnett, Jeffrey Jensen. 2007. "Emerging Adulthood: What Is It, and What Is It Good For?" *Child Development Perspectives* 1(2):68–73.

Becker, Howard S. 1960. "Notes on the Concept of Commitment." *American Journal of Sociology* 66(1):32–40.

Burke, Peter. J. and Donald C. Reitzes. 1991. "An Identity Theory Approach to Commitment." *Social Psychology Quarterly* 54(3):239–51.

Chen, Kevin K. and Denise B. Kandel. 1995. "The Natural History of Drug Use from Adolescence to Mid-Thirties in a General Population Sample." *American Journal of Public Health* 85:41-47.

Dworkin, Jodi. 2005. "Risk Taking as Developmentally Appropriate Experimentation for College Students." *Journal of Adolescent Research* 20(2): 219–41.

Faupel, Charles E. 1991. *Shooting Dope: Career Patterns of Hard-Core Heroin Users*. Gainesville, FL: University Press of Florida.

Glassner, Barry, and Bruce Berg. 1980. "How Jews Avoid Alcohol Problems." *American Sociological Review* 45(4):647–64.

Harrington, Brooke. 2003. "The Social Psychology of Access in Ethnographic Research." *Journal of Contemporary Ethnography* 32(5):592–625.

Hays, Robert B. and Diana Oxley. 1986. "Social Network Development and Functioning During a Life Transition." *Journal of Personality and Social Psychology* 50(2):305–13.

Heckert, Alex and Druann Maria Heckert. 2002. "A New Typology of Deviance: Integrating Normative and Reactivist Definitions of Deviance." *Deviant Behavior* 23(5):449–79.

Herman-Kinney, Nancy J. and David A. Kinney. 2013. "Sober as Deviant: The Stigma of Sobriety and How Some College Students 'Stay Dry' on a 'Wet' Campus." *Journal of Contemporary Ethnography* 42(1):64–103.

Hirschi, Travis. 1969. *Causes of Delinquency*. Berkeley, CA: University of California Press.

Hser, Yih-Ing, Douglas Longshore, and M. Douglas Anglin. 2007. "The Life Course Perspective on Drug Use: A Conceptual Framework for Understanding Drug Use Trajectories." *Evaluation Review* 31(6): 515-47.

Jackson, Kristina M., Kenneth J. Sher, and Aesoon Park. 2005. "Drinking among College Students: Consumption and Consequences." *Recent Developments in Alcoholism* 17:85–117.

Jessor, Richard. 1991. "Risk Behavior in Adolescence: A Psychosocial Framework for Understanding and Action." *Journal of Adolescent Health* 12(8):597–605.

Jessor, Richard and Shirley L. Jessor. 1977. *Problem Behavior and Psychosocial Development: a Longitudinal Study of Youth*. Waltham, MA: Academic Press.

Johnston, Lloyd D., Patrick M. O'Malley, and Jerald G. Bachman. 2003. *Demographic Subgroup Trends for Various Licit And Illicit Drugs 1975-2002*. Ann Arbor, MI: Institute for Social Research.

Lightfoot, Cynthia. 1997. *The Culture of Adolescent Risk-Taking*. New York, NY: Guilford Press.

Matsueda, R. L. 1992. "Reflected appraisals, Parental Labeling, and Delinquency: Specifying a Symbolic Interactionist Theory." *American Journal of Sociology* 97(6):1577–1611.

McCall, George J. and Jerry Laird Simmons. 1966. *Identities and interactions: An Examination of Human Associations in Everyday Life*. New York: Free Press.

Mead, George Herbert.1934. *Mind, Self, and Society*. Chicago, IL: University of Chicago Press.

Ravert, Russell D. 2009. "'You're Only Young Once' Things College Students Report Doing Now Before It Is Too Late." *Journal of Adolescent Research* 24(3):376–96.

Schulenberg, John E., Alison L. Bryant, and Patrick M. O'Malley. 2004. "Taking hold of some kind of life: How developmental tasks relate to trajectories of well-being during the transition to adulthood." *Development and Psychopathology* 16(4):1119–40.

Schulenberg, John E., Jennifer L. Maggs, and Klaus Hurrelmann. 1997. *Health Risks and Developmental Transitions during Adolescence*. New York, NY: Cambridge University Press.

Schulenberg, John E. and Nicole R. Zarrett. 2006. "Mental Health During Emerging Adulthood: Continuity and Discontinuity in Courses, Causes, and Functions." Pp. 135–72 in *Emerging Adults in America: Coming of Age in the 21st Century*. Washington, DC: American Psychological Association.

Sharp, Susan F. and Trina L. Hope. 2001. "The Professional Ex-Revisited Cessation or Continuation of a Deviant Career?" *Journal of contemporary ethnography* 30(6):678–703.

Substance Abuse and Mental Health Services Administration. 2010. *Results from the 2009 National Survey on Drug Use and Health: Volume I. Summary of National Findings*. Rockville: MD: Office of Applied Studies.

Sutherland, Edwin H. 1947. *Principles of Criminology*. Philadelphia, PA: Lippincot.

Van Maanen, John. 1977. *Organizational Careers: Some New Perspectives*. New York: Wiley.

Vander Ven, Thomas. 2011. *Getting wasted: Why college students drink too much and party so hard*. New York: NYU Press.

Zinberg, Norman E. 1986. *Drug, Set, and Setting: The Basics for Controlled Intoxicant Use*. New Haven, CT: Yale University Press.

Chapter Seven

The Self and Intoxication

College is a time when emerging adults learn how to live. In his classic research on the college experience, Howard Becker (1964) discussed the less acknowledged, yet equally important skills, learned in the university context. Becker states: "It may be that the important things that happen to students in college do not happen in the library, the laboratory, or in the classroom" (1964:14). This remark by Becker certainly rings true in many instances, to live and function as an adult today in modern society involves many skills and abilities that the experience of college can provide.

Modern society is a highly mobile one, and when people move, as is often in the trek to college, they do not take families and communities with them. Young adults moving off to college often find themselves leaving behind families, high school peers, neighborhood networks, and familiar communities. Instead of the familiarity of past friendships fostered by family connections, high school, or community relations, new friendships must be made without assistance. As Becker states:

> Going away to college provides a rehearsal for the real thing, an opportunity to be away from home and friends, to make a new life among strangers, while still retaining the possibilities of affiliation with the old. In the dormitory…one finds himself on his own but at the same time surrounded by strangers who may become friends. One has the experience of learning to shift for oneself and making friends among strangers (1964:15).

Still other tasks that involve independent everyday human life are often learned through the college experience. All the seemingly small chores once done by family members such as meals, cleaning, taxes, bills, laundry, and shopping now must be completed by the recently independent student. As Becker writes about college: "They are a kind of training for the passage from home...going away to college provides an opportunity to play at moving away from home for good and it prepares the [student] for the world in which they will have to live" (15).

College, Self, and Identity Development

The experience of university or college attendance is a pivotal period in the life of emerging adults. It is a time of growth, maturation, intellectual stimulation, and personality development. A distinct part of being human is the development of **personality** or the dominant attitudes, feelings, and behaviors of a person. Sociologists posit that personality is one facet of the **self**. While people often believe that the self (or personality) is genetically determined, sociologists understand the self to be a constant product of social interaction with others and wider society. Thus, from a sociological perspective, the self is a *somewhat* stable set of perceptions of who we are as individuals. The self is not fixed or permanent; it is in flux and changing over our lives; a social process in which we experience feelings about who we are, derived from how we see ourselves in the eyes of others. Ultimately, the self is the image we have of who we are. And this image, this self-feeling or self-perception, is a product of social interaction. As Vander Ven (2011:53) writes:

> Sociologists view the self as the active, reflexive process of being self aware...the self is not a thing; it's a process—a process of seeing oneself as both subject and object. The active self can be observed in the ways in which we watch ourselves, have private conversations with ourselves, manage others' impressions of us, and tailor our behaviors to meet other people's expectations.

In this sense, the idea of reflexivity or self-awareness refers to our ability to be both a subject (feelings and perceptions) and object (seeing ourselves as others do). This is derived from the process of role-taking; putting ourselves in the shoes of others or viewing ourselves through the eyes of others. This unique consciousness is frequently considered the quintessential feature of the human condition (Gecas & Burke 1995). The social process of role-taking and seeing ourselves through the eyes of others will be discussed in further detail later in this chapter.

Identity is essentially the most public aspect of self. Our identity is often tied to the status positions (I am a student) and associated role obligations (I study, write papers, earn grades) we hold within the structure of society. Identity can be derived from our membership in social groups or the shared meanings between us and those around us about "who we are" (e.g., I am a father, a student, a soccer player, a heavy drinker)" (Vander Ven:2011). According to Gecas and Burke (1995), identity refers to who or what one is, the various meanings attached to oneself by self and others, and the self-characterizations individuals make in terms of group memberships.

Thus, the self is the conscious understanding that you are a distinct individual within larger society. You experience self-feelings and perceptions of who you are (subject), yet the self is also derived from the reflexive process enabling you to be conscious and aware of yourself in relation to others (object). The self is "composed of various identities, attitudes, beliefs, values, motives, and experiences" in terms of which you define yourself (Gecas and Burke 1995:42). Identity is the most public aspect of self, filling social statuses, roles, and memberships in groups. Identity is related to who or what you are in relation to society, the meanings you and others attach to who you are. Self is thus a fundamental determinant of identity formation, yet identities are an important component of self.

Identities

Research conducted by Peter Kaufman and Kenneth A. Feldman (2004) provides an important example of the changes in conceptions of self (and identity) that can be experienced by college students. One of the first studies to take a sociological approach on the topic, the research focused on students' reported change in self and identity within three domains: **intelligence and knowledgeability, occupation and career**, and **cosmopolitanism**. The researchers examined changes in students' conceptions of self, the presentation of their identity to others, and the identity attributed to them by others (Kaufman and Feldman 2004). Overall, the researchers concluded that the "college experience plays an important and constitutive role in forming the identities of students" (Kaufman & Feldman 488:2004).

First, students in the study reported that college helped them form a sense of their own **intelligence and knowledgeability**; that since entering into college, and through various experiences and interactions, they attribute the acquisition of knowledge and intelligence to their sense of self (Kaufman & Feldman 2004). The researchers were not concerned if students were objectively smarter because they had attended college; "but the extent to which students saw their college experience as largely responsible for making intelligence and knowledge salient components of [who they were]" (2004:470). Students also reported that through their college experience they developed the ability to think critically. As Kaufman and Feldman noted; "their interactions in college produced a mindfulness of the world around them, and they recognized that the world goes beyond the local environment to which they have been accustomed for so long" (2004:471). Furthermore, college students learned to use their language or to "talk smart" to "convey to others who they are, how they want to be identified, and to which social groups they belong" (2004:473).

In the second domain, **occupation and career**, students reported perceiving themselves as fitting into certain occupations (**status positions**) with associated **role obligations**. Through social interactions with fellow students, class instruction, college clubs, and professors, students experimented with potential occupations for their future self. For students, the college environment allowed them the opportunity to "try on" different careers, thus experimenting with changing notions of self and identity.

The third aspect of identity development felt by students throughout the university experience was that of **cosmopolitanism**. According to Kaufman and Feldman (2004), students did not use that specific term, yet it represented their acknowledged change in their cultural tastes and awareness. Students reported feeling "college educated," becoming cultured and cosmopolitan as opposed to uncultured and provincial. The college environment provided cultivation of cultural understanding, empathy, and relativism. Students reported that their education and cultured interactions taught them to rethink normative ideas about race/ethnicity, gender, sexuality, and social class. College influenced the types of individuals with whom students interacted and provided them social interactions and experiences that may not be available to those outside the college realm. As stated by Kaufman and Feldman:

> College presents students with an opportunity to engage in activities that shape their tastes and hobbies…college gives students a breadth and depth of experiences that adolescents and young adults might be hard pressed to find elsewhere. By being offered many options, and by engaging in an array of new social activities, students may begin to form identities grounded in new social interactions (2004:485).

As we will see later in this chapter, these developments in self and identity are also related to developments and maturation in role-taking or the ability to view oneself through the eyes of others. Furthermore, students were increasingly locating themselves in the eyes of larger society with elevated knowledge, intelligence and critical thinking skills, understanding of potential status positions, and cultural awareness.

Alcohol Use and College Life

People react to their environment. This fundamental sociological fact is crucial in understanding the prevalence of heavy episodic drinking among American colleges students. Colleges and the surrounding communities provide the social context for students to drink. Campuses are often rife with bars, retailers, and distributors that set the stage for heavy drinking with their low prices and high-powered promotions. Furthermore, a "high concentration of bars in a relatively concentrated area breeds competition that forces owners to decrease prices or stage irresponsible promotions in order to endure economically" (Wechsler 2002:91).

Within the college culture of heavy drinking, alcohol is cheap, bar specials abundant, drinking games popular, and intoxicating beverages fundamental for a successful party. Furthermore, drinking generally begins early in the evening and ends late at night, involving expectations for students to engage in atypical extroversion and sociability. Students often drink consistently throughout an evening out, trying to keep up with the drinking of peers.

Furthermore, students do not enter college as blank slates, but are often bombarded with imagery about college life through the news media, Hollywood movies, peer networks, television, and collegiate recruiting strategies prior to their arrival on campus. The cultural messages from these sources shaped the perceptions, motives, and expectations of students that college is a time to drink and party. However, while the college environment and the life stage of emerging adulthood provide the context for students to drink, not all students drink or drink heavily, furthermore, those students who do drink often have distinct motivations and expectations for the consumption of alcohol.

Emerging Adulthood and Alcohol Use

As noted in chapter one, the developmental stage of emerging adulthood is a useful conceptual framework in which to understand substance use during the college years (Arnett 2005). The central features of emerging adulthood (the age of identity explorations, the age of instability, the age of self focus, the age of feeling in-between, and the age of possibilities) all offer explanations on why substance use and abuse may be prevalent during this time period.

Identity exploration: It is during emerging adulthood when young adults are figuring out their own identity (particularly in the realm of love and work). With love and relationships, individuals "begin to ask themselves more seriously what kind of person they wish to form a long-term relationship with, which requires them to know who they really are and what qualities are most important to them in a (hopefully) lifelong romantic partner" (Arnett 2005:239). With work, emerging adults ponder their long-term goals and career paths, which requires them to know themselves, their abilities, interests, and work they might aspire to as adults. During this time substance use may increase with an absence of commitment to love and work. Students may use alcohol and other substances to cope with identity confusion and students may crave "experience" or "sensation" seeking as they try out different identities and lifestyle options before settling into adult roles and relationships (Arnett 2005).

The age of instability: The college years are associated with great instability and is arguably the most unstable period of life (Arnett 2005). As students experiment with different identities, this stage is associated with "frequent changes in their lives in terms of love partners, jobs, and educational status (dropping in and out of college, changing college majors)" (Arnett 2005:241). The anxiety, stress, and even sadness associated with such instability often elevates substance use as students use to alleviate negative moods as a form of self-medication.

The self-focused age: To say emerging adults are self-focused does not mean they are selfish or egocentric (Arnett 2005). It is the fact that college students often gain independence from family, teachers, and past obligations and commitments of adolescence. Students are free to make independent decisions regarding their money, time, leisure, and relationships. In this context, free from family and past social groups, social controls that once constrained risk behaviors may weaken. Furthermore, students may spend more time with friends who promote substance use.

Feeling in-between: Students may have a "foot in both worlds," feeling neither fully adolescent or fully adult. Thus, emerging adults may feel that "because they are no longer adolescents, they are capable of deciding for themselves whether or not to use substances. But if they also feel that they are not yet adults, they may not feel committed to adult standards of behavior and an adult level of responsibility" (Arnett 2005:246). In this context, students may experience a feeling of freedom or "time-out" to engage in heavy alcohol use and other substances that will be less acceptable later in adulthood.

The age of possibilities: Emerging adulthood is a time when students can make dramatic changes in their lives, the future looks bright, and they experience optimism for success and happiness. In this context, students may participate in risky substance use because they do not understand or foresee the potential negative consequences of their present behavior.

Thus, for college students and emerging adults, self and identity exploration often entails a high degree of experimentation, including meeting different kinds of people, questioning their belief system, engaging in promiscuous sex, and using drugs (Arnett 2000; Dworkin 2005).

Who are the Drinkers?

Annually, roughly 5.4 million full-time college students (60.1 percent of this population) consume alcohol in the past month, with 3.5 million engaging in binge drinking (39 percent), and 1.2 million participating in heavy alcohol use (13.2 percent) (Lipari and Jean-Francois 2016). However, within these numbers there emerges a general pattern, with white male college students who started drinking in high school, consuming more alcohol and in greater frequency than women and racial and ethnic minorities (American College Health Association 2014). For the majority of college students, heavy drinking does not begin in college. Wechsler et al. (1995) "found in a study of 140 campuses, that frequency of heavy episodic drinking in high school was predictive of the frequency of heavy episodic drinking in college when controlling for a variety of other individual difference measures" (Baer 2002:43).

Furthermore, white male college students are more likely than any other group to engage in heavy episodic drinking. White males engage in binge drinking more than females, African American males, and above all, females of color (Johnston et al. 2013). Thus, for the vast majority of African American, Hispanic, and Asian students, drinking is not a strong tradition in the university setting (Wechsler 2002). According to O'Malley and Johnston (2002:32), "white students have the highest rates of heavy drinking, black students have the lowest, and Hispanic students are intermediate." One theory, is that white male college students consume more alcohol because they are the least concerned with health consequences during emerging adulthood. The concept "**White Male Effect**" (WME) was coined by Finucane et al. (2000) when the researchers found that across all intersections of race and sex, white men were the least sensitive to risk.

Recent scholarship has started to focus on the drinking experiences of transgendered students and students who identify as gay, lesbian or bisexual. To this point, results have been mixed. For example, data from the American College Health Association-National College Health Assessment (ACHA-NCHA) of 120 institutions (Coulter et al. 2015) found that "transgender students reported heavy episodic drinking more frequently than their cisgender peers, whose biological sex and gender identity are in congruence" (Tupler et al. 2017:3). In contrast, the Center for Collegiate Mental Health (CCMH 2016), drawing on data from 139 colleges and universities, reported that "transgender students less frequently engaged in heavy episodic drinking than their cisgender peers" (Tupler et al. 2017:3). Studies concerning sexual-orientation are also inconsistent. Some research suggests that lesbian, gay, and bisexual students are more likely to participate in heavy episodic drinking compared to their heterosexual counterparts, while others have found no differences in the prevalence of alcohol use or heavy episodic drinking by sexual orientation (Coulter et al. 2016; Schauer et al. 2013; Talley et al. 2012). Reasons for these divergent findings are related to context, as alcohol use varies widely by the campus environment and how these studies define and categorize transgender people, as well as lesbian, gay, and bisexual people.

Psychosocial Factors

Drinking motives are the specific reasons for consuming alcohol, also known as drinking motivation or the initial decision to consume alcohol. The four primary drinking motives identified by Cooper (1994) are **social** (e.g., drinking to improve parties or social events), **enhancement** (e.g., drinking to enhance mood), **coping** (e.g., drinking to dull or avoid mood), and **conformity** (e.g., drinking due to social pressure to fit in). A drinking motive typically involves a need or psychological function that alcohol consumption fulfills.

Research on the drinking motives of college drinkers consistently finds **social** and **enhancement** motives are most prevalent among students and predicts higher levels of alcohol use (Dvorak et al. 2016). Endorsing greater **social** motives relates to increasing levels of alcohol consumption, and in some studies, greater alcohol-related problems (Van Damme et al. 2013). Furthermore, higher **enhancement** motives also predict risky drinking and related problems. Higher **coping** motives are less common among college students, but research has found they predict later alcohol-related problems (Cooper et al. 2015). Conclusions on **conformity** motives are mixed; some studies suggest increased conformity leads to greater drinking and problems (Merrill and Read 2010), while others determine no relationship at all (Cooper 2010; Dvorak et al. 2016). Overall, given the norms of the collegiate drinking culture social and enhancement drinking motives are most salient among emerging adults during this time period (Cooper at al. 2015).

Alcohol expectancies are defined as "specific beliefs about the behavioral, emotional and cognitive effects of alcohol" (Baer 2002:45). Research has shown that heavier drinkers expected alcohol to have a more positive influence on sociability and sexuality and expected less influence on cognitive and behavioral impairment (Baer 2002). In a study of students who completed measures of drinking and alcohol expectancies during both their freshman and junior years, Werner (1995) found that "high-risk drinkers had the greatest positive expectations for alcohol effects at both time points. Participants who moved into a problem-drinking category had higher positive expectancies at both time points and developed less concern for negative outcomes over time (Baer 2002:46)."

Theoretical Perspectives

Through alcoholic intoxication and the gradual but sometimes sudden loss of control, certain cell assemblies become active in the body and excitations are magnified, while inhibitions are lowered. However, the process of intoxication is, similar to everything humans do, social in nature. The intoxicated individual is not only impacted by the chemical changes in the body, but of the self-perceptions and the definitions of others, or as we will see, taking the role of the other. Just as inhibitions are lowered through intoxication, so is the ability to take the role of the other. As a drinking episode continues there occurs a loss of control. It has been observed with respect to alcohol that there is a patterning of effects as drinking proceeds, with the most complex and recently acquired controls to be the first to weaken or deteriorate. The process of taking the role of the other is a crucial facet of the self, individuals are constantly taking the role of the other to make sense of their social environment and understand proper behavior in varying social contexts. So, in maintaining and generating a sense of self, the reflexive process of taking the role of the other is the most complex and recent social control mechanism, or the first to weaken or deteriorate as drinking progresses.

As the ability to take the role of the other is altered through intoxication, the individual loses the cognitive and social awareness normally offered through complex role-taking. Such controls and awareness refer to self-criticism, self-consciousness, shame, and behavioral contemplation, all products of reflexive role-taking. The following sections provide a theoretical framework to begin to understand this process and intoxication from a sociological perspective. The theories presented will be applied to the data collected and will inform the conclusions regarding student alcohol use and intoxication.

Reflected Appraisals

Reflected appraisal is the concept that people form an opinion of themselves, based on their perceptions, of other people's opinions about them. The idea behind the reflected appraisal process is derived from the work of sociologist Charles Horton Cooley who coined the term **looking-glass self**. According to Cooley (1902), our notion of self not only arises via social interaction, but based on our perceptions of how others see us.

According to Cooley there are three stages of the looking-glass self:

1. We imagine how we look to the other person.

2. We imagine that other person's reaction to our appearance and behavior.

3. We experience self-feeling such as embarrassment, pride, or happiness.

Cooley theorized that through this interactive reflected appraisal process we form a conception of self. That through the looking-glass self we frame feelings and ideas about who we are as a person. Thus, our concept of self is a reflective process as we learn to use the looking-glass to learn who we are, especially in the intimacy of primary groups. Basically, during our interactions in groups (primary, secondary, and reference groups) we monitor how others respond to us and we continually modify our self; our perception of who we are. It is important to note that this process is ongoing throughout life as we continually interact with different people and different groups.

The I, the Me, the Generalized Other

Continuing in the tradition of Charles Horton Cooley, George Herbert Mead (1934) contended that the self arises through a reflective process called **role-taking**. According to Mead, role-taking or taking the role of the other, is how we learn to, and when, we put ourselves in the shoes of others—to try to understand how someone else feels, thinks, and thus try to anticipate how that person will behave. The role-taking process (similar to the looking-glass self) develops throughout a person's life as one learns to take the role of significant others. A **significant other** is a person with whom one has knowledge of that person's thoughts, feelings, obligations, and potential behavior. The most advanced form of role-taking is the **generalized-other**. Taking the role of the generalized other entails not only taking the role of particular significant others, but of various social groups and community or society at large. At the stage of the generalized other, a person may take the role of various primary, secondary, and reference groups, as well as the norms, rules, and customs of his or her culture and society. Mead considers taking the role of the "generalized other" as a form of social control. In taking the role of the other, the individual sees him/ herself as an object in the social community; it is through this reflexive view that the individual becomes self-conscious. Through this feeling of self-consciousness, the individual develops self-criticism, and through this self-criticism from taking the role of the "generalized other," the individual develops behavioral choices. Thus, the generalized other represents the collection of statuses, roles, norms, and attitudes that people use as a reference to figure out how to behave in any particular situation.

In the development of self, Mead also introduces the constant reflective process between the "I" and the "Me." Essentially, the "I" is more spontaneous, in the present, while the "Me" is more past and future, more involved in contemplation. If an individual were to blurt out something ignorant, the "I" did the speaking, while the "Me" will ponder why such a statement was made. The "Me" is the facet of self that contemplates the "generalized other," while the "I" is the immediate reaction made by the individual regarding the attitudes of others toward the self, it is more liberated and incalculable.

Thus, taking the role of the other is a cognitive process, a reflexive interplay between the impulsive **"I"** and the contemplative **"Me"** (Mead 1934). The "I" reflects human agency, the acting response in interaction that attempts to manipulate and control the environment. The "I" is informed and regulated by the "Me," the reflexive, contemplative role-taking facet of the self that represents the **generalized other**. This role-taking process, as an imaginative rehearsal between the "I" and the "Me," begins to form a stable self as an individual refers to previous "Me's" to inform the present action of the "I." As this process is reproduced through learning and socialization, previous "I's" and "Me's" inform present and future behavior forming a stable set of perceptions and feelings about who one is. Taking the role of the generalized other occurs in the present, but applies past experiences to anticipated experiences; the "Me" is called upon to solve problems, and forms an important form of social control.

Role-Taking in the College Environment

Researchers have further distinguished two different yet interrelated forms or role-taking: **reflexive role-taking** and **empathic role-taking**. According to Crawford and Novak (2001), people who focus on others' responses to themselves as social objects display a tendency toward **reflexive role-taking**. Those people who regularly anticipate the needs and feelings of others demonstrate a tendency toward **empathic role-taking**. More complex and advanced forms of role-taking involves these two interrelated forms (emphatic and reflexive) in the same cognitive process. Role-taking at its cognitive peak should involve both a focus on peoples' responses to the self as an object in social situations, but also an imaginative idea of the anticipation of needs and feelings of others.

Factors associated with participation in college life often determine an individual's role-taking ability. Age is a factor that may affect the degree of role-taking able to be performed by an individual. Viewing the world from the perspective of another person, including their thoughts and feelings, (empathic role-taking) requires a level of cognitive ability that may not be acquired until late adolescence or early adulthood, the prime years of college participation (Crawford and Novak 2001). Furthermore, certain social environments that involve unfamiliarity and uncertainty may advance role-taking capability. The college setting provides emerging adults with new found freedoms, unfamiliar social groups, novel experiences, and exposure to controversial issues. Within this context, students may be especially prone to evaluation and criticism, of both themselves and the world around them, and this process develops more advanced forms of role-taking (Crawford and Novak 2001).

The Presentation of Self

The concept of self can also be examined through the theoretical framework of Erving Goffman (1959) and *The Presentation of Self in Everyday Life*. Goffman approached the self from a **dramaturgical approach**, viewing the world as a stage, where all individuals are social actors. Interaction is viewed as a "**performance**," shaped by environment and audience, constructed to provide others with "**impressions**" that are consistent with the desired goals of the actor.

Goffman stated that we, as social actors, are in a constant state of "**impression management**." That is, we are all actors on a metaphorical social stage, striving constantly to make a good impression on our audience (who also happen to be actors). The end game is not just to make the best impression on others; we often actively work to ensure that others will believe they are making a good impression as well. This helps keep society and social relations running smoothly.

According to Goffman, the process of instituting a social identity deals with what he terms **front-stage** behavior, or "the part of the individual's performance which regularly functions in a general and fixed fashion to define the situation for those who observe the performance (Goffman 1959:22)." As a "collective representation," the front-stage establishes proper "setting," "appearance," and "manner" for the self being presented by the actor. However, this presentation of self in the front-stage is practiced and perfected in the **backstage** realm where the individual does not deal with the social constraints of the front-stage. The back stage is a personal setting where the individual might behave in ways or exert particular traits or mannerisms that would not normally be exhibited in the front stage.

Motives and Accounts

A **motive** is an explanation for an individual's action that arises during "question situations" (Mills 1940). Coined by C. Wright Mills, motives are tools in which a person attempts to "explain away" their actions and realign their behavior with expected rules of conduct. When an individual behaves outside expected patterns of conduct, and when this conduct is called into question by others, the individual experiences crisis and criticism, and must account for their behavior in such a manner that is acceptable for their social groups.

Expanding upon the work of C. Wright Mills, Scott and Lyman examine how speech is used to realign conduct with social norms, rules, and expectations. An **account** is a linguistic device employed whenever an action is subjected to evaluative inquiry. Such devices are a crucial element in the social order since they "prevent conflicts from arising by verbally bridging the gap between action and expectation" (Scott & Lyman 1968:46). Defined by Scott and Lyman (1968:46), "an account is a statement made by a social actor to explain unanticipated or untoward behavior." The behavior in question could have arisen from the social actor, or that of others. And the account can come from the social actor or from someone else. Scott and Lyman refer to two types of accounts: **excuses** and **justifications**. "**Excuses** are accounts in which one admits that the act in question is bad, wrong or inappropriate but denies full responsibility… **Justifications** are accounts in which one accepts responsibility for the act in question, but denies the pejorative quality associated with it" (1968:47).

Research Methods

The data for this chapter is drawn from 106 surveys and 32 intensive interviews of undergraduates at a large, state university in the American Midwest. Respondents were asked to provide basic demographic information: age, sex, year, socioeconomic status, recent and past intoxication history, and to write a factual story detailing their most recent experience with alcohol intoxication. Respondents were recruited via introductory college courses and asked to complete surveys. Students were asked to write personal anecdotes about the last time they drank to intoxication.

Specifically, respondents were asked to write an in-class report about "the last time that they got drunk." Focusing on their most recent experience with intoxication served to randomize drinking experiences, which kept respondents from relating a story about their most "interesting, unusual, or eventful" drinking episode. Respondents were required to be at least 18 years old to participate. They were asked to outline the process: How they decided to drink, how they obtained the alcohol, a description of the drinking process, and an account of the aftermath (i.e., what happened after they got drunk? What happened the next morning?). Finally, the students were asked to describe how they felt they changed when intoxicated, how their self or personalities changed, and how they felt others changed.

Intensive interviews were arranged through snowball sampling of university students. Students were asked to provide the investigator's name and contact information to potential informants who contacted the investigators if they agreed to be interviewed. Interviewees were asked to refer other potential participants to the investigators. Intensive interviews were conducted with undergraduates who were identified through student informants. Specifically former students were asked to recruit friends, dorm-mates, housemates, class-mates, etc. to participate in a short interview (approximately one hour).

The 106 "drinking stories" and interviews were then coded for content. Both were coded in similar fashion. Special attention was paid to text related to how the respondent perceived that alcohol intoxication was intertwined with perceptions of the self and how intoxication altered the self. Guided by theory and research, stories and interviews were coded with an emphasis on how self and drinking relate. The basic sensitizing question was: "How is the self altered during a drinking episode?" Coding focused on terms and phrases such as: "I, me, I usually don't do this, it wasn't me, I wouldn't have done that if." Coding not only focused on key phrases and terms, but on depictions of the behavior of drinkers as well. Once the descriptions of drinking behavior had been identified, they were categorized accordingly (change in self, no change, accounts/excuses, reflected appraisals) in the margins and on special forms created specifically for coding this data.

Those who were involved in the surveys were not involved in an interview and vice versa. Interviews and surveys were both chosen as data collection methods as to ascertain the desired information under different circumstances and contexts. It was thought that during an interview, the interviewer could steer the conversation to open particular facets of information, find new directions, and ask the specific questions to discover desired data. Surveys were done first to inform the interviews. Essentially, the two methods were selected to level the strengths and weaknesses each held for the research project; to collect the data and explore the research questions in the most thorough and methodical manner.

Overall, the sample had a mean age of 19.25 and 63% were female. In terms of academic year the sample contained: 64% Freshmen, 19% Sophomores, 9% Juniors, and 5% Seniors. With regard to binge drinking episodes, 86% of respondents had consumed 4 or more alcohol drinks in a row at least once in the past two weeks.

The Self and Alcohol Intoxication

In the loss of control, often experienced under the effects of alcohol, the loss of inhibition is brought about by chemical influences which interact with self-perceptions and the definitions of others brought to bear upon the drinking individual (Lindesmith et al. 1991). It has been observed with regard to alcohol that there is a pattern of effects as drinking proceeds, with the most complex and recently acquired controls being the first to deteriorate or weaken. Drinkers often start to exhibit this phenomenon by becoming uninhibited in their speech, laughter and actions sometimes ending up in a general stupor (Lindesmith et al. 1991:24).

Role-Taking Sabotage

Through the content analysis of the narrative "drinking stories" and interviews collected from the university sample, it seems that many respondents drank to facilitate a persona, that sober, they do not exhibit. Many reported drinking to become more social, less shy, less caring of others, more outgoing, and more likely to do things they would not do when sober. In a sense, the respondents were drinking to hinder (or manipulate) the ability to take the role of the generalized other, the most complex form of role-taking that forms self-consciousness, self-criticism and social control. As one respondent reported:

> I think that when I am intoxicated I loosen up a lot more. I am not afraid to say something stupid. I feel like I can be myself and not worry about what other people think of me. When I am sober I am more of a shy person and I am always worrying about what people think of me (female, 18, freshman, survey).

Similarly, another female respondent claims that drinking changes her personality:

> At the dorms and at the party my personality changed a lot. I am normally a pretty shy person and try to watch what I say not to hurt anybody. When I drink I am a lot more open to give hugs to almost everyone I see on the

street, or at least talk to them. I also noticed that I confront people with things I normally would not say to them. Sometimes I drink just to have the guts to tell people things normally I would be afraid to say. I definitely change a lot when I drink and my friends say that they don't recognize me then. I turn to an open person (female, 20, sophomore, survey).

Another respondent states intoxication is a necessity in social situations:

I'm usually nervous in social situations, so this (drinking) is usually a necessity when going anywhere with a bunch of people (female, 19, sophomore, survey).

The previous three respondents seem very aware of themselves in social situations, aware that they are social actors surrounded by other social individuals who take notice of their actions and words. The respondents are very self-critical and shy, and they use alcohol as an escape from such a social barrier. While some respondents claim to be habitually shy in sober social contexts and use alcohol to become socially outgoing, other respondents simply seem to lose the fact that they are social actors in the midst of others. They lose the self-control and self-consciousness that comes with the ability and cognitive functioning to take the role of the generalized other. Such behavior is apparent in the descriptions offered from the next few respondents.

My plan for the night was to get "wasted" and have a good time…in about a time span of 5 hours I drank 14 beers…my personality and conversations changed rapidly while I was drinking. I had more to say. I also made more vulgar and sexual comments. I felt really relaxed and good, but I would have gotten into a fight if I needed to (male, 20, sophomore, male, survey).

As with the previous respondent, the next two survey respondents claim their behavior can steer out of their control while intoxicated. Both claim they behave in a manner or say certain things they would not if they were sober.

> When I am drunk I talk a lot more than when I am sober. I also say everything that I am thinking about even if I shouldn't. I am glad that I am a girl because if I wasn't I would probably get beat up. I think most people are like that and that is why guys get into so many fights (female, 19, freshman, survey).

> ...there we had a lot of shots and beer. I personally had two shots of Tequila and some beer to which I can't remember. When I am sober I usually act a little crazy, I lift weights a lot and like to talk too much. When I am drunk, my other side comes out, which I will try to cause trouble and be an asshole. I like to bottle my anger and I usually take it out on drinking because I don't like to be an asshole around other people. I have a sort of invisibility when drunk and I just stop caring (male, 19, freshman, survey).

The next interview respondent states that people simply lose consciousness of their actions:

> A: I think spontaneous decision making is made more frequently and your conscience is repressed a lot more. I guess you're a lot more selfish, you just do what you, you know, what works out best for you at that time, you don't think about other people. I guess it's just being conscious of your actions (female, 22, senior, interview).

As apparent from the previous four respondents, the self, as a social actor when intoxicated, is hindered in its ability to take the role of the generalized other. The intoxicated individual is less engaged in role-taking in its most complex form. Alcohol intoxication induces in the social actor a decreased perception of oneself in the eyes of others, the thoughts and feelings others may feel towards the social actor via their behavior and general demeanor. As exhibited in the subsequent response, social awareness begins to wane. While the individual my still hold the basic reflexive ability of social human functioning, the ability to comprehend consequences, shame, accidents, and the thoughts and feelings of those around them is inhibited.

Q: Okay, so when you see people drink, how do you think people change?

A: I think when people drink…it's a lot of their subconscious, or what they want to do when they are sober. When you are drunk, you do anything you want to do, your natural kind of instinct, your unconscious comes out and you do whatever you want to do…in the moment…right then and you really don't think about it, or have any rationale of what is right or wrong, you kind of feel good right now, and whatever you want to do, just kind of comes out, and a lot of people, that's when [they make] bad judgment calls, or sex, running around naked, or doing stupid things, all of that is what they feel in the moment, or to make a scene, or make other people like them, or feel more accepted (male, 21, interview).

It is suggested through such responses that individuals' are aware of the change intoxication has on themselves and others. Some may be more cognizant of their inebriated actions and discourse, while some simply may not care. However, the high of a drinking episode will eventually cease, and the previously intoxicated individual will have to take into account the reality that he or she was not the only social actor at the scene.

Accounts for the Booze

Accounts are a crucial element in the social order because they prevent conflicts from arising by verbally bridging the gap between action and expectation. An account is a statement made by a social actor to explain unanticipated or untoward behavior. Such accounts often result via college binge drinking due to the sporadic and aberrant behavior often times associated with such intoxication. Students often use intoxication as an excuse for untoward behavior since excuses are accounts in which one admits that the act in question was bad, wrong, or inappropriate but denies full responsibility. Accounts are important because they are thought of as socially acceptable, that is how they bridge and assist in placing blame elsewhere aside from the social actor. Alcohol use and intoxication are so prevalent in the university context, that alcoholic inebriation is often a socially acceptable excuse. In this sense the individual can blame their actions on the alcohol intoxication rather than the self.

> I've noticed when I drink, I drink very quickly and drink a lot...when I drink, I drink to get drunk...I am a very social person and talk to people that I would never talk to before, and say things I would never say when I am sober...when my friend drinks, she gets angry. She drinks until she's drunk, and feels she needs to keep going, she thinks it's okay to act that way because she's drunk. I guess we do things because in the morning, it's ok because we were drunk. We all use being drunk as an excuse to do stupid things we would never do when we're sober (female, 19, freshman, survey).

In the previous narrative alcohol is simply an excuse for any untoward behavior that may have occurred during the drinking episode. She states: "...it's okay because we were drunk. We all use being drunk as an excuse to do stupid things we would never do when we're sober." In this sense, once the cognitive process of the generalized other diminishes, there will be

no stress, no worries, because essentially "it was the alcohol's fault." The
individual may still be aware of themselves as social actors in a particular
social context, but they are less aware of the ramifications of their
intoxicated actions, which calls for the eventual need of accounts. Various
sorts of untoward behaviors occur while intoxicated, and while the
behavior may not seem like a bad idea while drunk, the sober self must
later take account for such action usually revolving around the excuse of
intoxication.

> A: …and I know a lot of people that do, and they're like 'oh, it's okay, we
> were just drunk' and I'm like, 'no, you know, I am really sorry for doing
> that' and I apologize.

> Q: Right. Have you ever regretted something you did so much that you
> said, 'I'm not, I'm never drinking again'?

> A: uh huh…those kinds of things are really embarrassing the next day, and
> that makes me want to really control my drinking. I can't remember what
> happened right before spring quarter last year, specifically what happened,
> but it made me not drink all quarter (female, 22, senior, interview).

Many students may realize through previous intoxicated incidents that
they have such accounts and excuses at their disposal to place the
inebriated behavior away from the sober self. The individual experiences
the need for **post-intoxication disassociation**, or the need or desire to
distance the **sober self** from the actions and behavior of the **intoxicated
self**; a product of the drinking episode. Many individuals make mistakes
and are unhappy or embarrassed concerning their intoxicated actions. The
intoxicated behavior of an individual may clash with the ideal image of self
the individual desires in normal social settings.

...so I just go out and have a good time watching everyone else be drunk and act like a fool. I don't like the way I am when I am drunk. I fight with my boyfriend and act stupid. I'm very quiet and laid back when I'm not drinking...I say things I normally would never say when I'm drunk, but I'm still not really bad like some people...I don't like feeling like I have no control over what I do. Last time I kept losing my balance, I knew it too, but there was nothing I could do (female, 18, freshman, survey).

While some students stated they enjoyed themselves intoxicated, citing they were more humorous, outgoing, social, and carefree, it seems that the presence of untoward behavior in such accounts changed the intoxicated outlook. And while some acknowledged the effects of intoxication on their self, they also enlisted excuses and justifications to downplay the aspects of the drunken self. Alcohol can also be used as an excuse in and of itself. Students may use alcohol deliberately to facilitate certain behavior. They may be cognizant that intoxication is a viable excuse in the college context, and understand how it can be used to account for intoxicated behavior, whether the behavior was deliberate or spontaneous.

I am a pretty laid-back guy and I don't think drinking changes my personality at all other than I'm more apt to say what's on my mind. I know people who will become super competitive when they drink. I have friends that grow beer muscles and want to fight after drinking. Most girls I know would be more willing to give consent for sex after becoming intoxicated. In my opinion intoxication is just an excuse to act the way you want too. You got this reason, you can just say I was drunk, but you can get away with what you want (male, 19, freshman, survey).

Reflected Appraisals of the Drunk Self

After a drinking episode, students experience reflected appraisals of their intoxicated behavior from friends and peers. Reflected appraisals refer to the process of seeing ourselves as we think others see us. An important dimension of building the self is taking cues from evaluations made of us by our social audience. College binge drinkers frequently receive reviews of drunken performances the next morning. Numerous times, after a drinking episode, the sober self must take into account the reflected appraisals from the behavior and the action of the intoxicated self.

> I hate being around people that drink. They always become aggressive and overly friendly and say and do stupid things. When I tell my roommate and neighbors things they said or did, they are always embarrassed the next day (female, 19, freshman, survey).

The previous respondent describes the appraisals she offers to her friends and neighbors. She states that they become aggressive, overly friendly, and stupid, and the next day they are embarrassed when she reminds them of their intoxicated behavior. The next respondent reminds her friend of her hurtful actions when intoxicated, yet her friend laughs it off, not understanding the ramifications of her behavior. She continues to explain she appreciates the appraisals received by friends when she does something wrong or hurtful while intoxicated, it reminds her not to become so inebriated in the future and act in the same manner.

> Q: And what happens the next day? Do people have to remind her of this?

> A: Many times I have.

> Q: So, how does that, how does that play out? [Do they say] 'Oh my God, do you, do you remember what you said last night?' Is it that sort of thing?

A: Uh huh, sometimes it's easier not to remind people of that though, because you could just, especially, depending on like, their reaction to it, if you tell them, you know, 'this is what you did' and then, you know, most of the time she'll just laugh at it. And you're bringing it up because it hurt you…it's almost like, you know, 'why do I even say anything?' Because I know when it's happened to me, it really upsets me to hear stuff about something that I said that just hurt someone else…I mean, it upsets me that, to hear what I've done, but at the same time, I'm glad they tell me so it's almost a constant reminder not to get that way in the future (female, 22, senior, interview).

As with the previous respondent the next interviewee receives appraisals from a friend that cause her embarrassment. She doesn't like her intoxicated behavior because it clashes with her desired self-image. However, she not only receives negative appraisals from a friend, but positive appraisals from another friend, for the same intoxicated actions.

A: I repeat myself a lot when I'm drunk and people say, 'You know how many times you told me this?' I'm like, probably about 8 and they're like, 'yep' and I'm like 'oh'…I get really embarrassed because, even though I drink on a fairly regular basis, I still get embarrassed because I feel like it's not how I should act. I need to be more distinguished, I have this image, this pristine image of myself is tarnished when I do that…

Q: Do people help you out then, on one hand someone would say, 'you wouldn't believe what you said last night, how you were acting.' Or someone might say, 'nah, don't worry about it, you're you, you were fine…

A: Yea, easily, I have a couple of best friends here and the one I was referring to earlier, that is very serious about watching out for me, she makes me feel really bad…because she was the one babysitting me…it's just so embarrassing hearing like, what I did. But my other best friend is like 'oh my god, we had the best time, you were hilarious'…and I'm going 'oh, I'm so embarrassed,' and she's like, 'no, don't be, it was funny. It's ok (female, 20, junior, interview).

The next respondent describes the intoxicated behavior of two friends. They both act in an undesirable manner when inebriated and are most likely aware of their untoward intoxicated behavior through appraisals from friends and acquaintances.

A: That sounds a little bit like everyone, but I do have a friend that is really quiet, she doesn't talk at all, she is completely silent and I try to have conversations with her and it is horrible, but when she drinks, she talks a lot, shares feelings and that kind of stuff. And I have another friend who is not very nice when he drinks, normally he refrains himself because I think he knows.

Q: Does he become violent?

A: Just mean.

Q: Is that something that you think he can control when he is sober, but he can't when he is intoxicated?

A: Yea.

Q: A part of himself that he restrains when sober, but can't when intoxicated?

A: Yea, I think that describes it pretty well.

Q: Do you think that happens with most people, they have restraints or…
to certain activities, but when they become intoxicated they…?

A: Definitely, but I think it is different for each person, but some people
will share secrets, other people get mean, and other people hit on other
people all the time.

A: Well, one person, I don't go out with her that much anymore, like every
time she got drunk she would bring a different boy home, and she never
knew him, never met him before, and we would have to send him home
because we knew it wasn't good for her and she would regret it in the
morning. And she told us before. Please don't let me do this anymore, and
she can't control herself.

Q: And she is not like that when she is sober?

A: No, not at all.

Q: Just after a few too many drinks?

A: Yea.

(female, 19, sophomore, interview).

The previous descriptions suggest that reflected appraisals can be both
positive and negative, the data also suggest that reflected appraisals can
predict future behavior. Reflected appraisals are very important to people
in society, specifically the college community because they often reflect the

thoughts and feelings of close friends, neighbors, or significant others. The reflected appraisal is essentially the dénouement of the drinking episode. Basically the individual is receiving a play-by-play of their intoxicated actions, whether slightly inebriated or completely blacked-out. Not only are they receiving information regarding their intoxicated behavior, but information regarding how such activity changed the thoughts, feelings and perceptions of those in contact with them during the drinking episode.

Conclusion

Through the systematic analysis of the 106 student surveys and the 32 intensive interviews, it seems that university students contain some knowledge of the effects alcohol will encompass upon their self. As stated in the previous pages, many students drink to the point of intoxication to become more outgoing, social, and carefree, to become a self that is normally inhibited during sobriety. While they may not be aware of the process in sociological terms, student drinking results in the diminished ability to take the role of the other, more specifically, the most complex form of role-taking, taking the role of the generalized other. They begin to lose their self awareness, and they become less conscious of themselves. This loss of self-awareness enables the individual to become more careless, less inhibited, and less aware of sober social restraints.

However, when the intoxicated self causes some form of embarrassment, rude behavior, unpleasant scene, or dire consequence, the notion of intoxication changes. Students blame the drinking and blame the alcohol through accounts consisting of excuses and justifications. The individual can reconfigure the blame away from a desired presentation of self, thus avoiding stigma and formulating impression management. The accounts serve as a vehicle in which the individual recalls the behavior as not his or her own, but that of an intoxicated self.

Students must also rely upon and withstand the reflected appraisals of others. Whether positive or negative, the individual will internalize the appraisals from friends and acquaintances due to the performance of the intoxicated self. Thus, the individual receives a sense of their drunk self from others, and will either denounce or embrace this self in terms of the self they wish to perform in the front-stage context.

While drinking to decrease self-awareness and self-consciousness may be the desired effect for many student drinkers, such action can entail negative consequences. These negative consequences are often registered through the reflected appraisals of witness testimony, be they friends or neighbors. However, the sober self is still involved in daily university life and must enact impression management, often times through excuses, that displace blame to another source, intoxication.

When discussing the effects alcohol has on the self, it is not as if the individual ceases to see him or herself as a social actor in a particular social context. The individual is aware, but views the self in a different framework, a framework where the individual is intoxicated. Many students acknowledged that alcohol did alter their personality in some manner, whether positive or negative, the student is now observing him or herself from an altered standpoint. The self is being viewed via an intoxicated lens, whether from personal experience or reflected appraisals; the sober view of the self begins to diminish.

As the drinking episode begins the individual has certain expectancies of how the self will change as intoxication intensifies. This knowledge of inebriated behavior may stem from personal experience or reflected appraisals, but, as many of the respondents stated, they were aware, or were under the impression they were going to be less shy, more outgoing, humorous, mean, flirty, or crazy. However, as the drinking episode continues and intoxication increases the individual begins to lose the most complex or recently acquired cognitive controls, or the ability to take the role of the generalized other. As this occurs the individual becomes less aware of the self as a social actor amidst other social actors. The individual becomes less cognizant of the thoughts, perceptions and feelings of those involved in the social scene and less aware of how the intoxicated self is being presented to other people. This is where the discrepancy seems to occur in the drinking episode. The individual becomes less aware of the self being presented and the information being relayed to others because of the gradual inability to take the role of the other in a manner that manages the self as the individual desires. When this occurs, and the individual behaves in an untoward, angry, or embarrassing fashion the individual seems to depend on reflected appraisals to make sense and define the intoxicated behavior. It is also at this point that accounts are enacted to realign the desired self, owning to the behavior in question, but transferring the blame to the alcohol.

There seems to be a four-stage process of self involved in the intoxicated context: the **ideal sober self**, the **ideal intoxicated self**, the **real intoxicated self**, and the **real sober self**. An individual may hold a desired image of the intoxicated self, and even contain the ability to maintain that desired self during certain points of a drinking episode, but as the intoxication process continues, and the ability to take the role of the generalized other gradually falters, the individual may lose control of the ideal intoxicated self. It is at this point the individual relies upon reflected appraisals from friends and neighbors to make sense of and contemplate this intoxicated self and enact accounts and excuses if the self in question conflicts too greatly with the desired image of the self.

Future Questions

First, many student respondents were aware of how their self and personality changed throughout a drinking episode. Some listed positive changes, such as becoming more social, humorous, and outgoing, while others cited negative outcomes, such as becoming mean, uncontrollable, and behaving in a regrettable manner. While many of the students were aware of how they changed, the difference between those who list positive characteristics while drunk compared to those who list negative characteristics should be examined. Have the students who cited positive outcomes learned their limits with regard to alcohol consumption? Have they learned how to drink in a deliberate and manageable manner to maintain control over intoxication?

Second, many of the respondents claim that people who are drunk become impulsive, act "right in the moment," and they reveal a true part of their subconscious. As discussed previously, many people seem to understand how intoxication will impact their self, they also understand that alcohol can be used as an excuse for untoward behavior once the drinking episode as ended. Do some students understand, and drink to the point of intoxication, to do bad things knowing full well they can simply blame alcohol? Is this subconscious revealed in a spontaneous drunken manner, or does the individual know full well that once they and others have had enough to drink it will then become socially acceptable to do and reveal things they cannot in a sober context?

Third, who are the students that can always use accounts as an excuse for their untoward behavior after a drinking episode? In the college drinking culture, alcohol operates as an acceptable excuse for bad behavior, yet why does the excuse of alcohol work for some students and not others? Is it their social groups? Is it simply the university context that allows for such excuses to emanate? Are their certain "problem" drinkers that seem to always be excused by their friends and peers? At what point in the life-course does alcohol cease to be an acceptable excuse?

Fourth, reflected appraisals may be essential in the persistence and desistence of student drinking and other forms of deviant behavior. Students often rely upon depictions from friends and acquaintances to make sense of their drinking behavior. Not only do they hear about their actions and words while intoxicated, but hear how their behavior changed the thoughts, feelings, and perceptions of other social actors privy to the scene. Ultimately, such appraisals play a crucial part in the building of the self, or the maintenance of an ideal self, especially since the college years are so important in self and identity formation. Seeing oneself through the eyes of others plays a crucial role in how an individual feels others see them. Yet, reflected appraisals are not simply how someone imagines others see them, but can take the form of direct discourse from friends and neighbors of how an individual was behaving while intoxicated and how others perceived that behavior. If a student receives numerous negative appraisals due to intoxicated behavior will the student persist or desist in drinking? Likewise, in what way do positive appraisals impact student drinking? Do they encourage the behavior and overlook or downplay possible problems the student experiences while drinking?

Last, the positive aspects of university drinking should be examined. Some researchers, such as Henry Wechsler, seem to only demonize the drinking that is involved in the university context. Yet, as mentioned previously, the heaviest drinkers consume the majority of the alcohol, leaving many students out of the heavy drinking category. Many students drink throughout their college years, do not cause problems to themselves and others, remain healthy, and eventually graduate. More research should be focused on these students, if not simply to level the field of research on college drinking, but to inform the public that not all college students are heavy dangerous drinkers. For example: What impact does alcohol have on building social relationships? How does it help build camaraderie? Does alcohol use in college help build responsibility through helping others, understanding limits and dangers, and developing a sense of right and wrong when under the influence of a legal drug? Certainly the abuse of alcohol can be dangerous to any individual, college student or not, but college drinking will always be, and understanding its implications on all sides of the social spectrum is definitely cause for further social inquiry.

Notes and Discussion Questions:

Appendix A: In-Class Survey

1.) Sex   Female_____   Male_____

2.) Age in years   _____

3.) Academic Class   Freshman ___ Sophomore___ Junior____ Senior_____

4.) Socioeconomic Class: Please estimate your parents' or guardians' annual family income in dollars._____

5.) Have you ever used alcohol to the point of intoxication?

6.) About how old were you the first time you drank beer, wine, or liquor?:

     Age in years when you first drank: _____

7.) About how many times, if ever, did you have 5 or more drinks in a row in the past two weeks? (Circle only one answer)

Never

Once

2-3 times

4-5 times

6-7 times

More than 7 times

Appendix B: Instruction for Anecdotes

On the papers provided, please provide a true anecdote or story about the **most recent** time that you used alcohol to the point of intoxication as a university student. **Do not use names for any of the people you describe in your account. Please use role titles instead (e.g., friend, resident advisor, fellow student).** Providing as much detail as possible, describe the entire process including:

1. How you decided to drink alcohol on this particular occasion.

2. How you obtained the alcohol.

3. What you drank (e.g., beer, wine, liquor) and where you consumed it (e.g., dorm, apartment, house, bar) and who you drank with.

4. How you consumed it (e.g., drinking games, leisurely consumption, specialized techniques like shotgunning beers, beer "bongs", etc.)

5. How did you avoid being detected by authority figures? (Police, resident hall officials, etc.)?

6. How did it feel? What were the rewards of drinking alcohol. If it was fun, how so? If it was a negative experience, how so? In rich detail, describe what ensued during and after the drinking event that day/night.

7. What were the consequences of this drinking experience? Describe what happened that night and the morning after. Did you have a hangover? How did you "treat" your hangover and did it affect your ability to attend to other responsibilities (e.g., school work, work, relationships, etc.).

8. Any other details that you would like to provide our welcome.

Completion and return of this survey implies consent. **You will have forty minutes to complete your anecdote. If you do not wish to participate, please write, "I do not wish to participate" on the paper provided.**

Appendix C: Potential Interview Questions

1. Tell me about one of the last times you drank to the point of intoxication. Meaning when you were noticeably not sober.

2. Why do you think you drink to the point of intoxication?

3. Do you think people change when they are intoxicated? Some examples.

4. How does your behavior change when you are intoxicated?

5. Do you feel you as a person are better represented while sober or intoxicated?

6. Do you like the way you act when you are intoxicated?

7. What mistakes have you made? Do you have any regrets that are directly related to intoxication?

8. Do you use alcohol differently in various social aspects?

9. Do you think your identity changes when you drink?

10. Do you feel your true self/identity is represented while intoxicated or sober?

11. Do you think people have a true self?

12. What have been some social consequences of your drinking to intoxication?

13. Do you feel sexual assault or victimization is a problem in university settings due to people drinking to intoxication?

14. Do you have any past experiences of such behavior or incidences?

15. Do you drink to become more social?

16. If you have suffered detrimental consequences from intoxication, why do you continue such behavior?

References

Arnett, Jeffrey Jensen. 2005. "The Developmental Context of Substance Use in Emerging Adulthood." *J. Drug Issues* 35(2):235–254.

Baer, John S. 2002. "Student Factors: Understanding Individual Variation in College Drinking." *J. Stud. Alcohol* (14):40–53.

Becker, Howard S. 1964. "What Do They Really Learn at College?" *Trans. Action.* 1(4):14–17.

Center for Collegiate Mental Health. 2015. Annual Report. 2016. Publication No. STA 15-108.

Cooley, C. H. 1902. "Human Nature and the Social." *Order* 184.

Coulter, Robert W. S., John R. Blosnich, Leigh A. Bukowski, A. L. Herrick, Daniel E. Siconolfi, and Ron D. Stall. 2015. "Differences in Alcohol Use and Alcohol-Related Problems between Transgender- and Nontransgender-Identified Young Adults." *Drug Alcohol Depend.* 154:251–259.

Coulter, Robert W. S., Miesha Marzell, Robert Saltz, Ron Stall, and Christina Mair. 2016. "Sexual-Orientation Differences in Drinking Patterns and Use of Drinking Contexts among College Students." *Drug Alcohol Depend.* 160:197–204.

Crawford, Lizabeth A. and Katherine B. Novak. 2000. "The Effects of Role-Taking and Embarrassability on Undergraduate Drinking: Some Unanticipated Findings." *J. Soc. Behav. Pers.* 15(2):269.

Lynne Cooper, M., Emmanuel Kuntsche, Ash Levitt, Lindsay L. Barber, and Scott Wolf. 2016. "Motivational Models of Substance Use." in *The Oxford Handbook of Substance Use and Substance Use Disorders: Volume 1*, edited by K. J. Sher. Oxford University Press.

Cooper, M. Lynne. 1994. "Motivations for Alcohol Use among Adolescents: Development and Validation of a Four-Factor Model." *Psychol. Assess.* 6(2): 117.

Cooper, M. Lynne. 2010. "Toward a Person$\times$ Situation Model of Sexual Risk-Taking Behaviors: Illuminating the Conditional Effects of Traits across Sexual Situations and Relationship Contexts." *J. Pers. Soc. Psychol.* 98(2):319.

Dvorak, Robert D., Nicholas J. Kuvaas, Tess M. Kilwein, Tyler B. Wray, Brittany L. Stevenson, and Emily M. Sargent. 2016. "Are Drinking Motives Associated with Sexual 'Hookups' among College Student Drinkers?" *J Am. Coll. Health* 64(2):133–138.

Dworkin, Jodi. 2005. "Risk Taking as Developmentally Appropriate Experimentation for College Students." *Journal of Adolescent Research* 20(2): 219–41.

Finucane, Melissa L., Paul Slovic, Chris K. Mertz, James Flynn, and Theresa A. Satterfield. 2000. "Gender, Race, and Perceived Risk: The'white Male'effect." *Health Risk Soc.* 2(2):159–172.

Gecas, Viktor and Peter J. Burke. 1995. "Self and Identity." *Sociological Perspectives on Social Psychology* 41–67.

Goffman, Erving. 1959. *The Presentation of Self in Everyday Life.* New York, NY: Doubleday.

Johnston, Lloyd D., Patrick M. O'Malley, Jerald G. Bachman, and John E. Schulenberg. 2013. "Monitoring the Future National Results on Adolescent Drug Use: Overview of Key Findings, 2012."

Kaufman, Peter and Kenneth A. Feldman. 2004. "Forming Identities in College: A Sociological Approach." *Res. High. Educ.* 45(5):463–496.

Lindesmith, Alfred R., Anselm Strauss, and Norman K. Denzin. 1999. *Social Psychology*. SAGE Publications.

Lipari, Rachel N. and Beda Jean-Francois. 2016. *A Day in the Life of College Students Aged 18 to 22: Substance Use Facts*. US Department of Health & Human Services, Substance Abuse and Mental Health.

Mead, G. H. 1934. "Mind, Self, and Society from the Standpoint of a Social Behaviorist (CW Morris, Ed.)." *Chicago: University of Chicago*.

Merrill, Jennifer E. and Jennifer P. Read. 2010. "Motivational Pathways to Unique Types of Alcohol Consequences." *Psychol. Addict. Behav.* 24(4):705–711.

Mills, C. Wright. 1940. "Situated Actions and Vocabularies of Motive." *American Sociological Review* 5:904–913.

O'Malley, Patrick M. and Lloyd D. Johnston. 2002. "Epidemiology of Alcohol and Other Drug Use among American College Students." *J. Stud. Alcohol Suppl.* (14):23–39.

Schauer, Gillian L., Carla J. Berg, and Lawrence O. Bryant. 2013. "Sex Differences in Psychosocial Correlates of Concurrent Substance Use among Heterosexual, Homosexual and Bisexual College Students." *Am. J. Drug Alcohol Abuse* 39(4):252–258.

Scott, M. B. and S. M. Lyman. 1968. "Accounts." *Am. Sociol. Rev.* 33(1):46–62.

Talley, Amelia E., Kenneth J. Sher, Douglas Steinley, Phillip K. Wood, and Andrew K. Littlefield. 2012. "Patterns of Alcohol Use and Consequences among Empirically Derived Sexual Minority Subgroups." *J. Stud. Alcohol Drugs* 73(2):290–302.

Tupler, Larry A., Daniel Zapp, William DeJong, Maryam Ali, Sarah O'Rourke, John Looney, and H. Scott Swartzwelder. 2017. "Alcohol-Related Blackouts, Negative Alcohol-Related Consequences, and Motivations for Drinking Reported by Newly Matriculating Transgender College Students." *Alcohol. Clin. Exp. Res.* 41(5):1012–1023.

Van Damme, J., L. Maes, E. Clays, J. F. M. T. Rosiers, G. Van Hal, and A. Hublet. 2013. "Social Motives for Drinking in Students Should Not Be Neglected in Efforts to Decrease Problematic Drinking." *Health Educ. Res.* 28(4):640–650.

Vander Ven, Thomas. 2011. *Getting Wasted: Why College Students Drink Too Much and Party so Hard.* New York, NY: NYU Press.

Wechsler, Henry and Bernice Wuethrich. 2002. *Dying To Drink: Confronting Binge Drinking on College Campuses.* Rodale: Emmaus, PA.

Wechsler, Henry, George W. Dowdall, Andrea Davenport, and Sonia Castillo. 1995. "Correlates of College Student Binge Drinking." *American Journal of Public Health* 85(7):921–26.

Werner, M. J. and J. W. Greene. 1992. "Problem Drinking among College Freshmen." *J. Adolesc. Health* 13(6):487–492.

Chapter Eight

Gender and Informal Control of Alcohol Use

Gender is a central component of the social order and is one of the major ways human beings organize their lives (Lorber 1994). Conceptualized as both a societal structure (Risman 2004) and a social institution (Martin 2004), gender constrains and facilitates behavior and action, involves normative expectations, informal rules, and is embedded in individuals throughout their social life. Gender is constantly created and re-created through human interaction, it textures and orders social life and controls our actions and decisions as we constantly work on "**doing gender**" appropriately (Lorber 1994; West and Zimmerman 1987).

Gender operates as a **normative control mechanism** in the college party scene because it streams men and women into certain forms of behavior. The influence of masculine norms on male drinking behavior is documented through the heavy and competitive drinking style among men (Christie-Mizell and Peralta 2009; Young et al. 2005). Researchers generally situate heavy drinking as a hegemonic masculine pursuit (Heath 2000; Montemurro and McClure 2005; West 2001), one that is "male dominated, male identified, and male centered" (Capraro 2000:307). Peralta (2007) observed that male drinking practices in the college party scene embody an athletic, competitive, powerful, and self-assured norm that is often used to accomplish dominant ideas about hegemonic masculinity.

In contrast, scholars have observed that femininity constrains women's drinking behavior. Women generally limit their alcohol use to avoid stigma, view heavy drinking as problematic and unbecoming of feminine accomplishment, and do not believe drinking symbolizes strength and power (Peralta 2007). Others have averred that women are drinking more akin to their male counterparts, regarding drinking, like men, as a way to gain power and equality in the college drinking scene (Young et al. 2005). Although research has documented the problems and disadvantages women experience in the college drinking scene (Armstrong, Hamilton, and Sweeney 2006; Peralta 2007), less is known about how gender operates as social control and funnels women into distinct patterns of behavior. In this chapter, I analyze the beliefs and behaviors of college women in a university drinking scene. I address how gender operated as an informal control mechanism and analyze the ways women negotiated femininity in a social climate dominated by a hegemonic masculine style of drinking. I focus on behaviors and norms of drinking, ways of doing gender, and the social controls women experienced and developed for themselves.

The Ideal Drinker

In this college drinking scene, alcohol was cheap, bar specials abundant, drinking games popular, and intoxicating beverages fundamental for a successful party. Furthermore, drinking generally began early in the evening and ended late at night, involving predictable expectations for participants to engage in atypical extroversion and sociability. However, it was the normative drinking ideals, women noted, that mainly contributed to a culture of heavy drinking. These drinking norms were rooted in a masculine value system (i.e. a masculine ideal), and women had to subscribe to them for successful participation in the college drinking scene. The drinking norms were geared towards men, and men were better able to meet them. However, female drinkers believed, as did most undergraduate men and women, that the ideal drinker embodied how students primarily drink. The ideal drinker was a person who could drink consistently throughout the evening, keep up with the drinking of peers, yet remain in some semblance of control and contribute to the necessary mood and spirit required in the collective drinking scene. The ideal drinker was abstract, separate from people, an "ideal type" that ultimately reflected heavy drinking norms that reflected masculine characteristics.

Drink Long and Strong

College women described "ideal" drinkers as undergraduates who consumed alcohol heavily, aggressively, and often competitively. Madeline, a 21-year-old senior discussed, "well, you have to be able to drink a lot, everyone knows that, otherwise you're cut from the team (laughing)." Stephanie, a 22-year-old senior noted, "you're expected to play beer pong; no matter how bad you are at it, you still have to play." This style of partying not only involved drinking games, but also taking shots when offered, always having a drink in hand, and maintaining pace with drinking mates. Elizabeth, a 22-year-old senior, noted, "having a high tolerance is godly, it shows strength, someone who can drink different drinks and can tolerate them throughout the night." Drinking games, "shot-for-shot," "shot-gunning," and "keg stands" were prevalent and reinforced norms of heavy drinking. Kerstin, a 20-year-old junior, remarked, "well, you have to able to drink, and then drink more. I guess that's where a high tolerance comes in. You can drink a lot, but still have fun."

Female drinkers also reported longevity and stamina as characteristics of ideal drinkers. Sarah, a 21-year-old senior, discussed the traits she considered indicative of good drinkers: "Someone who can drink all night, but still hold their liquor and be social, but still continue drinking until the party is over." Drinking generally began at a pre-party or "pre-game" stage where students drank with close friends before heading to the first party or bar. Beth, a 20-year-old junior, recounted a typical college night out: "we started drinking at Natalie's, we had some shots there, I guess it was around five o'clock…we went to a few parties later, got some drinks at a bar, and ended around 2 a.m. drinking at my friend Matt's apartment. Eventually we wandered home I guess."

Once the bars closed, or a party reached its end, students held after-hours parties where drinking continued into the early morning hours. Those students who could not meet the social drinking expectations of ideal drinkers were often viewed as weak or burdensome. Amy, a 22-year-old senior, noted, "you have to pace yourself, you don't want to ruin your friends' night out by being a mess…having to get walked home or babysat." These internalized conceptions of an ideal drinker served as **normalizing judgment** (Foucault 1977) as undergraduates often sanctioned or corrected those who did not conform to ideal drinking standards. Heavy consumption practices informally controlled drinking behaviors for women and the drinking culture generally.

Drink and Travel

For undergraduate women, the ability to travel and to socialize was also a central characteristic of ideal drinkers. Socializing, flirting, and potentially meeting romantic partners were very important to all the women with whom I spoke. Jane, a 21-year-old senior noted, "it's very expected that you, like, 'hop' groups. Clusters of people, you know. Like, you can't stick with the same person all night. You have to make the rounds and meet new people, I mean, why else would you be out drinking?" Traveling was intertwined with socializing, and entailed movement from party to party, bar to bar, or in some combination.

Through socializing, fun, and flirtatious interactions with fellow drinkers, women gained the attention and status they desired. Women believed that college was, as Janice, a 20-year-old junior, noted, "the time to meet new and often lifelong friends, maybe even a boyfriend." For undergraduate women, college was the central time and space to develop primary group friendships and identities (Arnett, 2004; Karp, Holstrom, and Gray 1998), and social interactions within the drinking scene provided opportunities to build both. These social outings were are an important facet of emerging adulthood, related to establishing and maintaining romantic and social relationships (West and Zimmerman 1987). Stephanie, a 22-year-old senior, talked about what she expected on a night out, "I want to have fun, socialize, you know, have some drinks. I like to go to a couple parties, and then usually hit the bars. It all depends on what's going on that night, where my different friends are going to be. If there is a boy I like I want to find where he is."

The women I interviewed did not want to drink and behave exactly like men, but they internalized and rationalized this heavy, masculinized drinking style to attain successful (i.e., participation, attention, status, romance) membership within the drinking scene. Although women had more freedom than men to maneuver between enacting femininity and masculinity when drinking (i.e., men *had to* drink like men), it was the masculinized drinking style that delivered the greatest sense of membership for female drinkers. However, when drinking women often violated the informal gender rules of femininity situated within the social order of the college drinking scene. It was not just the act of heavy drinking that was viewed as a gendered practice, but the manner in which men and women *accomplished* heavy drinking. Gendered rules existed for how men and women "do" heavy drinking, these rules guided and controlled behavior, and could be seen in the informal sanctions and stigmatization women could experience when drinking. Gender clearly operated as social control as women strove to accomplish heavy drinking, but in a more feminized manner.

Gender Rules and Heavy Drinking

Women within masculine dominated settings exist between sociocultural expectations of femininity and the inclusive membership norms of the masculine dominated scene. Women value their femininity and are normatively pressured to maintain it, but at the same time seek acceptance and status within these male-dominated contexts. Women who over-emphasize femininity, similar to women who over-emphasize masculinity, are often stigmatized, sanctioned, and denigrated. For women, the pressure to maintain behavior within the appropriate boundaries of masculinity and femininity operated as a potent social control mechanism within the college party scene.

Women followed the informal standards of ideal drinking, not only because these were the dominant norms of the drinking scene, but also because they had an emotionally fun and socially prosperous time doing it. As Stacey, a 22-year-old senior, discussed, "it's a blast to get drunk, let yourself go, talk to everyone, and get to dancing (laughing)." However, the drink "strong and long" mentality, when combined with expectations of social travel, caused problems for many of these undergraduate women. As women continued to drink throughout an evening, the possibility of losing control increased, destabilizing their ability to socialize coherently and to manage their behavior. Losing control can increase the potential for various negative outcomes that have recently been defined as a *drinking crisis* (Vander Ven 2011). A drinking crisis might include getting "pinched" by a cop, becoming ill, having relational conflicts with friends or partners, or engaging in a risky sexual hook-up. It was often an involved process of "do's" and "don'ts," as Stephanie, a 21-year-old senior, discussed:

> I guess for guys there's just one kind of drinker, they just get drunk you know. It's such a straight line for guys. Whereas with girls, there's more types, they are expected to keep up with the guys and be partying, but once they reach that point they are expected to stop. But guys can just keep going and it's hard to stop when everyone's still partying, but you don't want to be so wasted it's a problem. For girls it's just more complex...so many more factors to it.

Although men drank more than women in the college drinking scene, women drank and often drank heavily. The vast majority of undergraduate women discussed the complexities of negotiating drinking benefits versus drinking problems, and it was the pursuit of benefits and the avoidance of problems that ultimately operated as informal control. For women, drinking problems could ruin their drinking benefits. Women encountered problems when they drank too much and/or violated the informal gender rules that governed how they were supposed to "do" heavy drinking as women.

Presentation and Femininity

College women were often meticulous and deliberate with regard to dress and appearance on a night out drinking. For female drinkers, presenting oneself as feminine was a central rule for accomplishing heavy drinking in a feminine manner. On any traditional party night, women could be seen frequenting parties and bars wearing heels, skirts, and carefully done hair and makeup, exhibiting a deliberate physical presentation of femininity. For women in American culture, conforming to emphasized or stereotypical femininity in practice often involves being sexually attractive and available, fashionable, thin, busty, White, tan, supportive, flirtatious, enthusiastic, and even wealthy (Armstrong et al. 2006; Deirdre, Pomerantz, and Currie 2005; Grindstaff and West 2006) Female drinkers deployed these emphasized feminine characteristics under a **double gaze**; women judged other women's appearance and behavior, but status and attention from men were central. This internalization of the double gaze contributed to the development of a subcultural specific "**generalized-other**" (Matsueda 1992; Mead 1934), one that operated as an informal control mechanism concerning gender and alcohol use. This generalized other reflected the norms, rules, and expectations of this subcultural context as women started to apply their past experiences to anticipated events involving drinking and gender presentation. Women's internalization of the double-gaze formed an important locus of informal social control. However, it was not just the outward appearance of femininity that concerned female drinkers. The development of this subculturally specific generalized other exhibited the fact that successful gender adaptations were complex and elusive. Genevieve, a 22-year-old senior, discussed:

A: Well, there's three types of girls. There's the really girly girl, there's the drinking and being like the guys girl, and there's the one that can do both…and I've realized that the ideal one is the one that can do both.

Q: And why is this?

A: Well, because the really feminine girl, she's fun to date…but she's not good when it comes to just hanging out. And the girl who is just one of the guys, well she is just that, one of the guys. Whereas the one that can do both is ideal because she is someone you can go out and drink with, she can hang out and watch the game or can do the typical dating things. *But* she can keep up with all the drinking, which in college is a very big deal.

Q: Is it hard for girls to find this middle-ground, to do both things?

A: You're either that way or you're not. If they try and do it on purpose they fail, they either go too girly, or they go too manly.

Q: But girls try this kind of performance?

A: Well, if I go out drinking with the guys, I try and wear girly clothes to try and maintain a visual femininity, but I'm still acting like the guys. Whereas with my girls, girls night out, I'm fine to go out in jeans. But with the guys, I don't want to seem too manly, so I prefer to be wearing something like a skirt, so there is some balance.

Undergraduate women were not only interested in achieving status through appearing feminine (i.e., "hot" but not "slutty") (Armstrong,

Hamilton, and Sweeney, 2006), or in meeting men's preferences through their drinking behaviors (i.e., drinking with the guys) (Young et al., 2005), but sought a meticulous balance of the two. The development of this **generalized other**, based from heavy drinking and stereotypical gender norms, streamed women into certain ways of acting as female drinkers sought to balance culturally valued feminine presentations with their accomplishment of heavy masculine drinking standards. As female drinkers discussed, this could prove difficult. Danielle, the 21-year-old senior, noted, "well, when you drink a lot and you start to lose control, it is hard trying to stay sexy and attractive when your make-up is all messed up because you are wasted, trying to talk to boys." Brittany, a 21-year-old junior, elaborated, "well, honestly they fail, I feel like girls who are really drunk make themselves look so stupid, falling down or crying, especially when they wear skimpy stuff where you can see everything when they fall." Their feminine performance did not end until they reached a safe **backstage** location at the end of the evening, Kerstin, the 20-year-old junior, noted: "we have to stay pretty until we get home." The previous respondents reported a clear breakdown in control as heavy drinking often interfered with the reflexive functioning of their **generalized other**. For women, this served an important learning tool and control function used to reassess and align future behavior with the gender expectations of the college party scene.

Gendered Drinking Consequences

Though college women rarely regarded the act of drinking as problematic, it was being drunk, or too drunk, that presented issues for them. Women were often perceived by fellow drinkers as annoying, "slutty," irresponsible, careless, or unladylike for drinking heavily or being drunk. For women, drinking was far too often a behavioral tightrope. To a certain extent, women and all participants in the drinking scene were expected to consume alcohol, to lower their inhibitions, to lose control, and to contribute to the collective scripted sentiments of the party. Grace, a 22-

year-old fifth-year senior, noted, "girls are just expected to be dancing and flirting." For female drinkers, the boundary line between acceptable drunken behavior and undesirable drunken behavior was often a gray area. Women were expected to lose some control, but too much "loose" behavior could end in stigmatization. For college women, embodying masculine drinking standards not only had the potential to ruin their desired presentations of femininity, but to lose them the status and attention from peers and friends they hoped to attain.

For example, walking home alone at night, a masculine privilege, was viewed as inappropriately feminine within the college drinking scene. Fear of victimization and harassment were of central concern. Women often implemented a safety-in-numbers style of travel, never walking alone and watching over friends. Anna, the 21-year-old senior, noted:

> If you go off by yourself to the bars or walk home alone and you don't tell anybody it's not treated the same. I mean I personally don't consider it safe. Girls worry; we worry all the time when we're drinking. Whereas guys I know, they don't worry.

Female drinkers viewed walking alone at night as dangerous and irresponsible. Women were supposed to travel like women. They had to plan ahead for buses, taxis, Uber or Lyft. Women berated themselves for being irresponsible when walking alone at night. They stressed always "having a plan" or developing a "buddy system." Others discussed the fact that they had seen other women "in situations they wouldn't want to be in." Yet getting drunk with the guys often reduced the fear of walking alone at night, and women became less cautious.

Women also reported that trying to "keep up" with guys could prove problematic. Young et al., (2005) have suggested that women in the college drinking scene might drink in a masculine manner, as it has become appealing to men and offers them an elevated social position; however, it was also a way to demonstrate their worthiness for this inclusive social position. Brittany, a 21-year-old senior, remarked, "I think girls like to prove that they can drink as much as guys…it's a way to prove themselves, to fit into the group." Although drinking with men might offer women attention and status, it was also fun to partake in the collective and exciting sentiment of the drinking scene. Jenny, a 21-year-old senior, discussed her participation in drinking games at parties, "I like to compete; it's fun. I like to be part of the group. I don't do it to impress a guy. It's just being part of the atmosphere, playing a game and not being below the male competitors." However, for women, acting too competitively, chugging beer, or taking whiskey shots could be viewed as overly masculine behavior, and such a drinking style could lead to an undesired level of drunkenness.

In contrast, drinking like girls could also prove problematic. Students' drinks of choice were gendered. With some exceptions, women mostly drank hard alcohol in the form of vodka or rum, often flavored, sometimes simply as a shot or in a mixed drink. Fruity drinks and flavored liquors were viewed as feminine by students, while beer and whiskey were the masculine counterpart. Although women certainly drank beer, liquor was the norm and often reserved for women at private parties. Christina, the 21-year-old senior, noted, "I think there is definitely a difference between girls and guys in terms of alcohol. Girls drink vodka, guys drink beer… girls grew up taking shots, drinking Bacardi." The feminine style of drinking could prove problematic for female drinkers on three levels. First, women disproportionately reported limiting their food consumption and favoring shots and mixed drinks to restrain their ingestion of calories on a night out drinking. Women used this tactic to maintain control over their desired body image, but it also "served the added benefit of requiring less alcohol to become intoxicated" (Peralta 2002:31). This allowed for heavy alcohol use with less fear of gaining weight. Second, the majority of the "girly" drinks were designed to be "strong and tasty," drinks that were able to be drunk quickly with little if any notice of the taste of alcohol. Anna, now a 21-year-old senior, remembered when she first started attending bars after she received her first fake ID:

> I would order these great tasting mixed drinks and I could never taste the alcohol. I would drink them so fast, one after the other. When I would drink beer, it would be slower because I didn't really love the taste. With the liquor drinks, they would catch up to me before I knew it and I would just be wasted.

Finally, women would often take shots or drink quickly to avoid constantly having a drink in their hands. Women used this style of drinking when they wanted to dance, were bar hopping with friends and had to stay with the group, or had to account for restroom options and availability. Kerstin, the 20-year-old junior, talked about the nights she became more intoxicated than she intended:

> I think it has to do with liquor. Beer spreads out your drinking and it's more of a gradual process, so you can kind of keep check on where you are at. The girly drinks are faster. I'll take a shot and then five minutes later I'll take another one. The beer drinking style is slower; you're not just going to power through every single beer really intensely.

It is important to note that although drink types and drinking styles were categorized by undergraduates as appropriately masculine or appropriately feminine, these drinking norms were subordinate to the drinking standards that fostered a "drink long and strong" sentiment, regardless of what style of drinking (i.e., masculine or feminine) undergraduate women enacted.

Social and Emotional Consequences

Emotional **dramaturgy** was a facet of the drinking order for undergraduate students. Undergraduate women reported that certain emotional displays were revered within the college drinking scene (i.e., happiness, extroversion, sociability, humor), but emotional displays that denigrated the collective spirit of the party were frowned upon and stigmatized. Although it was understood by undergraduates that emotions, combined with heavy alcohol use, could run awry for college drinkers (i.e., crying, fighting, screaming, anger), improper displays of emotions could ruin the party. Jill, a 21-year-old senior, noted, "if a girl is drunk, she might get more emotional, like more sensitive, more like 'what do my friends think?' and she'll just start crying. Then people, like her friends and other people there, have to deal with it. It's just annoying."

For female drinkers, feelings of intoxicated happiness, euphoria, and carelessness usually dominated during a night of drinking, but women often felt a sense of embarrassment or guilt the next morning, especially if they violated their comfortable level of intoxication or preferred gender performance. For women, the behavioral and bodily control often lost through drunkenness was the central reason for these emotional consequences. Christina, the 21-year-old senior, noted how she often felt after a night of excessive drinking:

> I wake up and I feel guilty, because girls have these social norms we have to follow. We are supposed to be put together. We are supposed to have our shit together. And you know you make a lot of mistakes when you are drunk. I think girls have guilt; I feel guilty sometimes because of the way girls are supposed to look and behave.

Sometimes these infractions could be as trivial as crying at a party or falling in heels; other times they could involve drunk texting or dialing or hitting on a man. Other examples were more serious acts, such as having unprotected sex, not remembering sex, starting a fight, or losing a friendship. Janice, the 20-year-old junior, also noted, "you re-live it. You lay in bed the next morning and you're like 'oh shit.' And guys are like, whatever. We over-analyze everything."

Women partly developed these emotional responses on their own through self-reflection. They anticipated how they appeared to others while drinking and experienced varying degrees of embarrassment and guilt from their behavior. Stacey, the 22-year-old senior, noted, "I mean, I know how I judge, so I know how other girls judge, it's not hard to imagine how they're talking about you." Often the reflexive dynamic of seeing oneself through the eyes of others (i.e., **reflected appraisals**) was enough for college women to feel judged or condemned (Cooley 1902). Beyond their internal reflections, female drinkers also noted direct judgment from peers and friends. Elizabeth, the 22-year-old senior, noted:

> Girls don't want to have that judgment, so they don't drink as much. Guys don't get as much negative feedback. What do they care if everyone is hearing these stories? For women it's like, "do you realize this is what happened last night?" Maybe you want to think about that for the next time.

Sarah, the 21-year-old senior, explained that certain actions could be seen as "amusing" or "hilarious" at the time, but would later be sanctioned. Although a direct confrontation might never occur, women sometimes experienced passive aggressive forms of condemnation for their behavior. A woman could lose friends, become the subject of jokes, be pitied or ignored, and ultimately earn a tarnished reputation. Women were well aware of how they could be judged for certain types of drunken comportment and did not want to be "that girl" or be associated with "that girl," the one who gets drunk and sleeps around, cries, fights, falls, vomits, ruins the night for others, or simply causes embarrassment to herself or her friends. Women were ultimately worried about being labeled, thus altering their reputation and identity among fellow students. As (Wilkins 2004:31). noted, "the power of the label is that it can be applied at any time for any reason...to avoid the potentially ruinous label young women must constantly manage their self-presentation."

Constructing the Limit

For college women, participation in the male-dominated drinking scene presented a performative problem, as Amber, a 20-year-old junior, noted: "It's hard for girls to fulfill that expected party role, be fun and loose, without being too loose." If female drinkers over-emphasized femininity, over controlling and limiting their behavior, they could be viewed as the "girly-girl," occupying a tertiary "cheerleader" status within the drinking scene. Yet if women over-emphasized masculinity by drinking too much, or too much like the guys, they could be viewed as "slutty," "out-of-control," annoying, manly, or problematic. These women not only risked being lower than men in the status hierarchy, but also lower than women who could maintain both femininity and the hegemonic masculine drinking standards of this scene.

Controlling Drinking

At some point along their university careers, women realized that if they wanted to participate successfully in the drinking scene, they needed to develop a practical strategy to maintain desired femininity within this masculine drinking scene. This solution is what I refer to as **"the limit."** For college women, the essence of the limit involved negotiating a fluid boundary that regulated personal alcohol consumption and gender performance. The limit was developed through women's maturation, drinking consequences, and learning experiences that produced and reproduced an increasingly effective generalized other within the college drinking scene. The limit evolved as women entered into new primary relationships and their close friends provided emotional support, information diffusion, and learning techniques that formed "a stable and organized set of generalized others" (Matsueda 1992:269). Female drinkers used the limit to control their intoxication and subsequent behavior, and to adhere to the expectations of femininity within the drinking scene. For example, the limit could refer to intoxication, gender performance, and even sex. Malorie, a 22-year-old senior, noted, "getting drunk is only half the problem, then it's what you did, what you looked like, and who you went home with…too many guys and you're slutty…but they could also call you, like, a prude." Thus, the limit operated as a personal and subculturally specific boundary maintenance device for women, controlling their own behavior and enabling other women to understand and learn what types of behaviors were acceptable. For upper class women who had experienced and learned from their younger college years, their behavior operated as a reference group for younger and inexperienced female drinkers. As such, it offered a route to social and behavioral success for female drinkers. A narrative tool, the limit also represented a belief system among women as *they matured through college*, that *as women*, they were *supposed* to control and to limit themselves to some extent. Not having limits was viewed as irresponsible, dangerous, and unfeminine.

For college women, this limiting or self-control was important. Women were concerned about maintaining agency over their intoxication and the social situation, as it was easy to lose oneself in the collective effervescence of the party. This form of control was crucial for female drinkers as it not only enabled them to accomplish heavy drinking physically, but to socialize and travel. Self-control was also a central facet of the ideal drinker. Danielle, a 21-year-old senior, discussed the importance of control when partying, she remarked, "if you are going to drink, you need to stay in control. It's fine to be more social, funny, and lower inhibitions, but not in an obnoxious way." Kerstin, the 20-year-old junior, reflected similar sentiments, "if you are a college student, especially a girl, well, people just have to know their limits, but in college, limits can be pushed. I think people in college expect you to have a few-slips ups or go crazy one night, but not necessarily all the time."

The inability to hold a conversation, to play drinking games, to walk, to speak, to make eye contact, to hook-up, or to respect the personal space of others provided negative examples of self-control. The limit emanated from women's desire to control their bodies, to control their behavior, and to control their gendered performances. As such, it was a necessity for balancing a hegemonically masculine style of drinking with their desired emphasized feminine presentations. Krane et al. (2004) has suggested that in American society, women who appear heterosexually feminine are privileged over women perceived as masculine, and my data suggest that female drinkers not only went to great lengths to appear feminine, heterosexual, and sexually attractive, but to balance these feminine attributes with a masculine style of drinking. The social atmosphere of the drinking scene did allow female drinkers to test acceptable boundaries of femininity, but maintaining femininity was still crucial as they understood that men were not simply attracted to women who could drink heavily, but valued women who could balance femininity with heavy drinking.

Learning the Limit

Constructing a limit was ultimately a learned experience for women, one they often developed through practice and the consequences of heavy drinking. Krissy reflected on the development of her learning experiences from her freshman year to her senior year:

> I had no tolerance or any idea of what I was doing my freshman year. I definitely didn't have a limit. I had drunk some in high school, but college was different with all the freedom and alcohol. I just would drink and drink. I remember it was dangerous and often embarrassing. Those experiences really taught me something. I'm just better at drinking now.

Women discussed building a tolerance to alcohol's effects, learning to pace themselves by slowing down, or drinking water or soda for a brief period. Others drank alcohol with which they were familiar, or shied away from shots or drinking games. These tactics were not common knowledge, but were acquired through subcultural learning and primary groups as women implemented others' drinking successes and failures into their own lives. Women often discussed different drinking strategies and tactics. Ashley, a 22-year-old senior, noted, "ee would talk about what happened the next day, and who did what when drinking. Most things are funny, but if someone got out of control we would talk about what she could do different next time not to embarrass herself, or not to be in that same situation." For women, the direct and indirect judgment they received from friends, their embarrassment over a drunken night, demeaning experiences (Boswell and Spade 1996), or the "walk of shame," also served to perpetuate thoughts about personal drinking limits.

Female drinkers used various tactics to track their level of intoxication on a given evening. Some women reported a drinking limit marked by a preferred number of drinks. Janice, a 20-year-old junior, noted, "I know girls who have done the marker thing, where you do tallies on your arm." Natalie, a sophomore, noted:

> I usually cut myself off around five, I tend to be at a good level, and if I go over five, I tend to be drunker that I would like. Well, it's usually around five. It's not like I took five and I can't have anymore, it's more like this level and the level I like to be around is five drinks.

However, it was far more common for women to rely on a personal comfort level of intoxication or a "buzzcheck" (Vander Ven 2011). As a subjective experience influenced by social and environmental circumstances, using a preset number of drinks on a particular evening was not always practical. Danielle, a senior, remarked:

> Girls will do checkpoints, every now and again throughout the night; they will check in with themselves, about how much they've drunk. But I think a lot of them use feelings of drunkenness, more than a certain number. Because I mean that changes so often, how much you drink versus how drunk you get.

Checkpoints could be about physical indicators, such as difficulty walking in heels, texting on cell phones, drunk dialing, or having blurry vision. Chelsea, a 21-year-old junior, remarked, "well, when I start feeling quiet and uncomfortable I know I need to stop, or when I can't find the words or thoughts to hold a conversation." For female drinkers, learning the limit was not just about directly controlling intoxication. Women faced a gendered disadvantage when drinking with their male peers (Young et al. 2005). It was not their level of intoxication *per se* that caused them trouble, but the fact that their intoxication could conflict with their desired presentations of socioculturally "appropriate" forms of emphasized femininity.

Contexualizing the Limit

For female drinkers, the limit was typically premeditated. Women often decided before a night out how much they were going to drink, how they were going to present themselves, and the locations where they planned on drinking. Such things were set through women's application of past experiences and the anticipated events of the college party scene into their generalized other. However, the limit was also fluid, often environmentally driven by the context and the company of the party scene. Female drinkers attempted to manage themselves in relation to the atmosphere, the location, and those in attendance at a party or bar. The university drinking scene predominantly occurred in two social milieus: the house/frat party and the bar scene. Drinking with close friends or attending a friend's party fostered an environment where women felt freer to drink more heavily. Sarah noted: "If you go to a friend's party, for a girl, you're comfortable drinking what you want…if you go to a stranger's party, you don't drink at the same level at all, even if you're with friends."

The feelings of comfort undergraduate women derived from being around trusted company and in familiar locales often served to destabilize their limit, creating an environment where the stigma of being drunk or "unfeminine" was not so intense. Some women renegotiated their limit when they changed their location or their company. If a group of friends suddenly left or arrived at a party, or the party moved to a different place, women might reevaluate their limit for that evening. Being with close or established friends rendered a *perceived* level of safety and mutual trust among female drinkers. Danielle, a 21-year-old senior, discussed a situation where she was careful to limit her consumption with unfamiliar peers, "I controlled myself that night, because I didn't know them that well. I wasn't ready for them to see me in a really drunk state; I didn't feel as safe, as comfortable." Safety was of particular concern, especially when among unfamiliar men in unfamiliar places. Women reported that passing out on couches or simply "crashing" was often unacceptable and another privilege for men. Furthermore, men could "sketch-out" whenever they pleased, but women could not because of the gendered norms of the setting. Christina, the 21-year-old senior, expressed her views on planning a night out drinking: "I gauge how much I drink on where I'm going, who is there, and how I'm getting home."

As participants in the college drinking scene, women were complicit in reinforcing a dominant and heavy style of alcohol consumption. Like women in other male-dominated settings who perform masculinity for successful membership, undergraduate women drank like the guys, but were expected to accomplish heavy drinking in a feminized manner.

Gender operated as a powerful social control mechanism as female drinkers were sanctioned and stigmatized by men and women when they breached the gendered rules of alcohol consumption. From this, women realized that optimal success in this male-dominated scene required learning to limit their alcohol consumption and to control their gendered behavior to perform forms of masculinity through drinking, but to do so in a manner regarded as appropriately feminine.

Conclusion

Peer groups played a primary role in the potency of gender norms. Although students experienced gender behavior through **reference groups** (i.e., upperclassmen and popular culture), they primarily learned gender norms through **sanctions** and discussions with close friends. Cultural conceptions of how masculinity and femininity were done ordered university life and functioned as a powerful form of manifest and latent social control. Men adapted to masculine drinking norms (e.g., drinking heavily, frequently, and competitively), while women were streamed into presentations, beliefs, and behaviors that reflected both femininity and masculinity. Gender constrained and facilitated students' drug and alcohol use and fostered a specific gender enactment for women who had the sociocultural resources and party capital to accomplish this gender enactment.

For women to navigate this male-dominated scene better than their female peers, they learned to enact a *party femininity* that combined masculine characteristics of collegiate drinking with culturally valued attributes of femininity. Undergraduate women embodied masculinity behaviorally (i.e. they drank "long and strong") and ideologically (i.e., they internalized masculine drinking norms), but were careful to exude femininity through the deliberate deployment of appearance, dress, and conduct. Female drinkers embodied this party femininity because they profited both symbolically and materially. Similar to the idea of "trading power for patronage" (Schwalbe et al. 2000), these women adapted to the masculinity of this scene because they were rewarded within their peer networks with compensatory benefits (i.e., status, attention, dating opportunities) through their relationships with the men and other women. Women were not constantly doing this type of femininity; rather, it was *available* to women with certain sociocultural assets who *could* deploy it as a gender adaptation. This depended on their sociocultural resources.

For college women, their youth and student status freed them from childcare and other family responsibilities allowing them the time and freedom to participate in the drinking scene. Their middle- to upper-class ideals of career and self-development before starting a family catered to a lifestyle free from serious relationships, allowing women to go out and drink, to flirt with men, and to present themselves as sexually available. Identification with heterosexuality allowed women to participate in the hook-up scene, dress provocatively for men, and use their sexuality to gain valued status and attention from male peers (Armstrong, Hamilton, and Sweeney 2006). Their class status provided them with the monetary resources to purchase alcohol and to perform femininity through appropriate appearance and dress (i.e., clothing, makeup, hairstyle). Finally, their Whiteness provided them comfortable and implicit inclusion in the drinking scene, as minority students generally experience alienation and disinterest in the college drinking scene (Peralta 2005).

These women represented the privileged and powerful strata of society and they had the ability to enact a feminine adaptation that might continue to resonate throughout the remainder of their work, family, and social lives. Thus, these conceptions of "appropriate" gender enactments would continue to control behavior and order society, producing and reproducing dominant norms of masculinity and femininity in relation to drug using behaviors. This form of informal control was extremely potent as undergraduate women learned the norms and behaviors of this gender enactment from **primary groups** and **reference groups** and passed it on to subsequent classes.

Notes and Discussion Questions:

References

Armstrong, Elizabeth A., Laura Hamilton, and Brian Sweeney. 2006. "Sexual Assault on Campus: A Multilevel, Integrative Approach to Party Rape." *Social Problems* 53(4):483–99.

Arnett, Jeffrey Jensen. 2004. "Emerging Adulthood: The Winding Road from the Late Teens Through the Twenties." New York: Oxford University Press.

Boswell, A. Ayres and Joan Z. Spade. 1996. "Fraternities and Collegiate Rape Culture: Why Are Some Fraternities More Dangerous Places for Women?" *Gender & Society* 10(2):133–47.

Capraro, Rocco L. 2000. "Why college men drink: Alcohol, adventure, and the paradox of masculinity." *Journal of American College Health* 48(6):307–15.

Christie-Mizell, C. Andre and Robert L. Peralta. 2009. "The Gender Gap in Alcohol Consumption during Late Adolescence and Young Adulthood: Gendered Attitudes and Adult Roles." *Journal of Health and Social Behavior* 50(4):410–26.

Deirdre, Kelly M., Shauna Pomerantz, and Dawn Currie. 2005. "Skater Girlhood and Emphasized Femininity: 'You Can't Land an Ollie Properly in Heels'." *Gender and Education* 17(3):229–48.

Foucault, Michel. 1977. *Discipline and punishment.* New York: Pantheon.

Grindstaff, Laura and Emily West. 2006. "Cheerleading and the Gendered Politics of Sport." *Social Problems* 53(4):500–18.

Heath, Dwight B. 2000. "Drinking occasions: Comparative perspectives on alcohol and culture."

Karp, David A., Lynda Lytle Holstrom, and Paul S. Gray. 1998. "Leaving Home for College: Expectations for Selective Reconstruction of Self." *Symbolic Interaction* 21(3):253–76.

Krane, Vikki, Precilla Y. L. Choi, Shannon M. Baird, Christine M. Aimar, and Kerrie J. Kauer. 2004. "Living the Paradox: Female Athletes Negotiate Femininity and Muscularity." *Sex Roles: A Journal of Research* 50(5-6):315–29.

Lorber, Judith. 1994. *Paradoxes of Gender*. New Haven, CT: Yale University Press.

Martin, Patricia Yancey. 2004. "Gender as Social Institution." *Social Forces* 82(4):1249–73.

Matsueda, R. L. 1992. "Reflected appraisals, Parental Labeling, and Delinquency: Specifying a Symbolic Interactionist Theory." *American Journal of Sociology* 97(6):1577–1611.

Mead, George Herbert.1934. *Mind, Self, and Society*. Chicago, IL: University of Chicago Press.

Montemurro, Beth and Bridget McClure. 2005. "Changing Gender Norms for Alcohol Consumption: Social Drinking and Lowered Inhibitions at Bachelorette Parties." *Sex Roles: A Journal of Research* 52(5-6):279–88.

Peralta, Robert L. 2002. "Alcohol Use and the Fear of Weight Gain in College: Reconciling Two Social Norms." *Gender Issues* 20(4):23–42.

Peralta, Robert L. 2005. "Race and the Culture of College Drinking: An Analysis of White Privilege on Campus." Pp. 127-41 in *Cocktails and Dreams: Perspectives on Drug and Alcohol Use*, edited by Wilson R. Palacios. Upper Saddle River, NJ: Prentice Hall.

Peralta, Robert L. 2007. "College Alcohol Use and the Embodiment of Hegemonic Masculinity among European American Men." *Sex Roles: A Journal of Research* 56(11-12):741–56.

Risman, Barbara J. 2004. "Gender as a Social Structure: Theory Wrestling with Activism." *Gender & Society* 18(4):429–50.

Schwalbe, Michael, Sandra Godwin, Daphne Holden, Douglas Schrock, Shealy Thompson, and Michele Wolkomir. 2000. "Generic Processes in the Reproduction of Inequality: As Interactionist Analysis." *Social Forces* 79(2): 419-52.

Vander Ven, Thomas. 2011. *Getting wasted: Why college students drink too much and party so hard.* New York: NYU Press.

West, Candace and Don H. Zimmerman. 1987. "Doing Gender." *Gender & Society* 1(2):125–51.

West, Lois A. 2001. "Negotiating Masculinities in American Drinking Subcultures." *The Journal of Men's Studies* 9(3):371–92.

Young, Amy M., Michele Morales, Sean Esteban McCabe, Carol J. Boyd, and Hannah D'Arcy. 2005. "Drinking Like a Guy: Frequent Binge Drinking among Undergraduate Women." *Substance Use & Misuse* 40(2):241–67.

Chapter Nine

Marijuana and Social Control

Illicit polydrug use is a common behavior among American college students (Feigelman, Gorman, and Lee 1998; Martin, Clifford and Clapper 1992; McCabe et al. 2006; Quintero 2009; Schorling et al. 1994). Recent studies suggest that increasing numbers of university students are experimenting with a variety of psychoactive substances such as cocaine, hallucinogens, MDMA, and prescription drugs (Ford and Schroeder 2009; Gledhill-Hoyt et al. 2000; Mohler-Kuo, Lee, and Wechsler 2003; O'Grady et al. 2008; O'Malley and Johnston 2002). On an average day during the past year, 1.2 million full-time college students drank alcohol, 703,759 used marijuana, 11,338 used cocaine, 9,808 used hallucinogens, 4,570 used heroin, and 3,341 used inhalants (Lipari and Jean-Francois 2016). Although illegal drug use among college students pales in comparison to alcohol consumption, marijuana is still a popular drug of choice.

Next to alcohol, marijuana is the most widely used drug on college campuses. When this research started in 2009 marijuana was the most commonly used illicit drug in the United States with 16.7 million past month users (SAMSHA 2010). Furthermore, marijuana was used by 76.6 percent of current illicit drug users in the U.S. and was the *only* drug used by 58 percent of them (SAMSHA 2010). Among full-time university students aged 18-22, 20.2 percent reported current (i.e. in the past month) marijuana use, while 63.9 percent considered themselves current drinkers, 43.5 percent identified themselves as binge drinkers, and 27.1 percent reported current tobacco use (SAMSHA 2010).

Although marijuana is prohibited and criminalized throughout the majority of the United States, several states have passed laws decriminalizing the possession of small amounts of the substance, and as of 2012 when this research was ongoing, 16 states and the District of Colombia had removed criminal sanctions for its medical use (Eddy 2010; Procon.org 2011). As of 2018, 31 states have passed legislation permitting medical marijuana, while nine states including California, Washington, Oregon, Nevada, Colorado, Maine, Vermont, Alaska, Massachusetts and the District of Columbia have legalized cannabis for recreational purposes (ProCon 2018).

This legal-medicalization of marijuana has shifted the drug into a therapeutic framework, as it is increasingly defined and treated medicinally rather than criminally (Conrad 1979; Conrad 2007). Similar to shoplifting, mental illness, gambling, drug abuse, and sexual dysfunction, medicalization increasingly destigmatizes cannabis use (Zola 1972). These shifting designations of marijuana are controversial as the methods of social control, the legal statuses, and the social meanings attached to the drug are being transformed. Forces on opposing sides of the prohibition-legalization debate view medical marijuana laws as a route to its legalization and in 2012 Washington and Colorado became the first to legalize marijuana at the state level (Clark 2000; Schrag 2002; Stein 2002).

In this chapter, I investigate changes in social control within an illicit marijuana market as it shifted into a **legal-medicalized framework**. I examine this policy shift in relation to students' marijuana use, their shifting perceptions of power and agency, and the associated impact on social control. I focus on students' entrance into this regulated and monitored marijuana scene that distanced them from a criminalized marketplace and redefined their patterns and beliefs concerning cannabis use and fostered a shift toward informal control methods.

Escaping Criminalization

Marijuana markets are different from the open-air markets for drugs such as heroin and cocaine (Caulkins et al. 1999; Caulkins and Reuter 1998) and research suggests that marijuana is most likely purchased indoors through friends and acquaintances (Caulkins and Pacula 2006; Mohamed and Fritsvold 2010). Marijuana is a traditionally prohibited substance and students interacted with the drug in an illegal/underground market context. Furthermore, the structural and cultural placement of marijuana in the underground setting also located students in a **deviant learning environment** (Akers 2009). As marijuana moved from the illicit shadows to a regulated and controlled marketplace, student cannabis users experienced a fundamental shift in self-control and social control as they were resocialized into this novel drug scene.

Using Unlicensed Providers

Students discussed the power held by the illegal marijuana dealers from whom they had traditionally made their purchases. These distributors controlled every aspect of the transaction from the time, location, price, and amount of the purchase. It is attractive to dealers "to be able to work when they want, where they want, and to have complete freedom to control prices and quantities in their transactions" (Tewksbury and Mustaine 1998). Madeline was critical of the illicit marijuana marketplace. A 21-year-old, junior psychology and sociology double-major from New Jersey, she stated:

> In the illicit market you are at the hands of the dealer, they decide the time and the place and you really don't have any say unless it's your friend or something. You might have to wait for your dealer to go pick it up, wait for them to weigh it all out, and have to wait for them to come and meet you or wait until they get home, and it's like four hours before you get any marijuana.

A dealer could increase prices based on unsubstantiated claims of "boutique" or high potency strains, or refuse to sell "eighths" or "quarters" [of an ounce] and distribute only in ounces, "QP's" [quarter pounds], or pounds, leaving a buyer no alternative but to comply with the terms of sale. In the illicit market, students were subject to **informal controls** that operated below the state (Innes 2003) and outside of formalized and codified rules and practices. As social actors, students were continually controlling and being controlled through their interactions, but in the illicit market they were subject to **deviant norms and routines** dictated by dealers and the rules of the underground economy.

The distribution process of the dealer further dictated power and control through the length of the transaction. Students reported that some marijuana distributors had organized and proficient operations, citing minimal conversation and pre-weighed grams that fostered a timely and efficient purchase. In contrast, participants discussed other marijuana dealers who plagued the transaction with tardiness, disorganization, undesired conversation, or unnecessary rituals. An unwritten rule of purchasing marijuana is that one may be encouraged to "smoke-out" the dealer as a token of appreciation or to experience and discuss the "high" of the product. A certain degree of lingering is almost required so as not to offend the dealer and potentially jeopardize a good source of marijuana, and students typically viewed this ritual as a display of good faith by both parties involved in the transaction (Mohamed and Fritsvold 2010). The process is necessary in establishing "membership" in **closed marijuana markets** where dealers generally sell to people they know or to customers vouched for by other buyers. Ethan, a 21-year-old, senior and finance major from a wealthy and conservative Midwest town, noted with a smile:

> It's hard to think back to those primitive days when I was buying illegally. You know, where you go in to some place you might not want to be, maybe they have a scale, and you basically buy whatever pot they have to smoke. I never really liked having to smoke with the guy I buy it from either, you know smoke out your connect for good measure or because

they were nice enough to sell you some weed. It's not always a bad thing, but it I'm buying at 1 PM in the afternoon and I have shit to do, I don't want to feel obligated to get high just because I want some marijuana to have at home.

Students further discussed the location and atmosphere of purchasing marijuana illegally as they lacked personal control over the location of transactions. Although illicit transactions typically occurred in private residences from friends or peripheral acquaintances, participants reported buying in situations where they felt uncomfortable and anxious. Although **closed-drug markets** are often touted as offering both dealers and customers security and some degree of quality guarantee over the product, participants discussed their potential apprehension in behind-the-scenes transactions. Sarah, a 20-year-old sophomore and communications major from New York City, discussed transactions where she felt nervous and insecure:

I have had some shady experiences buying weed, and that is never the case with the dispensary. I feel safe in a dispensary. I'm in a public place. I'm not saying you're always buying weed in strange places, but when I was back in New York, I had to buy weed from this guy in his 40s. He lives on this really sketchy street and I was the only one allowed to go inside. He had the weed in shopping bags and it was super awkward. A bunch of his friends were just staring at me. Sometimes it just sucks having to go over to some dude's house to get it.

With a legal-medicalized industry a fundamental shift occurred away from *illicit informal controls* dictated by drug dealers and an illegal market, to a **social order** that reflected conventional society. Students touted the efficiency of buying marijuana from the dispensaries. They felt that purchasing cannabis in this **legal marketplace** enhanced their control over the transaction. Similar to other legitimate businesses, the marijuana shops had advertised business hours and a public location that allowed participants agency over the logistics of the interaction. Jarrod, a 22-year-old senior sociology major and manager at a dispensary, noted:

> It's just more efficient. I just go to my dispensary, and I've shopped around so I know the best prices and what dispensary has what I'm looking for. You get your pot in a nice bag, you're in and out in 10 minutes and you just don't have to worry about buying crap or having to stock up with bulk. The dispensary will be there.

Purchasing cannabis from the dispensaries "fit" into the fabric of normative society and conventional routines. Marijuana sales resembled a business transaction, much like alcohol, and students did not have to track down sellers, call their cell phone, wait for a callback, and meet at the dealers' behest. Medical marijuana dispensaries resembled Amsterdam coffee shops, bohemian espresso bars, or high-end delicatessens. Patrons were greeted and identified in comfortable waiting rooms adorned with couches, fish tanks, literature, flat screen televisions, Internet workstations, and espresso bars. The social and physical environment of the marijuana shops fostered a sense of well-being among students. Jack, a 19-year-old sophomore and open-option major, noted:

> Dispensaries present a warm and welcome environment. You feel comfortable. Even if you bring a friend who isn't a cardholder, they might not be able to come into the back room, but they can sit and wait and still enjoy the atmosphere. These places are clean; sometimes they provide drinks, always magazines and books to read while you wait. I just don't feel weird or in harm's way, like I'm intruding. Everybody is just super cool and upfront.

Although the illegitimate marijuana community around Campus University was not typically associated with violence or danger, students reported that the dispensary system reduced the harm and the problems associated with unregulated transactions. John, a laid-back 21-year-old senior and environmental studies major who grew marijuana for personal use, elaborated:

> None of the trouble that actually does hurt people would be around under this type of system. You don't have to buy from some shady dealer because your dealer left town for two weeks. You don't have to carry around a bunch of money and buy quantity because you have a small purchasing window or the transaction scares you. You're buying legit.

The social environment of the marijuana shops was a significant benefit that students contrasted with the illicit marketplace. This legal-medicalized system enhanced social control for students as it removed *systemic hassle*, indicative of an underground market, from their interactions. Students who once bought marijuana within a criminal social order were distanced from informal norms and rules dictated by drug dealers and gained agency in the transaction over the time, place, and amount of the purchase.

Attaining Economic Legitimacy

The legalization of medical marijuana moved employment opportunities out of the market and into a regulated dispensary system. Licensed providers needed employees to work in the dispensaries and "grow warehouses" and participants lauded this emerging job market. Ethan, the senior finance major, discussed:

> I just think about all the jobs this industry provides and that everyone has
> a chance to get hired. I have a friend who is a major caretaker and he owns
> a warehouse where he grows and harvests everything. Me, my girlfriend,
> and about six friends work for him, $20 an hour, just clipping plants,
> taking care of the grow, and doing what he needs. I've learned a lot. Tons
> of jobs have popped up, jobs you won't get arrested for doing.

In the illicit marijuana market, students reported a **differential
opportunity structure** (Cloward and Ohlin 1960), with employment open
to those with the necessary connections and qualifying characteristics.
According to students, marijuana sales were typically a masculine
enterprise, further limited to those with knowledge of the industry rules of
distribution and those networked into a supply chain. The legalization of
medical marijuana extended employment opportunities for women and
individuals who may not have had connections to the illegitimate
economy. In the dispensary system, women were owners, managers, and
retailers. Madeline, the junior psychology and sociology major, noted:

> My friend she is working at the dispensary. No risk. I know some
> girlfriends who are going to be working for their caretaker who is actually
> a former grower, they will be trimming plants and preparing weed for
> dispensaries. It's so funny that when it's out in the open all the sketchiness
> disappears.

For those involved in the underground economy, the medical marijuana
industry provided an avenue into legitimate employment. The legality of
marijuana cultivation and sales fostered conventional business practices
and retail skills and this gave some the opportunity to quit their
involvement with the illicit economy. Although participants reported this
could be a tenuous move for friends or dealers who had learned to
navigate and thrive in the illegal industry, many valued the opportunity to
work legitimately. Dave, a 21-year-old, junior marketing major, stated:

> My friend who used to grow illegally filed his paperwork and now he's a
> legit caretaker and a grower for a few patients. Ever since high school he's
> loved growing. Now he can do it legitimately. I know he stresses about all
> the paperwork and changing laws, but I think I might work with him too.

As the dispensary system expanded, participants reported a substantial
decrease in the number of people they knew selling or growing marijuana
illegally. The legalization of medical marijuana significantly reduced the
immense earnings available to those willing to risk distributing illicit
drugs. Similar to Mohamed and Fritsvold (2010), my informants noted that
college-level dealers "make a ton of money, with minimal work." Ethan, a
finance major from the Midwest, stated:

> I have seen the medical marijuana industry cut into the illegal market, and
> if anything proves that legalization will work it's that. There just isn't the
> money to be made. I can name eight people right now who have been shut
> down in the last six months because their clientele base has gotten their
> card.

The primary motivators for drug dealers include a desire to maintain a
personal supply, economic gain, and the attraction to the drug dealing
lifestyle (Mohamed and Fritsvold 2010: Tewksbury and Mustaine 1998).
Participants noted that the operation of the dispensary system diminished
these opportunities. Marijuana sales resembled alcohol sales and did not
require a connection and made transactions a routine and mundane
activity. Some students discussed their dismay in the ego gratification and
power some dealers cherished from selling drugs and were happy to see
the end of such self-importance. Dave, the junior marketing major, noted:

The illegal market is basically done. And some people at the dispensaries were once dealers, and now they are legal and they are getting taxed by the government. People are going to be getting pot anyway, so why would I give it to my friend the drug dealer to go to Europe or buy a Beamer when I could give it to a local business owner. Some of these businesses are donating to cancer research and stuff like that.

In contrast to the illegal market, students valued that their money was providing tax revenue and that the dispensary system saved public money. They noted the savings for citizens through the reduction of costs associated with marijuana arrests, court appearances, incarceration, and mandated treatment. Participants also discussed the microeconomy of businesses and professionals that catered to the industry, such as web design and advertising firms, chefs, lawyers, doctors, tax consultants, plumbers, carpenters, and business owners. They increasingly viewed the medical marijuana industry as another functional and contributing piece of late modern society. Students did not always applaud the high taxes and were not altogether against forking over money to dealers, but they preferred the legal-medicalized system of legitimacy and control.

Ultimately, by locating cannabis sales and employment in increasing salience and legitimacy, the legal-medicalized system held dispensary workers to norms and rules that reduced the systemic hassle of an illegal market. Disputes and norm violations that arise within the illicit market, no matter how trivial, cannot be resolved through traditional business strategies. The dispensary system reduced any anxieties and discomforts students and sellers might have experienced when transactions occurred in a criminalized setting. This shift in human interaction altered methods of informal control as the norms, rules, beliefs, and values related to marijuana sales now aligned with normative and agreed upon patterns of the interaction order (Goffman 1983).

Avoiding Arrest and Career Damage

With licensed providers and legitimate transactions, a medical marijuana license offered students insulation from the law. Just as the legal-medicalized system shifted control away from dealers, it also reduced the power of the police to arrest card-carrying students. As cardholders, undergraduates evaded the risk of arrest, fines, and potential incarceration for possessing marijuana. Once subjected to punitive **formal controls** through the city and the university for their marijuana use, student's chances of becoming embroiled with the criminal justice system were significantly reduced. Anthony, a 21-year-old senior and accounting major who had once been threatened with suspension by campus judiciaries for smoking in his dorm, noted:

> I got my license partly for legality purposes. That way if I get caught I'm not getting fined and arrested. It's a $150 insurance policy. I like to smoke every now and again. Should that fuck my life up? I mean really? People might say that I don't have AIDS or glaucoma, but I still shouldn't be arrested or suspended for relaxing.

Participants reported personal scrapes with law enforcement or had first-hand knowledge of friends who had been arrested. They viewed the medical marijuana license as a valid tool to circumvent such life-changing events. Ben, a 20-year-old junior and psychology major who was distrustful of the criminal justice system, noted:

> Why take the risk? If you can get a card to protect you from getting arrested, fired, or kicked out of school, it just makes sense. If I get stopped, I have my license. I can't be hassled. I don't think I should be arrested or even fined for smoking a bit of bud. I've had a few friends who have had their lives turned in different directions for just having some marijuana.

I'm not saying they went to prison or anything, but it really changed their plans.

Although protection from law enforcement may not have been the primary factor motivating students to apply for their medical license, it was a benefit to everyone discussed. They were aware of the high number of arrests for nonviolent marijuana possession and the consequences of an arrest. Participants reported denial of student loans, suspension or expulsion from school, being fired from part-time jobs, losing financial support from their parents, or having to use their own funds (which they often lacked) to finance fines or legal representation. John, the 21-year-old senior and environmental studies major, stated:

> I know people that have gotten busted and had to go to court, pay a ton of money. My good friend got suspended from school. So, I saw the doctor, paid my money and now I don't have to buy or carry illegally.

Having a card freed students from the stress and worry of doing something illegal. They viewed the license as a welcome reprieve from the unjust laws and policies prohibiting marijuana. The legal-medicalized shift distanced students from formal controls and sanctions, and similar to the to the reduced power of illegal dealers, placed control mechanisms into the fabric of conventional interaction and civil society. Students were given the opportunity to monitor themselves rather than be subjected to police power and the criminogenic model of control. As Mark, a 20-year-old sophomore and economics major who participated in club sports and student government, discussed:

> For me it was a big sigh of relief. For my whole life I was doing something illegal for as long as I could remember, something my friends and I never

thought was that bad. Now the cops can't bother me. I have the right to smoke some weed. It's a huge weight off my shoulders. You can't get arrested unless you're being ridiculous, driving maybe, which is fine.

Although marijuana is a mass market drug, and large numbers of arrests mean that an individual user is at low risk of being apprehended (Room et al. 2010), students were wary of the **formal and informal labels** attached to a drug arrest and a criminal record. They were critical of being designated as criminals or lawbreakers by parents, employers, university officials, or the criminal justice system for simply possessing marijuana. The dispensary system shifted the social and interpersonal designations of their actions. As marijuana users, they were no longer relegated to a criminal subculture, but were increasingly moving into conventional realms of society.

The dispensary system was not a flawless industry in the eyes of students. Some were critical of the costs of access (i.e., getting the card), the limited business hours of dispensaries, or the requirement of State registration as a marijuana user. Others were fearful that the industry would be completely commandeered by the state or big bnusiness (i.e., pharmaceutical companies). Furthermore, participants were not entirely disapproving of the illicit marketplace. They were accustomed to the lack of control and security involved in the informal rules of illegal marijuana sales involving unlicensed dealers and unregulated cash flow. But in contrast to the illicit market, the dispensary system emerged as a preferred arrangement as students touted the power and self-control it gave them.

For participants, buying marijuana legally from licensed businesses with qualified employees placed the substance into a social context of increasing legitimacy and into a new framework of control. Much like alcohol, marijuana shifted into a legal but regulated substance. Students visited dispensaries tucked in among traditionally legitimate businesses that included coffee shops, retail stores, and company offices. They used the coupons and followed the advertisements marijuana shops placed in local magazines and newspapers. Students were **socialized** into the rules and expectations of the medicalized system. They learned why (i.e., security, regulation, lawfulness) to purchase marijuana with proper identification from licensed providers and how to use the drug responsibly. Marijuana became ordinary and routine as its cultivation, distribution, and use was part of the normative interaction order. Although these elements provided the foundation for the new control mechanisms attached to marijuana, the medicalization process further transformed the deviant social order associated with prohibition and criminalization.

Discovering Medicalization

Although students sought entrance into the medical marijuana dispensaries with expectations of expanded product options, increased agency, and insulation from the law, they found the **medicalization** process had further shifted the definitions previously attached to marijuana. Within this legal-medicalized framework, a medical perspective regarding marijuana use became dominant over other viewpoints (e.g., marijuana is criminal, dangerous, addictive, or unhealthy) as medical norms and beliefs defined the drug. Medical marijuana **ideology** and **language** was advanced through advocates, politicians, and medical professionals; and doctors operated as gatekeepers as their signature and recommendation provided entrée. Marijuana began to connote a substance that could cater to myriad needs and desires, which were only available through a legal-medicalized framework. Mark, the 20-year-old sophomore and economics major, stated:

> I think it's great how many different strains I have to choose from. I have different options for how I'm feeling or what I'm doing. I had this strain the other day, and it gave me a smile and some energy, which is what I wanted. You buy from your friend, he's got one strain, maybe two if you're lucky, and you think whatever, I guess this will do the job, I'm sure I'll get

high. But with the dispensary options you can go in with an agenda of how you want to feel or what you want out of the marijuana. It's almost like your mood, wine or beer, red or white, stout or lager, like that.

The variety of strains available to students were exhibited in the countless brand names such as "Bubble Gum," "Sour Kush," "God's Gift," "Grand Daddy Purp," and "Blue Skunk." Student cardholders learned to distinguish between the countless brands as each contained a depth description of the strain and its effects. For example, "Citrus Haze" was described as possessing a sweet citrus aroma with amazingly high trichome density, resulting in an excellent analgesic effect as well as a strong, fast, energetic high that lasts. "Matanuska" was described as extremely potent, sativa dominant, with an incredible cerebral high and a spicy and smooth taste with a pungent flavor. Students embraced the variety of smokable strains, with indica, sativa, and hybrid cannabis options and the power to control their drug experience. They came to define their marijuana experience through the different effects of these distinct strains. Madeline, the psychology and sociology double-major from New Jersey, noted:

> Dispensaries have options I'd never seen. I used to buy from this guy with one kind. With the dispensaries if you don't like some strain, you've got like 10 others to try out. If I buy an indica that I should smoke before bed to relax, I look for that aspect in the effects. I know when to use it and why I'm using it; it's just a whole new spin on marijuana.

They were also appreciative of the consistency and safety of these smokable varieties. Professional laboratories provided dispensaries with reliable reports on the levels of THC and cannabinoids of their strains and also tested products for potential infections of root aphids, fungus gnats, mildew, mold, and spider mites. William, a senior who had spent most of his high school days selling marijuana in Washington D.C., noted:

> The dispensary cuts down on all the crap. You're never getting seeds or
> dirt, brown weed. The dispensary is accountable to you as a patient and as
> a customer. I've had friends who have smoked weed they were convinced
> was laced with something. I mean you can't really cut marijuana with
> other substances like dealers do with ecstasy or coke, but you never worry
> with the medical stuff.

Students also learned about the range of options and effects contained in
edible marijuana products. In the illicit market, edible products were rare,
often baked by close friends or by oneself. Potency was ambiguous and
consistency was relatively nonexistent. Participants touted the benefits of
edible marijuana options and the branding of products for reliable potency
and effects. Emily, a 22-year-old business major and prospective law
student, stated:

> The selection is enormous; you've got candy, brownies, ice cream, olive oil,
> something for all tastes. I like the tincture. I put it in my tea or just drop it
> on my tongue. I don't like to smoke, really. It hits me really quick and I
> cough and stuff. The edibles are more gradual and I don't get as paranoid
> if I just eat a little bit. Sometimes I like to eat a little and watch a movie,
> and so I go buy a brownie or something. I don't have to drive across town
> and buy a 50 dollar eighth of weed from my friend Steven, which is what I
> had to do before.

Students did not learn this information in a vacuum. They were initially
novices in the medical marijuana scene, accustomed to the language and
interactions of the illicit market. While some learned aspects of this new
system through friends or even advertisements and websites, the central

gatekeepers of knowledge were dispensary employees. Josh, a 20-year-old marijuana enthusiast majoring in physiology with future plans as a medical doctor, discussed:

> It's nice for me to go into a place where people are very knowledgeable about the product. I mean dispensaries want to put people behind the counter who are educated on the products, strains, effects, strength and all that stuff. I used to just have some idiot that sold me weed. I know how to get high, but you can ask questions and learn new information you would never learn anywhere else. Just learning about indica and sativa and how they're different, that's never happened before buying marijuana. With honest information you can make good decisions about how you use marijuana; knowledge is power.

Budtenders are the bartenders of the medical marijuana dispensary system, they offered product information, recommendations, and guidance to licensed customers. They provided new ways to think and talk about marijuana that could only be available through a legal system. With this shift to legal-medicalization, the **status** position and associated **role** behaviors of marijuana distributors mirrored those of conventional employees working in retail, sales, or the food industry. Budtenders were there to educate, inform, and make a sale. The customer could visit another dispensary if service, information, or products were subpar and this emerging dynamic placed power and control in the hands of student cardholders. Brooke, a 22-year-old senior and geography major who worked as a receptionist at a local dispensary, discussed:

> I think the amount of knowledge a budtender needs to have to help customers and patients is really crucial, and what is really different with the dispensaries. Because if you go to an illegitimate drug dealer and you're like "Hey what bud do you have?" They can throw out lies of names

to boost their prices, they may have smoked it and they can kind of tell you what the high is like, but you're not expecting that. All you are really expecting from a drug dealer is to walk in somewhere and get a certain amount of bud and hope it's not shitty. But when you go to the dispensary, they can tell you exactly how the high is supposed to feel and what issues it will address, what's going to work better for you. You can come back and say "oh, my high was too intense," or "this didn't really help me," and they can direct you and recommend something different. It's like *Pineapple Express*, where they talked about how you really can't be friends with your dealer. It's just someone you interact with momentarily and then jet. People aren't best friends with dispensary budtenders, but the relationship is more warm. They are eager to make suggestions, offer information, throw in a free candy to try, or talk with you about what product will make you feel better.

Medical dispensaries and budtenders provided students the medicalized language to define and label marijuana products in ways never available. The dispensary system also gave students increased control over their marijuana experience, from product options, educational information, desired high, and customer agency.

New Justifications and Rationalizations

As students were socialized into the medicalized system, it allowed them to control their **justifications** and **rationalizations** for using and buying cannabis that were previously unavailable in the illicit economy. Participants did not use with more frequency or create new reasons for using marijuana, but the increased legitimacy of medical marijuana provided institutional support for their personal motivations. Madeline stated:

I use if for relaxation, I always have, to lose some stress, and to laugh. I don't have cancer or glaucoma. The State doesn't have relaxation as a medical condition, which I guess is why everyone has their card for chronic pain, but the dispensary system gives my reasons more authority.

Students were typically not using medical marijuana for traditionally accepted conditions such as glaucoma, cancer, AIDS, or Multiple Sclerosis, but they **denied that using marijuana for other reasons was wrong, and explained how it was appropriate** (Sykes and Matza 1957). The reordering and reconceptualization of marijuana within society validated students reasons for using cannabis. They were critical of the small scope of acceptable medical uses written into law and used the increasing authenticity of marijuana as medicine to justify the personal health benefits they experienced from it. Jason, a 21-year-old, international affairs major from Boston, noted:

I think it's a shame that people narrow the definition of medical or medicinal to suggest it can only help you if you are going through chemotherapy or if you have multiple sclerosis. In the limited research I've seen, there are at least 200 things it can be used for. I'm sure if you went around and interviewed people, in addition to what it's prescribed for, it helps them with other things. I use it to help me sleep and for my headaches. But I'll also use it to laugh or get into a movie. That makes me happy, and that's healthy.

Students also justified obtaining their license to support social change. This legal regulation of marijuana had completely changed the social, political, and economic climate surrounding the drug and they viewed this as a shift toward a more pragmatic policy direction. Ben, the junior psychology major, elaborated:

I got my card to support the cause. If I get taxed it sucks, but I could care less. If tax money gets the support of people who don't support medical marijuana, it's a good reason. I would rather have my money going into taxes or social services or whatever than to dealers.

Participants may have been reluctant to advocate for marijuana openly in the past, but its increasing legitimacy in portions of mainstream society made getting a card a political statement. Andrew, a 22-year-old senior computer science major, stated:

A lot of people are getting their card to support the movement. I feel like the more people that get cards they can't take it back or they will finally be forced to legalize. To take it away now would be like alcohol prohibition, just a huge mistake.

Students were opposed to the continued prohibition of marijuana and medicalization provided an avenue to support change that was previously unavailable.

Salient Community of Users

The growth of the medical marijuana industry **defined deviance down** (Moynihan 1993) and moved marijuana users and cannabis shops into an increasing position of legitimacy. **Subcultures** of drug users form where drugs are illegal or users face disapproval (Faupel, Horowitz, and Weaver 2010) and the legal-medicalization process diminished the utility of a deviant marijuana subculture. This shift in the criminal designation of marijuana users served to increase students' visibility of them in their community. As marijuana cultivation and sales shifted from the shadows to legitimate storefronts, they witnessed for the first time the demographic span of people around them who used and supported marijuana. Mark elaborated:

I go into a dispensary and I see old ladies, college kids, business people. I mean you can see that so many people are using marijuana, adults that want good stuff and no hassle. I think it really shows everyone there is a large community of like-minded marijuana users.

This new awareness of users enhanced the legitimacy of medical marijuana by showing people that normative and functioning members of society use marijuana, dispelling stereotypical myths of cannabis as amotivational or a gateway to abuse. For students, this opened up practical discussions about marijuana in a manner never experienced under the umbrella of criminalization. Jason, the international affairs major from Boston, noted:

I think the more people see it accepted around here, in this community, by their neighbors and friends, the more legitimate and accepted marijuana becomes. I think legitimacy is important for older people, for parents and people to be able to talk about it and even use it. Legitimacy opens the door for communication. I can say, "hey it's medicine, it helps me relax and feel better," or "what about the tax dollars and the law?"

For students, the dispensary system channeled them away from the rubric of prohibition and criminalization. The marijuana community was now intertwined with conventional society, and this normalization process further reduced the cultural anxiety and negative labels attached to marijuana. People were less inclined to guard information about their drug use; they were less likely to lose status through sanctions from authorities or to offend non-users who might disapprove (Hathaway, Comeau, and Erickson 2011). Anthony, the senior accounting major with past legal issues, elaborated:

I think the biggest thing is that people that couldn't or didn't want to, or were afraid to say, was that they smoked, but now they can. Now you start to see the true numbers of people who use marijuana. I mean before, they were behind closed doors, maybe worried about the cops or their jobs, and I'm sure there is still some of that, but people are getting away from that fear. People are finally being able to say I do this. We all do something to relax, de-stress, have fun, feel better, whatever, now it's just out.

The dispensary system increasingly illustrated the similarities between marijuana users and non-users, rather than the differences between them. Participants watched as medicalization placed marijuana into the normative system of community life, distancing it from previous associations with an underground market of criminals.

Marijuana dispensaries provided students with an efficient and secure environment for the purchase of cannabis. By holding a registry card, they distanced themselves from the criminal justice sanctions handed down to those who illegally possessed and distribute the drug. Students experienced fundamental social control shifts as a result of this emerging legal-medicalized industry. First, **control shifted away from the informal rules and norms** of the illicit industry. The power held by drug dealers decreased as the demand for illicit market marijuana declined and medical marijuana gained popularity and a significant customer base. Furthermore, they were no longer subjected to the business practices of illicit dealers, they could control the time and location of their transaction, and they could dictate the drug experience they desired (i.e., edible, smokable, potency, strain, or brand). The dispensary system allowed student cardholders, over the age of eighteen, to exert a level of control and agency over their substance use that was unavailable to them with alcohol. Second, the legal-medicalized industry **shifted control away from the criminal justice system** and university security forces. Although students could not use marijuana on school property, they could possess the drug legally throughout the state and this legality of possession effectively insulated them from criminalization and formal sanctions.

Finally, modes of social **control shifted into civil society and reordered society**. The medicalization process placed some power with doctors (i.e., as gatekeepers) and professional interest groups and the state collaborated with medical practitioners, lawyers, and law enforcement to draft medical marijuana laws and policies. However, the responsibility of control rested primarily in the **civil sphere**. Medical dispensary owners, cultivators, students, bakers, and employees, along with local officials and affiliated business owners, remained bound to state laws and policies. The industry was heavily proctored by the state, but expected to sustain and maintain social control over itself. Thus, these groups produced and sustained a system of informal control that reflected changes in both formal law and medical regulations. Student cardholders were subjected to these informal rules and norms of the legal-medicalized industry as marijuana entered the normative order of society.

Conclusion

In contrast to the zero-tolerance and prohibitionist formal controls surrounding alcohol use that students experienced through Campus University, they encountered a fundamental shift in social control as they entered a legal dispensary system for medical marijuana. Similar to the punitive policies at Campus University, the control of marijuana has historically been concerned with formal control agents such as the police, the courts, and the prisons. Drug policy in the U.S. is primarily criminogenic and emphasizes a punitive and "law and order" stance. The U.S. criminal justice system relies on deterrence and aims to control marijuana possession and distribution through arrest and incarceration (McBride et al. 2009; Robinson and Scherlen 2007; Shelden 2010). **Deterrence theory** contends that swift, certain, and harsh formal punishments will eliminate or at least minimize deviant behavior such as drug use (Akers 2009; Shelden 2010; Thomas and Bishop 1984). These social control policies have resulted in a dramatic increase in drug arrests (especially for marijuana) and contributed to the mass incarceration rates in the U.S. (Benavie 2009; Shelden 2010). Policymakers have anticipated that a shift away from formal, criminogenic control methods (Benavie 2009; Global Commission on Drug Policy 2011; Nadelmann 2004) would reduce the costs and problems caused by drug prohibition.

Through the growing legal-medical marijuana industry in the area surrounding Campus University, the state, the community, and students experienced an unprecedented shifting of controls. The change from blanket prohibition transferred social control to a regulatory framework that fostered legal-medical controls. Norms and rules flowed through social life and human interaction, as student cardholders were socialized into a legitimate and conventional system of obtaining and using their drugs. Medical marijuana dispensaries provided participants eighteen years of age and older with an efficient and secure environment for the purchase of cannabis. In contrast to their collegiate experiences with alcohol, where students lacked party capital, by holding a registry card marijuana users distanced themselves from the criminal justice sanctions handed down to those who illegally possessed and distributed the drug.

In a twist on Becker (1963), students entered a **socialization process** that taught them new social meanings attached to marijuana. They learned the language, definitions, and motivations of the legal-medical marijuana industry and reaped the benefits of a regulated, controlled market. Students internalized this new information about health benefits, strain effects, and reliable branding, and transmitted it to others in their social networks. By embracing a legal-medicalized industry that provided them with agency and power over their drug experience, students demonstrated the effectiveness of regulation over blanket prohibition. Social control and power shifted away from both the police and the underground market and operated instead through the conventional norms, values, beliefs, and business practices of a legal-medicalized framework. State regulated and formal intervention was still possible, but only under circumstances when the supervisory legal-medical controls were no longer sufficient.

The medicalization of cannabis defined deviance down significantly (Moynihan 1993) and effectively reduced the demands placed on the state's criminal justice agencies. At the same time, the state increasingly embedded social controls into the fabric of society, rather than inserting them from above in the form of sovereign command (Garland 2001). Medical dispensary owners, cultivators, investors, students, and employees, along with local politicians and affiliated business owners, remained bound to state laws and policies and were expected to proctor themselves while government powers watched at a distance for a breakdown in control. The state was unable to manage the illicit marijuana market alone and redirected its control efforts away from the sole authority of the police, the courts, and the prisons. The dispensary industry provided the state with a situation in which it governed, but did not coercively control marijuana and its users. Instead, the government managed the drug *through* the actors involved in the legal-medical industry, and effectively mandated them as active partners in sustaining and enforcing the formal and informal controls of the dispensary system. The state controlled at an ostensibly distant fashion, but did not resign its power. On the contrary, it retained its traditional command over the police and the prisons while expanding its efficiency and capacity to regulate marijuana and its users. This new reality in crime control deemphasized traditional formal controls (i.e., police, course, and prisons) and emphasized legal-medical mechanisms. Students, as well as other marijuana users within the dispensary system, experienced this control shift at the structural, cultural, and interactional level of their lives. While users gained power and agency over their marijuana experience, the state extended greater control over this particular drug subculture.

At the *structural* level, the legal-medical model reduced the strain of a substantial segment of society by institutionalizing acceptable and lawful means of accessing marijuana, effectively shifting students and users into an ecological position where they could be watched and controlled. The groups once involved in the illicit market became visible, and the laws that governed the use, distribution, and production of cannabis became enforceable by the state. Marijuana users were patients and subject to medical control as they required a physician's recommendation to consume the drug lawfully. The state mandated what medical conditions warranted a registry card, and monitored people through licensing applications, doctors' files, government paperwork, and the medical marijuana registry. Dispensary owners were required to grow 70 percent of their own product, to provide live 24-hour surveillance camera feeds of their cultivation and distribution warehouses, and to subject themselves to periodic inspection. Dispensary owners and employees were fingerprinted and underwent extensive background checks, and marijuana businesses only operated in state zoned locations.

At the *cultural* level, the legal-medical system provided a greater degree of **social order, stability, and integration** by relocating marijuana users into the fold of conventional **norms and values**. Cultural cohesion and conformity were fostered through legitimate business operations that catered to conventional lifestyles and work hours, quelled concerns over safety and lawfulness, and reduced the alienation of a subculture of users. The state effectively aligned a once criminal population of people with dominant ideals of **normality** (Goffman 1983) and dismantled a framework of **deviant organization** (Best and Luckenbill 1980) with distinct ideologies and norms concerning marijuana sales and use. The government incorporated the norms and values of conventional society into the processes of distributing and using cannabis and now assisted in controlling marijuana through the cultural transmission (Shaw and McKay 1942) of rituals and sanctions now aligned with the normative social order.

At an *interactional* level micro-level processes mediated people's **differential associations and social learning processes** (Akers 2009; Sutherland 1947; Sutherland and Cressey 1955) as students were increasingly socialized into a conventional drug lifestyle. Marijuana users in the dispensary system decreased their contacts with deviant others and increased their contacts with legitimate associations by purchasing lawfully from licensed distributors. Dispensary owners interacted with contractors, real estate firms, tax specialists, and lawyers because they existed in legitimate occupational associations and lawful community relations. This legal-medical model allowed the state to further monitor interactional processes through receipts, taxes, and video surveillance. Zoning laws mandated where transactions occurred, distribution laws defined how much could be purchased, and monitored business hours controlled the time sales occurred. The government also strengthened **individual bonds to society** (Hirschi 1969) as a medical license protected users' conventional investments (i.e., education, career, and family) and catered to their time-consuming activities as they decided the time, speed, and location of their purchases. Finally, the medicalization of marijuana prompted people to endorse society's rules as progressively more politically and morally correct, since users were typically critical of cannabis prohibition.

The benefits to the state were numerous. The legal-medical system reduced illegal marijuana sales, typically impervious to law enforcement, that occurred consensually within personal social networks (Caulkins and Pacula 2006). The state gained a substantial revenue stream from licensure and taxation, saved money once spent on arresting, adjudicating, and imprisoning non-violent marijuana offenders, reduced the "gateway effect" by decreasing users' contact with "harder" drugs, and released a substantial segment of the population from the criminal label, effectively lowering the crime rate. Finally, marijuana became increasingly ordered through regulated controls that reflected conventional society, rather than the deviant norms of an illicit market or the formal control agents of the criminal justice system.

The shifting state laws regarding marijuana fostered an emergent medical ideology. Marijuana was increasingly defined as medicinal, viewed through a medical framework, and discussed using health terminology. Furthermore, the medical industry operated as "gatekeeper" because students were required to get a physician's recommendation to legally consume the drug. Marijuana took on a different meaning for students within this emerging medicalized framework (Conrad 1979). As a form of control, medical ideology adopts medical imagery and vocabulary, and further imbues medical authority over the situation (Conrad 2007). Through this medical authority, the use of marijuana became associated with divergent designations from simply "getting high" or "getting fucked up." For students, the use of the drug came to be *legitimately* associated with a conventional way to relax, de-stress, laugh, have fun, or relieve pain. Although students experienced resocialization into medical ideology through the legal marijuana dispensary industry, Campus University continued punitive responses to students' substance use.

Notes and Discussion Questions:

References

Akers, Ronald L. 2009. *Social Learning and Social Structure: A General Theory of Crime and Deviance*. New Brunswick, N.J.: Transaction Publishers.

Becker, Howard S. 1963. *Outsiders*. New York: Free Press.

Benavie, Arthur. 2009. *Drugs: America's Holy War*. New York: Routledge.

Best, Joel and David F. Luckenbill. 1980. "The Social Organization of Deviants." *Social Problems* 28(1):14-31.

Caulkins, Jonathan P., Bruce Johnson, Angela Taylor, and Lowell Taylor. 1999. "What Drug Dealers Tell Us About Their Costs of Doing Business." *Journal of Drug Issues* 29(3):323-40.

Caulkins, Jonathan P. and Rosalie Liccardo Pacula. 2006. "Marijuana Markets: Inferences from Reports by Household Population. *Journal of Drug Issues* 36(1):173-200.

Caulkins, Jonathan P. and Peter Reuter. 1998. "What Price Data Tell Us About Drug Markets?" Journal of Drug Issues 28(3):593-612.

Clark, Peter. A. 2000. "The Ethics of Medical Marijuana: Government Restrictions vs. Medical Necessity." *Journal of Public Health Policy* 21(1):40–60.

Cloward, Richard. A., and Lloyd E. Ohlin. 1960. *Delinquency and Opportunity*. New York: Free Press.

Conrad, Peter. 1979. "Types of Medical Social Control." *Sociology of Health and Illness* 1(1):1–11.

Conrad, Peter. 2007. *The Medicalization of Society: On the Transformation of Human Conditions into Treatable Disorders*. Baltimore: Johns Hopkins University Press.

Eddy, Mark. 2010. *Medical Marijuana: Review and Analysis of Federal and State Policies*. Congressional Research Service Report for Congress RL33211. Washington D.C.: Congressional Research Service.

Faupel, Charles E., Alan M. Horowitz, and Greg S. Weaver. 2010. *The Sociology of American Drug Use*. New York: Oxford University Press.

Feigelman, William, Bernard S. Gorman, and Julia A. Lee. 1998. "Binge Drinkers, Illicit Drug Users, and Polydrug Users: An Epidemiological Study of American Collegians." *Journal of Alcohol and Drug Education* (44)1:

Ford, Jason A. and Ryan D. Schroeder. 2009. "Academic Strain and Non-Medical Use of Prescription Stimulants Among College Students." *Deviant Behavior* 30(1):26-53. 47-69.

Garland, David. 2001. *The Culture of Control: Crime and Social Order in Contemporary Society*. Chicago, IL: University Of Chicago Press.

Gledhill-Hoyt, Jeana, Hang Lee, Jared Strote, and Henry Wechsler. 2000. "Increased Use of Marijuana and Other Illicit Drugs at U.S. Colleges in the 1990s: Results of Three National Surveys." *Addiction* 95(11):1655-67.

Global Commission on Drug Policy. 2011. "The War on Drugs: A Report of the Global Commission on Drug Policy." Retrieved September 9, 2011 (http://www.globalcommissionondrugs.org/Report).

Goffman, Erving. 1983. "The Interaction Order: American Sociological Association, 1982 Presidential Address." *American Sociological Review* 48(1): 1–17.

Hathaway, Andrew D., Natalie C. Comeau, and Patricia G. Erickson. 2011. "Cannabis Normalization and Stigma: Contemporary Practices of Moral Regulation." *Criminology and Criminal Justice* 11(5):451–69.

Hirschi, Travis. 1969. *Causes of Delinquency*. Berkeley, CA: University of California Press.

Lipari, Rachel N. and Beda Jean-Francois. 2016. *A Day in the Life of College Students Aged 18 to 22: Substance Use Facts*. US Department of Health & Human Services, Substance Abuse and Mental Health.

Martin, Christopher S., Patrick R. Clifford, and Rock L. Clapper. 1992. "Patterns and Predictors of Simultaneous and Concurrent Use of Alcohol, Tobacco, Marijuana, and Hallucinogens in First-Year College Students." *Journal of Substance Use* 4(3):319-26.

McCabe, Sean Estaban, James A. Cranford, Michele Morales, and Amy Young. 2006."Simultaneous and Concurrent Polydrug Use of Alcohol and Prescription: Prevalence, Correlates, and Consequences." *Journal of Studies on Alcohol* 67(4):529-37.

McBride, Duanne C., Yvonne Terry-McElrath, Henrick Harwood, James A. Inciardi, and Carl Leukefeld. 2009. "Reflections on drug policy." *Journal of Drug Issues* 39(1):71–88.

Mohler-Kuo, Meicho, Jae Eun Lee, and Henry Wechsler. 2003. "Trends in Marijuana and Other Illicit Drug Use Among College Students: Results From 4 Harvard School of Public Health College Alcohol Surveys: 1993-2001." *Journal of American College Health* 52: 17-24.

Mohamed, Rafik A. and Erik D. Fritsvold. 2010. *Dorm Room Dealers: Drugs and the Privelees of Race and Class*. Boulder, CO: Lynne Rienner.

Moynihan, Daniel P. 1993. "Defining Deviancy Down." *American Scholar* 62(1):17–30.

Nadelmann, Ethan A. 2004. "An End to Marijuana Prohibition: The Drive to Legalize Picks Up." *National Review.*

O'Grady, Kevin E., Amelia M. Arria, Dawn M.B. Fitzelle, and Eric D. Wish. 2008. "Heavy Drinking and Polydrug Use Among College Students." *Journal of Drug Issues* 38(2):445-66.

O'Malley, Patrick M. and Lloyd D. Johnston. 2002. "Epidemiology of Alcohol and Other Drug Use Among American College Students." *Journal of Studies on Alcohol* 14:23-39.

ProCon.org. 2011. "16 Medical Marijuana States and DC: Laws, Fees, and Possession Limits." Retrieved November 16, 2011 (http://medicalmarijuana.procon.org/view.resource.php?resourceID=000881).

ProCon.org. 2018. "33 Legal Marijuana States." Retrieved November 28, 2018 (https://medicalmarijuana.procon.org/view.resource.php?resourceID=000881).

Quintero, Gilbert. 2009. "Controlled Release: A Cultural Analysis of Collegiate Polydrug Use." *Journal of Psychoactive Drugs* 41(1):39-47.

Robinson, Matthew B. and Renee G. Scherlen. 2007. *Lies, Damned Lies, and Drug War Statistics: A Critical Analysis of Claims made by the office of National Drug Control Policy.* New York: SUNY Press.

Schorling, John B, Margaret Gutgesell, Paul Klas, Deborah Smith, and Adrienne Keller. 1994. "Tobacco, Alcohol, and Other Drug Use Among College Students."*Journal of Substance Abuse* 6(1):105-15.

Schrag, Peter. 2002. "A Quagmire for our Time: The W ar on Drugs." *Journal of Public Health Policy* 23(3):286–98.

Shaw, Clifford R. and Henry D. McKay. 1942. *Juvenile Delinquency and Urban Areas*. Chicago, IL: University of Chicago Press.

Shelden, Randall G. 2010. *Our Punitive Society*. Long Grove, IL: Waveland Press.

Stein, Joel. 2002. "The New Politics of Pot: Can It Go Legit?" *Time* 4:56-61.

Substance Abuse and Mental Health Services Administration. 2010. *Results from the 2009 National Survey on Drug Use and Health: Volume I. Summary of National Findings*. Rockville: MD: Office of Applied Studies.

Sutherland, Edwin H. 1947. *Principles of Criminology*. Philadelphia, PA: Lippincot.

Sutherland, Edwin H. and Donald R. Cressey. 1955. *Principles in Criminology*. Philadelphia, PA: Lippincott.

Sykes, Gresham M. and David Matza. 1957. "Techniques of Neutralization: A Theory of Delinquency." *American Sociological Review* 22(6):664–70.

Tewksbury, Richard and Elizabeth Mustaine. 1998. "Lifestyles of the wheelers and dealers: Drug dealing among American college students." *Journal of Crime and Justice* 21(2):37-56.

Thomas, Charles W. and Donna M. Bishop. 1984. "The Effect of Formal and Informal Sanctions on Delinquency: A Longitudinal Comparison of Labeling and Deterrence Theories." *The Journal of Criminal Law and Criminology* 75(4):1222-245.

CPSIA information can be obtained
at www.ICGtesting.com
Printed in the USA
FSHW011052250620